Media and the Politics of Offence

Anne Graefer
Editor

Media and the Politics of Offence

Editor
Anne Graefer
Birmingham Centre for Media
and Cultural Research
Birmingham City University
Birmingham, UK

ISBN 978-3-030-17573-3   ISBN 978-3-030-17574-0 (eBook)
https://doi.org/10.1007/978-3-030-17574-0

© The Editor(s) (if applicable) and The Author(s) 2019
This work is subject to copyright. All rights are solely and exclusively licensed by the Publisher, whether the whole or part of the material is concerned, specifically the rights of translation, reprinting, reuse of illustrations, recitation, broadcasting, reproduction on microfilms or in any other physical way, and transmission or information storage and retrieval, electronic adaptation, computer software, or by similar or dissimilar methodology now known or hereafter developed.
The use of general descriptive names, registered names, trademarks, service marks, etc. in this publication does not imply, even in the absence of a specific statement, that such names are exempt from the relevant protective laws and regulations and therefore free for general use.
The publisher, the authors and the editors are safe to assume that the advice and information in this book are believed to be true and accurate at the date of publication. Neither the publisher nor the authors or the editors give a warranty, expressed or implied, with respect to the material contained herein or for any errors or omissions that may have been made. The publisher remains neutral with regard to jurisdictional claims in published maps and institutional affiliations.

Cover image: stilllifephotographer/Getty images
Cover design by eStudioCalamar

This Palgrave Macmillan imprint is published by the registered company Springer Nature Switzerland AG
The registered company address is: Gewerbestrasse 11, 6330 Cham, Switzerland

Acknowledgements

The idea to this book emerged out of a prior project on offence that I have conducted with Ranjana Das (2015–2017). Like so many other books, it changed significantly from the first draft that was euphorically discussed and written in Bedford, up until the final stages that I am concluding in Munich. I am extremely thankful to the authors of this volume for bearing with me through the different stages, and for sharing their inspiring ideas, their words and their energy at a time when, at least in the UK, the 'REF-ability' of book chapters is questioned and academic staff is encouraged to prioritise other forms of knowledge production. All contributors for this volume have been nothing short of fantastic, and I am forever grateful for this.

I would also like to thank the numerous reviewers who carefully read and reread specific book chapters of this collection, giving thoughtful feedback and input to the authors. Hazel Collie, Gemma Commane, Kirsten Forkert, Inger-Lise Kalviknes Bore, Allaina Kilby, John Mercer and Karen Patel have been amazing colleagues at my former workplace, thank you so much for your support and solidarity. Not only for this project but also for countless other reasons, I am forever indebted to my dear friend and colleague Suzan Meryem Kalayci whose kindness, generous support and sheer endless creativity, continuously encourage me to be courageous. Special thanks to Carolyn Pedwell for her thought-provoking work on affect and her feedback on the introduction of this book.

I am also grateful to Jean Morris for her thorough copyediting, Antje Helch for her proficient help with the cover of this book, as well as

Mala Sanghera-Warren and Lucy Batrouney from Palgrave for their generous support, patience and editorial advice. The biggest thank you goes, as always, to my partner Jon who, with great sensitivity and unwavering commitment, believes in me and supports me—in true feminist fashion. This book is dedicated to Finn and Tate, with my ridiculous love.

Contents

1 Introduction to Media and the Politics of Offence   1
   Anne Graefer

Part I Offence, Politics and Protest

2 Political Offensiveness in the Mediated Public Sphere:
   The Performative Play of Alignments   23
   Martin Montgomery, Michael Higgins
   and Angela Smith

3 Creating an Emotional Community: The Negotiation
   of Anger and Resistance to Donald Trump   47
   Karin Wahl-Jorgensen

4 Unruly Women and Carnivalesque Counter-Control:
   Offensive Humor in Mediated Social Protest   65
   Anne Graefer, Allaina Kilby and Inger-Lise Kalviknes Bore

5 Changing Visual Politics in South Africa: Old
   and New Modes of Exclusion, Protest and Offence   91
   Marietta Kesting

Part II Offence, Representations and Popular Culture

6   Other Bodies Within Us: Shock, Affect and Reality Television Audiences   109
    Jacob Johanssen

7   'Period Sex': *Crazy Ex-Girlfriend* and the Feminist Politics of Offence   127
    Katrin Horn

8   Fans at Work: Offence as Motivation for Critical Vidding   147
    Sebastian F. K. Svegaard

Part III Offence, Media Ethics and Regulation

9   Blocked Access: When Pornographers Take Offence   165
    Susanna Paasonen

10 Regulatory Expectations of Offended Audiences: The Citizen Interest in Audience Discourse   187
    Ranjana Das and Anne Graefer

11 Negotiating Vulnerability in the Trigger Warning Debates   207
    Katariina Kyrölä

12 Gruesome Images in the Contemporary Israeli Mediated Public Sphere   233
    Tal Morse

Index   253

List of Contributors

Inger-Lise Kalviknes Bore Independent Researcher, Oslo, Norway

Ranjana Das Senior Lecturer in Media and Communication, University of Surrey, Surrey, UK

Anne Graefer Birmingham Centre for Media and Cultural Research, Birmingham City University, Birmingham, UK

Michael Higgins Senior Lecturer Journalism, Media and Communication, University of Strathclyde, Glasgow, UK

Katrin Horn Assistant Professor in American Studies. University of Bayreuth, Bayreuth, Germany

Jacob Johanssen Senior Lecturer at the Faculty of Education, Humanities and Social Sciences, St. Mary's University, Twickenham, UK

Marietta Kesting Junior Professor of Media Theory, Academy of Fine Arts Munich, Munich, Germany

Allaina Kilby Lecturer in Media & Communication, Swansea University, Swansea, UK

Katariina Kyrölä Lecturer in Media Studies, Åbo Akademi University, Turku, Finland

Martin Montgomery Professor at the Department of English, University of Macau, Zhuhai, China

Tal Morse Instructor in Media Ethics, Hadassah Academic College, Jerusalem, Israel

Susanna Paasonen Professor of Media Studies, University of Turku, Turku, Finland

Angela Smith Professor of Language and Culture, University of Sunderland, Sunderland, UK

Sebastian F. K. Svegaard Doctoral Student, Birmingham Centre for Media and Cultural Research, Birmingham City University, Birmingham, UK

Karin Wahl-Jorgensen Professor at the School of Journalism, Media and Culture, Cardiff University, Cardiff, UK

List of Figures

Fig. 4.1	Poster from Women's March 2018 New York, Central Park (*Source* Instagram)	72
Fig. 4.2	Users commenting on the circulated image from the protest (*Source* Instagram)	76
Fig. 4.3	Photo of protest poster depicting Trump's face as a bottom (*Source* Twitter)	77
Fig. 4.4	"If you don't support DACA you're [caca]". Woman with protest poster, Women's March 2018 New York (*Source* Instagram)	78
Fig. 4.5	"Little bitch you can't fuck with me" (Photo of protest placard posted by Cardi B on Instagram)	81
Fig. 5.1	*Goldendean* (2015) Artwork by Dean Hutton (© Dean Hutton)	98
Fig. 5.2	Fuckwhitepeople at IZIKO Gallery. Sitting in front of the installation that was vandalised and drew hate speech charges from a white separatist party in 2016 (© Dean Hutton)	100

CHAPTER 1

Introduction to Media and the Politics of Offence

Anne Graefer

Thinking about the media and offence is a tricky task because offence is relative. It implies, as Chiara Bucaria and Luca Barra argue, always 'reference to a specific context' (2016, 7): Offensive to whom? In what situation? Furthermore, offence is slippery so that offending others happens not only deliberately but also inadvertently. At the time of writing this book, the media is ripe with content that invites offence. On the one side, there are those who seem to delight in offending others: Right-wing commentator Katie Hopkins, for instance, builds her popularity on her outspoken offensive statements against poor people and immigrants. Former UK Foreign Secretary Boris Johnson writes that Muslim women wearing burkas 'look like letter boxes' and US president Donald Trump rails in interviews and on Twitter against 'politically correct fools' that hold back the country. On the other end of the spectrum are those who claim to offend others inadvertently and go to great lengths to apologise afterwards, hoping to limit the damage that might have been done. Case in point is H&M's press release after the retailer issued a controversial advert which showed a black child wearing a hoodie printed with the

---

A. Graefer (✉)
Birmingham Centre for Media and Cultural Research,
Birmingham City University, Birmingham, UK
e-mail: anne.graefer@bcu.ac.uk

© The Author(s) 2019
A. Graefer (ed.), *Media and the Politics of Offence*,
https://doi.org/10.1007/978-3-030-17574-0_1

slogan: 'coolest monkey in the jungle'. The image was widely criticised online for its reference to a monkey, an animal that has long featured in racial and ethnic slurs. The press release reads:

> [O]ur product and promotion were not intended to cause offence (...) This incident is accidental in nature, but this doesn't mean we don't take it extremely seriously or understand the upset and discomfort it has caused. We have taken down the image and we have removed the garment in question from sale. It will be recycled. (H&M press release after controversial children's sweater promotion, Newsroom, 9 January 2018)

Even though the above examples seem to suggest a clear distinction between deliberate and inadvertent offence, this is not so easy to determine. Claims of non-deliberate or inadvertent offence often depend on willful ignorance. Or claiming to be surprised by offence caused can itself be a political or PR strategy that does not necessarily reflect the fact that the offence was indeed unintended. It may be, for instance, in the interests of corporations and PR campaigns to provoke offence, to the extent that this generates publicity for their product. Thinking about offence requires us, then, to make a distinction between what is intended or not intended, on the one hand, and between the claims made around such discursive acts, on the other.

This book was written in the context of Trump's America, Brexit Britain, and the rise of far-right movements across the globe. A particular point in time where the so-called 'right to offend' is often seen as a legitimate and even necessary weapon against a political correctness that arguably stifles the free speech. This backlash against political correctness creates unusual allegiances: Conservatives, right-wing populists and some white liberal feminists alike, use the media to rail against a generation of 'snowflakes' that depend on political correctness only because they are 'whiny', 'overtly sensitive' and 'too easily offended'.[1] Paradoxically, this is also the point in time where the right to produce or consume 'offensive' media content becomes increasingly policed and diminished through corporations, policy-makers and regulators that rigidly define the borders of appropriate media content (see Paasonen in this volume). These ideas are often based on narrow notions of 'media

---

[1] Paradoxically, political correctness becomes here precisely what offends those who argue that 'generation snowflake' is too easily offended—the claimed 'victims' of political correctness.

effects', where particular media content (such as pornography or violent images) is regarded as inherently harmful. The result is therefore often a call for greater regulation and censorship, independent of viewing context and diversity within audiences (Attwood et al. 2012, 2). Offence is also carefully policed in instances where the discomforting feeling could get in the way of pleasurable consumption or conviviality. Social media giant Facebook, for instance, is increasingly under an ethical and legal pressure to make its platforms Facebook, Instagram and WhatsApp 'positive' and 'safe' spaces where the giving and taking of offence is avoided.[2] Tagg et al. found in their study about offence on social media, that Facebook users *themselves* work hard to avoid offence: Despite the fact that Facebook provides numerous instance where users were likely to be offended (namely, political, religious, sexist or racist opinions with which they disagreed) many strived for online conviviality, that is 'the desire for peaceful coexistence online through negotiating or ignoring difference and avoiding contentious debate' (Tagg et al. 2017, 4). Such considerations illustrate that the media are one crucial channel through which the current 'offence culture' takes shape and is renegotiated.

In order to better understand the current mediated 'offence culture', this book aims to generate a productive dialogue among scholars working in a variety of intellectual disciplines (sociology, cultural studies, media & communications, gender studies, applied linguistics), geographical locations and methodological traditions. Their differences notwithstanding, all the contributors share a concern about the complex and ambiguous nature of offence as well as about the different ways in which this so-called 'negative affect' comes to matter in our everyday and socio-political lives. Through a series of instructive case studies of recent media provocations, the authors illustrate how being offended is more than an individual feeling; indeed, it is closely tied to politics and power relations. For instance, while offending those in power can be seen as a rebellious and liberating practice, offending those who are relatively powerless or subordinated, is often perceived as problematic, since

---

[2] It is important to note here that the company's use of censorship has long been under critique. Many have pointed out that content of breastfeeding mothers or period stains (famously in the work of artist Rupi Kaur) is banned for violating community standards (inappropriate content), while some extreme and white nationalist content was—until very recently—deemed an acceptable form of expression and therefore not censored or removed (BBC News, 2019).

offence is indeed a powerful discursive and affective force that can further exclude and silence marginalised groups.[3]

The following chapters theorise offence not as one distinct emotive state, but rather as a messy affective fabric that encompasses a varied collection of sensations, relations and experiences which shape people's attitudes, opinions, beliefs and perspectives and therefore our social, economic and legal realities. While offence is often seen as a spontaneous, authentic reaction that we feel reflexively when encountering something 'offensive', it is precisely this spontaneity, seemingly without consciousness or will, that requires critical analysis, not least because of its pervasive and largely unquestioned influence on the conduct and quality of our lives. The relationship between offence and affect is here conceived in an elastic manner, acknowledging that embodied sensations, psychic experiences and cognitive understandings are constitutively intertwined in complex ways (Ahmed 2004 as cited in Pedwell 2017). Offence is thereby used as an umbrella term that can encompass such diverse and contradictory emotions and feelings as anger, pain, distress and shock, but also joy, titillation and glee, while also referring to emerging and shifting intensities that escape distinct categorisations. While many chapters in this book draw attention to the emotive and affective site of offence, there is no intent to divert attention away from the analysis of wider structures of power. In other words, the authors of this volume do not understand offence as apolitical or as outside cultural discourses and practices, but rather 'as one important (embodied) circuit through which power is felt, imagined, mediated, negotiated and contested' (Pedwell and Whitehead 2012, 176).

By interrogating the power relations through which offence is produced and mobilised, the different chapters ask: who is the target of offence and who should offend 'us'? Whose feelings matter and feature in the media, and whose feelings are silenced? Other key questions guiding this book are: what makes something offensive, to whom and in what context? Why is offence felt so differently? How can we understand the circulation of offence as an intrinsic part of wider structures of power? And what are some of the critical implications if offence is avoided at all costs? Rather than dismissing offence as an uncomfortable feeling that we need to overcome individually, this collection aims to map some of its

---

[3] Sharon Lockyer and Michael Pickering (2008) make a similar argument of the right to offend and hierarchies in the context of humour.

limiting and mobilising potentialities, and how these in turn animate our social and political lives.

Examining the complex workings of offence is important for understanding the media and processes of mediation because it can tell us a great deal about the construction of social and cultural norms and taboos, the workings of censorship and regulation, and the potential value of discomfort and anger in engaging with provocative media content. Understanding the attention-grabbing power of offence is essential at a time where the scarce commodity of 'attention' is the determining currency of an online media landscape with increasingly abundant and immediately available content.

Theorising and Defining Offence

According to the Oxford Dictionary of English Online (2018), offence originates from the Latin word *offensa*, which translates as transgression, misdeed, injury, wrong, affront. Early attested usage in the fourteenth century indicates four senses of offence that are still in use today: (1) attacking or assailing; (2) causing or experiencing a negative emotional state; (3) moral (and legal) transgression; and (4) the sources of these negative emotional states. These definitions illustrate the multifaceted nature of offence and explain why it has been a keen point of interest for researchers across a wide range of disciplines. Scholars of law, philosophy, moral education and linguistics, as well as of film, media and audience studies, have long theorised offence, but they offer, by default, only a partial understanding of this complex territory, precisely because of the detailed cultural contextualisation that such a 'touchy' issue necessitates.

On an abstract, structural level we could say that offence requires at least two components: the giving and the taking of offence. Yet, as Martin Montgomery et al. point out in this volume, these categories of giving and taking offence are not strictly symmetrical: for example, offence can be taken where none was intended. A case in point would be Kendall Jenner's appearance in a controversial Pepsi advertisement. In the advert, Jenner leaves a photoshoot to join protesters calling for love and peace, before handing a can to police as a peace offering. The officer smiles and the crowd cheers. This was criticised for undermining the Black Lives Matter movement and painting a privileged, white model as a peacemaker between civil rights activists and police. The backlash was so strong that Pepsi pulled the advert less than 24 hours after releasing it. Subsequently, Jenner apologised in tears in an episode of her family's reality television show, *Keeping Up with the Kardashians (season 14 premiere)*, claiming that she never intended to offend or hurt anyone. Independently of how we read this performance (genuine apology or publicity stunt), her words signalled that she had not intended to give offence. But just as offence can be taken where none was intended, offence can also be intended only for none to be taken. These cases are difficult to trace and document, and easier to show are cases where offence has been taken by proxy, on behalf of the ostensible target. For example, 'white' rapper G-Eazy ended his partnership with H&M after its online store featured an image of a black child model wearing a hooded sweatshirt that said, 'coolest monkey in the jungle'. Showing his offence on behalf of the black community, the rapper wrote on Instagram: 'Whether an oblivious oversight or not, it's truly sad and disturbing that in 2018, something so racially and culturally insensitive could pass by the eyes of so many (stylist, photographer, creative and marketing teams) and be deemed acceptable' (g-easy). These examples highlight the complex relationship between the giving and the taking of offence, illustrating that offence does not necessarily have foreseeable effects and consequences.

The elusive nature of offence is often summarised by the truism that almost anything (and nothing) can be offensive or offend someone in a particular context (Tagg et al. 2017; Bucaria and Barra 2016; Das and Graefer 2017). This banal yet pivotal observation has often led to a depoliticisation of offence whereby *feeling offended* is relegated to a question of personal sensibilities that need to be overcome and do not justify *taking offence* (in any formal sense). For instance, in his provocative lecture, *On the Duty of Not Taking Offence*, Robin Barrow has stated that 'people take offence too easily and are encouraged to do so by, e.g., institutional harassment policies' (Barrow 2005). Rather than recognising that registering and sanctioning offence can be a way of challenging systemic oppression and discrimination, Barrow posits that 'the current climate of political and moral correctness has led to a complete failure to make the distinction between what someone finds offensive and what is inherently offensive' (Barrow 2005, 270). In this vein, he challenges the view that 'jokes or unflattering generalizations about ethnic or gender groupings are inherently offensive' and goes as far as to argue that it is 'morally wrong to take offence' in these instances since this is only about *feeling offended* rather than *objectively being offensive*.

Barrow's perspective links to a much longer tradition of conservative and libertarian framings of 'political correctness' and the defence of 'free speech', where offence is sidelined as seemingly not causing direct harm to another individual (Mill 1859). Joel Feinberg's 'offense principle' challenges such understandings by declaring that some forms of offensive behaviour and/or speech are so serious that we can rightly demand legal protection from them even at the cost of other persons' liberties (Feinberg 1985). This is the case when offence, the disliked state of mind (disgust, shame, hurt, anxiety, etc.), is caused by the wrongful (right-violating) conduct of others. From his perspective, it is the wrongful behaviour of others, not the victim's feeling offended, which makes something really offensive: 'It is necessary that there *be* a wrong, but not that the victim *feels* wronged' (1985, 2; emphasis in original).

The question of whether something *is wrong* and therefore *inherently offensive* has longstanding roots within the philosophical study of morality and pragmatics (Haugh 2015; Barrow 2005; Haydon 2006). So, while Barrow posits that not words but rather 'intolerance and suppression of freedom of speech' are inherently offensive, Haydon challenges this essentialist view by pointing out that 'what counts as intolerant (...) or unjustified restriction of freedom, will often if not always be open to interpretation and dispute. Sometimes people will take offence at what they consider to be intolerance towards themselves while an observer will consider that it is the objectors who show intolerance' (Haydon 2006, 26). Thus, rather than invoking a *duty of not taking offence*, he proposes a *duty of educating respect* that regulates offence-giving and enables people 'to judge when it is and when it is not appropriate actively to take offence' (ibid.).[4]

Work on impoliteness (Culpeper 2005, 2011) has focused on the relationship between language and offence, and returns to the same questions as asked within moral education and philosophy: can offence be an inherent function of language? While some scholars have tended to assume that utterances are inherently polite or impolite (such as Herring 1994; Vinagre 2008), others have argued that acts of politeness or impoliteness can only be judged as such with reference to contextual factors such as local communicative norms, speaker intentions and hearer interpretations. Using a number of social-psychological studies, Culpeper

---

[4]Actively taking offence means here to file some sort of formal complaint. Thus, while we often do not have a choice or consciously decide to take offence, 'actively taking offence', i.e. filing a complaint, requires decision-making.

posits, for instance, that the perception of impoliteness is dependent on personal and cultural norms which determine whether or not an utterance or depiction is offensive.

Cultural theorists point out that offence occurs when something is perceived as going beyond the limits of 'acceptability', or transgressing what is deemed 'appropriate' within a specific sociocultural context (Attwood et al. 2012, 3). These notions of what is acceptable and appropriate are culturally constructed and therefore contingent, changing over time and place. Thus, our understanding of what makes something offensive has been, and continues to be, complex and fluid.

Although feeling offended involves a judgement that someone, or a group, has crossed a line, this cognitive appraisal of the situation cannot be separated from our bodily senses. As Haydon notes, 'our sensibilities, even our moral sensibilities, are (as the word suggests) not entirely divorced from our senses' (2006, 22). To illustrate his claim, he argues that we may find the public beheading of an innocent victim immoral (because our moral sensibilities have been by cultural convention educated and developed in this way), but we find it offensive also because of the sight and sound (even in imagination) of the event. The importance of our bodily senses for the experience of offence has also been highlighted by much work in media- and film studies. While some have turned to studies of the abject (Kristeva 1982) and of disgust (Kipnis 1996; Miller 1997) to explore this relationship, others have investigated how so-called 'body genres' (Williams 1991) such as horror films (Halberstam 1995; Laine 2006; Carroll 1980), on-screen violence (Abel 2009; Hill 1997; Schlesinger 1992), pornography (Paasonen 2011) and comedy are experienced as 'offensive' precisely because of the way they depict the body and because they have an arousing or other physical effect on the body.

Furthermore, acts of offence are affective in the sense that they can be felt in the body when they occur. As Lisa Baraitser notes, 'causing (or giving) offence is always tinged with a certain jouissance, and being offensive in public is a political act brimming with psychic investments' (2008, 424; see also Graefer et al. in this volume). Yet registering offence can also go with 'feeling bad', which may include emotions such as displeasure, annoyance, hurt or anger (Haugh 2015, 37; Culpeper 2011, 69). In reaction to hate speech, for instance, the target can experience a state of 'semi-shock', nausea, dizziness or even an inability to articulate a response (Boler 2001, 324–325). As critical race theorist Charles

R. Lawrence III comments, 'The experience of being called a "n**", "spic", "Jap" or "kike" is like receiving a slap in the face. The injury is instantaneous' (quoted in Lloyd 2007, 109). Experiences like these demonstrate not only the performative character of offensive language (generating the abuse and inequality named); they also bring to the fore one of the most significant conundrums in discussions about offence: the tension between the democratic right to speak freely and the right to live in a society where offensive communication is monitored and regulated.

Whereas for some giving and taking offence are simply the price of living in a democratic society, others (especially conservative and populist radical right voices) invoke the right to free speech in order to secure for themselves the right to offend members of minority cultures. But the right to free speech is also claimed, for entirely different reasons, from antipodal ideological positions. In *Excitable Speech* (1997), Judith Butler opposes censorship through state intervention and contends that a politics of resignification is a preferable political strategy for combating linguistic injury because it is vitalised by the instability inherent in all language. For Butler, offensive language such as hate speech does not necessarily have foreseeable consequences (i.e. hurting others), but it can also have other effects, such as providing an opportunity for defiant speech— and it is this defiant speech, not legal regulation, that has the capacity to defuse the power of hate speech. However, Butler also states that new (media) technologies urge us to rethink the limits of 'freedom of speech' because 'new technologies, or new uses of technology, produce new possibilities for incitement, harassment, and the commission of illegal activities' (2017, n.p.), thereby crossing the line between expressive activity and threat.[5]

While some contributors to the present volume explore the possibilities of resignification of offence in different contexts, they also draw attention to the fact that the principle of free speech is deeply mediated by unequal power structures which ensure that not all voices carry the same weight (see, for instance, Kersting in this volume). Thus, it matters who is giving offence and who is the intended or unintended target. As Megan Boler writes,

[5] Judith Butler's blog post was written in the context of Milo Yiannapoulos' planned lecture at UC Berkeley in February 2017. Butler refers here to a previous lecture of Yiannopoulos at the University of Wisconsin-Milwaukee where the writer had posted a photo of Adelaide Kramer, a trans student of the University, on the backdrop screen of his lecture and then not only jeered at her, but encouraged others to do the same.

> Different voices pay different prices for the words one chooses to utter. Some speech results in the speaker being assaulted, or even killed. Other speech is not free in the sense that it is foreclosed: our social and political culture predetermines certain voices and articulations as unrecognisable, illegitimate, unspeakable. Similarly, neither are all expressions of hostility equal. Some hostile voices are penalized while others are tolerated. Hostility that targets marginalised person on the basis of her or his assumed inferiority carries more weight than hostility expressed by a marginalized person towards a member of the dominant class. (Boler 2001, 321)

Similarly, to Joel Feinberg's 'offense principle', referred to above, Boler's considerations suggest that freedom of speech must have limitations in order to enable a free and democratic society.

While the thin line between the right of free speech and offence have been a touchy issue within the realm of politics and ethics, in the corporate world, some media and advertising companies try to profit from playing with the boundaries of offence. For example, in a 2014 Snickers commercial from Australia construction workers shout positive things at passing women, such as 'Have a lovely day', and even chant for gender equality: 'What do we want: equality!' The reason? These men 'aren't themselves' because they are hungry. Humour is supposedly provoked by inverting the classist stereotype that all male manual labourers are by nature prone to sexist behaviour, such as catcalling, and that sexual harassment is actually funny because 'boys will be boys'. This strand of advertising is excused, even celebrated, through recourse to the explanatory power of 'post-PC' irony—the naughty pleasure of returning to the 'good old days' (Gill 2007). And yet the backlash that Pepsi and H&M experienced from the above examples illustrate how offence can damage brand loyalty and the client–agency relationship. It is therefore not surprising that the study of offence has long been a keen point of interest for scholars of advertising and marketing communication (Phau and Prendergast 2009; Christy 2006; Chan et al. 2007; Waller et al. 2013; Barnes and Dotson 2014). Research in these fields has shown that ads may be perceived as offensive due to the nature of the product they depict (condoms, sanitary napkins, etc.) or due to their creative execution (use of derogatory depictions, expletive language or sexual appeals/nudity). Studies have also found that it matters where the advert is displayed (direct mail, internet, outdoor poster or television) and who the audience is. These four offence components need to intersect in particular ways in order to cause or avoid offence. As Christy writes: 'the use of nudity by itself may be offensive to some, but if nudity is used to promote a product associated with sex to certain audiences in a medium that includes sexual content, the likelihood of offense is lessened' (Christy 2006, 16). Empirical studies like these illustrate once again the contextual character of offence.

The importance of context, in the form of genre, audience expectation or viewing situation, for the experience of offence has also been considered in much empirical work in media and audience studies. In media studies, 'offensive material is, in principle, distinguished from that which is illegal (obscenity, child abuse images, incitement to racial hatred, etc.)' (Livingstone and Millwood Hargrave 2009, 26) and media content is judged to be offensive when it contains offensive language, violence or depictions of sexual activity. Intrusive images of suffering, or racist, classist or sexist depictions that contribute to stereotyping or to bias or inaccuracy in news reports and documentaries are also often reported as offending audiences (ibid.). And yet, it remains difficult to define the boundaries in a robust and consensual fashion because of the contextual nature of offence. In *Provocative Screens: Offended Audiences in Britain and Germany* (2017), Ranjana Das and I show that genres such as reality television are perceived as offensive when found in public broadcasting, but as less so when found on private channels where audiences expect low-budget content (see also Das and Graefer in this volume). The importance of context and audience expectation for the experience of offence is also highlighted by Livingstone and Millwood Hargarve who note:

> In the United Kingdom research has shown consistently that context, by which we mean the portrayed context within the programme, is key to the way in which audiences consider content (see also Ofcom's set of contextual variables, Ofcom, 2005). If a violent scene is thought to be editorially justified and appropriate to the scene, or appropriate to the genre, then the audience is far less likely to take offence to that scene, as opinion polls and other qualitative social research show. (2009, 73)

Further, in his work on television comedy programmes and regulation, Brett Mills demonstrates 'how insignificant actual content is compared to the context within which it is placed, for audiences seem to insist that there is no material that is definitively offensive or not, and the appropriateness of comedy is fundamentally affected by the context within which it occurs' (Mills 2016, 214).

Against the backdrop of these considerations, this book aims to engender a nuanced debate about offence in the media and its role in social and political life. Authors of this collection explore the ambivalent force of offence, delineating when meditated offence is debilitating and when it can operate to unsettle normative, ordinary and perhaps comfortable ways of thinking. They offer thereby a corrective to the simplistic, often psychological, theories of media effects that underpin popular journalistic discussions of our interactions with offensive content and illuminate new ways of thinking about offence.

STRUCTURE OF THE BOOK

The book is organised along the three dimensions in which offence has often been theorised: Part I 'Offence, Politics and Protest' explores the role of offence in the public sphere and socio-political protest, Part II 'Offence, Representation and Popular Culture' investigates the equivocal workings of so-called 'offensive' media representations in the context of entertainment and pleasure. Part III 'Offence, Media Ethics and Regulation' is concerned with questions about the visibility and regulation of 'offensive' media content.

The first part of this volume is introduced by Martin Montgomery, Angela Smith and Michael Higgins's Chapter 2 on 'Political Offensiveness in the Mediated Public Sphere: The Performative Play of Alignments'. The authors explore in this chapter developing concerns about the rise of offensiveness in the political public sphere and social media. Through an analysis of political discussions on social media, this chapter contends that the production of offensive discourse in the political domain is enacted within definable 'participation frameworks'. The structured performance of offence is constituted by such key components such Offence Giver, Offence Taker, Target of Offence and Audience. However, these are modulated in late modern societies, such that digitalisation and social media platforms allow re-semiotisation to initiate differences in the terms within frameworks are activated in subsequent reiterations, especially in the transition between private or face-to-face offensiveness or between connected individuals and publicly oriented offensiveness. Moreover, while claims to authenticity dominate in the rationalisation of such offence, its direction against the groups and priorities associated with progressive politics has implications for the conditions of the contemporary public sphere.

Chapter 3, by Karin Wahl-Jorgensen, explores the role of anger and offence in Donald Trump's politics. The chapter argues that Trump's rise heralds a shift in the prevailing 'emotional regime' (Reddy 2001) towards what the author refers to as 'angry populism' that does not shy away from offending. Based on an analysis of the role of anger and offence in media coverage of Trump since his election victory, the chapter shows that the president and his supporters are constructed as essentially angry—often about nothing in particular. The widespread emphasis on Trump's performative anger—and his appeal to an aggrieved public through this anger—has had significant consequences in shaping public debate over the presidency. It suggests the salience of angry populism, implying that anger is a viable interpretive framework for understanding political discourse and its performance. But it also appears to be an 'umbrella emotion', one which covers a wide variety of grievances and disaffections. The chapter suggests that Trump's populist anger is dangerous because it fosters negative and exclusionary feelings (bigotry, intolerance, hate) which are incommensurate with democracy. This, indeed, may explain why Trump's anger and will to offend is newsworthy in and of itself: his anger is seen to be one which closes down constructive debate and invites fascism in through the back door.

In Chapter 4 Allaina Kilby, Inger-Lise Kalviknes-Bore and I investigate the role of 'vulgar' and 'offensive' humour in mediated social protest. Through the example of the 2018 Women's March, the chapter provides insight into the ways in which offensive humour can function as a mobilising force, without glossing over its limitations in the realm of civic engagement. At the Women's March in January 2018 many protest posters featured offensive jokes at the expense of Trump's body and behaviour: images of his signature hairstyle, his 'tiny hands', his 'orange taint', but also more vulgar placards that compared Trump to faeces, were often spotted at protests and shared widely online, much to the amusement of the movement's supporters. Through a close analysis of posts on Instagram and Twitter, we illustrate that the online circulation of humorous (yet offensive) protest posters creates forms of 'polysemic undertow' (Waisanen and Becker 2015, 261) that both contest and confirm normative assumptions about white masculinity and the political public sphere. For this reason, the meanings of these protest posters are not so coherent as to reflect either transgression or backlash politics exclusively. Rather, the contradictory nature of offensive humour holds these circulating online images in tension, thereby enabling what Reilly and Boler (2014) call 'prepoliticization'—a novel form of civic participation that can mobilise citizens who would not otherwise explicitly participate in civic life, thereby creating new political sensibilities and desires.

Chapter 5 extends considerations about the subversive potential of 'offensive' images in the cultural and political context of South Africa. In 'Changing Visual Politics in South Africa: Old and New Modes of Exclusion, Protest and Offence' Marietta Kesting analyses to what extent visual representations of white and black bodies have changed after the official end of apartheid in 1992. Whereas some photographers have long tried to move people with their photographs of suffering black bodies, Kersting argues that nowadays artists use different techniques to move their audiences and instigate political change. Through the artwork of Zanele Muholi and Dean Hutton, two queer artists in South Africa, Kesting asks how their 'offensive' image creations work here as a mode of protest, empowerment and provocation that is significantly different from during the struggle.

Part II, 'Offensive Media Representations', explores the affective and ambiguous workings of 'offensive' media representations in popular culture. Rather than perceiving these representations as merely negative, harmful and limiting, the authors of this section aim to tease out how offence always moves between abjection and affection, and what the potential value of taking offence and feeling offended might be.

In Chapter 6, 'Other Bodies Within Us: Shock, Affect and Reality Television Audiences', Jacob Johanssen draws on Freudian psychoanalysis to analyse some qualitative interview data from a research project on audiences of *Embarrassing Bodies* (Channel 4, UK, 2007–2015). In this medical reality programme patients were diagnosed and treated by a team of doctors. It often featured graphic and detailed surgical sequences, as well as rare or tabooed medical conditions which were shown in front of the camera. The chapter demonstrates that offence, and specifically its articulation, may in some instances function as a defensive act whereby that which offends the speaker is split off from them. For many interviewees, offence thus functioned as a defence mechanism in order not to engage with functions or aspects of the body that we all share or may all potentially be confronted with one day. The chapter further highlights how viewers also took pleasure in feeling shocked, offended and disgusted by what they saw. Johanssen conceptualises such modes of engagement as a perverse form of voyeurism. Rather than only figuring as a way of creating boundaries between audiences and content, such modes of engagement also legitimise the viewing of a programme that may otherwise be ethically problematic or 'trashy'.

Chapter 7 '"Period Sex": *Crazy Ex-Girlfriend* and the Feminist Politics of Offence', by Katrin Horn, extends these considerations about the ambiguous nature of offensive material by analysing the musical dramedy *Crazy Ex-Girlfriend* (CEG). The chapter untangles Crazy Ex-Girlfriend's (The CW, 2015–2019) several strands of crudity and overall offensiveness to make the case for the show's complex commentary on postfeminism and contemporary media culture. Rather than looking at its musical interludes or comic elements as clashing with the show's exploration of feminist issues, the chapter positions these as essential to the biting critique that has made this portmanteau-hyphen television outlier—a female-lead dramedy-cringe-musical series—a critical, if not commercial, success. It outlines the show's critique of 'abject postfeminism,' before tracing its rejection of the romanticising of 'crazy women' in US-American popular culture. Exemplary readings of select scenes detail how the series employs different levels of offence to push the limits of female representation in contemporary television.

Chapter 8, 'Fans at Work: Offence as Motivation for Critical Vidding' by Sebastian F. K. Svegaard, adds another layer to our discussions about mediated offence by illustrating how feeling offended can work in productive ways, enabling a critical reading of mainstream popular culture. Svegaard explores the complex affective quality of vids produced by 'offended' fans. Vids are short remix videos made by fans that show the individual vidder's path through the text. While many of them celebrate the text other seem to critique it quite harshly. Yet, as Svegaard notes, even those critiques are often firmly rooted in feelings of intimacy and connection. Thus, fans can be said to be critiquing with love, their feelings of offence being a response to being let down by a text they are invested in; or, when taking the form of anti-fandom, where dislike of the text is the guiding emotion. Through analysing examples of critical vids, he explores how offence might be considered a motivator for fannish critique, and how this emotion is expressed in these particular cases. The metatext around the vids, such as vidders' comments on their work as well as debate in comment sections on postings, is part of the analysis. Utilising these online responses, this chapter explores the myriad feelings, bodily sensations and emotions used by commentators to describe their feelings of offence at these media texts and the ways in which their expressions of dislike suggest also the pleasures of being outraged. With this the author complicates our understanding about the affective nature of offence by illustrating how it mingles with both disappointment and love.

Part III of this volume 'Offence, Media Ethics and Regulation' is concerned with the ways in which 'offensive' content in the form of pornography, 'trash', or violence and death is regulated, warned about and made visible. Chapter 9, 'Blocked Access: When Pornographers Take Offence' by Susanna Paasonen, investigates the complexities of offence connected to sexuality, politics and sexual politics in the context of contemporary pornography. While pornographers are traditionally assumed to cause, rather than take to offence, porn video aggregator sites, production studios and individual professionals do indeed regularly engage in protests against internet policies and legislative measures connected to sexual equality. In many instances, this has involved porn companies protecting their own financial interests whereas the economic rationale has remained less lucid in others. Focusing on moments of pornographers acting out in protest, this chapter examines the political economy of offence connected to contemporary pornography. It explores how porn companies make use of social media visibility to articulate their case, how their forms of protest function as PR, as well as how the shift of porn distribution to online platforms has changed the political stakes that all this involves.

In Chapter 10, Ranjana Das and I analyse fieldwork with 90 people in the UK and Germany, exploring the expectations audiences articulate about regulatory processes behind television content they find offensive. The chapter demonstrates that, mapping people's responses on to the conceptual pairing of citizens and consumers, audiences tend to align themselves with citizen interests, even when, often on the surface, they respond to media regulation and institutions with suspicion. We illustrate further that complaints that make it to media regulators are just the tip of iceberg as most people do not feel encouraged to complaint. After carefully investigating people's expectations of actors and institutions in their responses to television content that startles, upsets, or just offends them, we note that it is crucial to treat a conversation on free speech and censorship with caution simply because people have very different ideas about what these concepts mean.

In Chapter 11 'Negotiating Vulnerability in the Trigger Warning Debates' Katariina Kyrölä, extends our thinking about offence and regulation by considering the (counter)productivity of trigger warnings. In the last few years, the language and politics of trigger warnings have spread all over the Internet and academic classrooms. The question of whether warnings should be given about content that may be upsetting, offensive or trigger post-traumatic stress responses has been heatedly debated in feminist, queer, and anti-racist discussions online. This chapter examines and contextualises these debates, asking how they both negotiate and generate experiences of vulnerability and agency in relation to controversial media content. The chapter analyses the differences and overlaps between three key sites of the debate: feminist discussion groups where the use of warnings is a required and normalised practice; feminist critique of trigger warnings emphasising the value of negative affect; and anti-feminist online spaces where trigger warnings are ridiculed.

Chapter 12 'Gruesome Images in the Contemporary Israeli Mediated Public Sphere', by Tal Morse, considers how technological changes have influenced Israel's mediated thanatopolitics that is, the different ways in which representations of death have been put to work in the service of political life. Morse argues that these changes require us to rethink our understanding of offensiveness. The chapter traces how the conservative approach of news organisations to protecting those who are dear to 'us' from the offensiveness of gruesome death images has gradually been replaced by a non-journalistic approach that utilises such images in order give offence to 'the Other'. This contemporary practice challenges common perceptions about the offensiveness of death imagery and the ethics of its circulation.

REFERENCES

Abel, Marco. 2009. *Violent Affect: Literature, Cinema and Critique After Representation*. Lincoln: University of Nebraska Press.

Attwood, Feona, Vincent Campbell, and I. Q. Hunter. 2012. *Controversial Images: Media Representations on the Edge*. Basingstoke: Palgrave.

Baraitser, Lisa. 2008. "On Giving and Taking Offence." *Psychoanalysis Culture & Society* 13 (4): 423–427.

Barnes, James H., and Michael J. Dotson. 2014. "An Exploratory Investigation into the Nature of Offensive Television Advertising." *Journal of Advertising* 19 (3): 61–69.

Barrow, Robin. 2005. "On the Duty of Not Taking Offence." *Journal of Moral Education* 34 (3): 265–275.

Boler, Megan. 2001. "All Speech Is Not Free: The Ethics of Affirmative Action Pedagogy." In *Philosophy of Education 2000*, edited by Lynda Stone, 321–329. Urbana, IL: Philosophy of Education Society.

Bucaria, Chiara, and Luca Barra, eds. 2016. *Taboo Comedy: Television and Controversial Humour*. London: Palgrave Macmillan.

Butler, Judith. 1997. *Excitable Speech: A Politics of the Performative*. New York: Routledge.

Butler, Judith. 2017. "Limits on Free Speech?" *Academe Blog*, December 7. https://academeblog.org/2017/12/07/free-expression-or-harassment/.

Carroll, Noel. 1980. *The Philosophy of Horror or Paradoxes of the Heart*. New York: Routledge.

Chan, Kara, Lyann Li, Sandra Diehl, and Ralf Terlutter. 2007. "Consumers' Response to Offensive Advertising: A Cross Cultural Study." *International Marketing Review* 24 (5): 606–628.

Christy, Timothy P. 2006. "Females' Perceptions of Offensive Advertising: The Importance of Values, Expectations, and Control." *Journal of Current Issues & Research in Advertising* 28 (2): 15–32.

Culpeper, Jonathan. 2005. "Impoliteness and Entertainment in the Television Quiz Show: The Weakest Link." *Journal of Politeness Research: Language, Behaviour, Culture* 1 (1): 35–72.

Culpeper, Jonathan. 2011. *Impoliteness: Using Language to Cause Offence*. Cambridge: Cambridge University Press.

Das, Ranjana, and Anne Graefer. 2017. *Provocative Screens: Offended Audiences in Britain and Germany*. Cham, Switzerland: Palgrave Macmillan.

Feinberg, Joel. 1985. *Offense to Others: The Moral Limits of the Criminal Law*. Oxford: Oxford University Press.

Gill, Rosalind. 2007. "Postfeminist Media Culture: Elements of a Sensibility." *European Journal of Cultural Studies* 10 (2): 147–171.

Halberstam, Jack. 1995. *Skin Shows: Gothic Horror and the Technology of Monsters*. Durham: Duke University Press.

Haugh, Michael. 2015. "Impoliteness and Taking Offence in Initial Interactions." *Journal of Pragmatics* 86: 36–42.

Haydon, Graham. 2006. "On the Duty of Educating Respect: A Response to Robin Barrow." *Journal of Moral Education* 35 (1): 19–32.

Herring, Susan C. 1994. "Politeness in Computer Culture: Why Women Thank and Men Flame." In *Cultural Performances: Proceedings of the Third Berkeley Women and Language Conference*, edited by Mary Bucholtz, Anita Liang, Laurel Sutton, and Caitlin Hines, 278–294. Berkeley, CA: Woman and Language group.

Hill, Annette. 1997. *Shocking Entertainment: Viewer Response to Violent Movies*. Luton: University of Luton Press.

Kipnis, Laura. 1996. *Bound and Gagged: Pornography and the Politics of Fantasy in America*. New York: Grove Press.

Kristeva, Julia. 1982. *Powers of Horror: An Essay on Abjection*. New York: Columbia University Press.

Laine, Tarja. 2006. "Cinema as Second Skin." *New Review of Film and Television Studies* 4 (2): 93–106.

Livingstone, Sonia, and Andrea Millwood Hargrave. 2009. *Harm and Offence in Media Content: A Review of the Evidence: LSE Research Online*. Bristol: Intellect.

Lloyd, Moya. 2007. *Judith Butler. From Norms to Politics*. Cambridge: Polity Press.

Lockyer, Sharon, and Michael Pickering. 2008. "You Must Be Joking: The Sociological Critique of Humour and Comic Media." *Sociology Compass* 2 (3): 808–820.

Mill, John Stuart. 1859. *On Liberty*. Oxford: Oxford University Press.

Miller, William. 1997. *The Anatomy of Disgust*. Cambridge and London: Harvard University Press.

Mills, Brett. 2016. "A Special Freedom: Regulating Comedy Offence." In *Taboo Comedy: Television and Controversial Humour*, edited by Chiara Bucaria and Luca Barra, 209–227. London: Palgrave Macmillan.

Paasonen, Susanna. 2011. *Carnal Resonance: Affect and Online Pornography*. Cambridge and London: MIT Press.

Pedwell, Caroline. 2017. "Mediated Habits: Images, Networked Affect and Social Change." *Subjectivity* 10 (2): 147–169.

Pedwell, Caroline, and Anne Whitehead. 2012. "Affecting Feminism: Questions of Feeling in Feminist Theory." *Feminist Theory* 13 (2): 115–129.

Phau, Ian, and Gerard Prendergast. 2009. "Offensive Advertising: A View from Singapore." *Journal of Promotion Management* 7 (1–2): 71–90.

Reddy, William M. 2001. *The Navigation of Feeling: A Framework for the History of Emotions*. Cambridge: Cambridge University Press.

Reilly, Ian, and Megan Boler. 2014. "The Rally to Restore Sanity, Pre-Politicization and the Future of Politics." *Communication, Culture & Critique* 7 (2): 435–452.

Schlesinger, Philip. 1992. *Women Viewing Violence*. London: British Film Institute.

Tagg, Caroline, Philip Seargeant, and Amy Aisha Brown. 2017. *Taking Offence on Social Media: Conviviality and Communication on Facebook*. Cham, Switzerland: Palgrave Macmillan.

Vinagre, M. 2008. Politeness Strategies in Collaborative E-mail Exchanges. *Computers & Education* 50 (3): 1022–1036.

Waisanen, Don J., and Amy B. Becker. 2015. "The Problem with Being Joe Biden: Political Comedy and Circulating Personae." *Critical Studies in Media Communication* 32 (4): 256–271.

Waller, David S., Sameer Deshpande, and B. Zafer Erdogan. 2013. "Offensiveness of Advertising with Violent Image Appeal: A Cross-Cultural Study." *Journal of Promotion Management* 19 (4): 400–417.

Williams, Linda. 1991. "Film Bodies: Gender, Genre and Excess." *Film Quarterly* 44 (4): 2–13.

PART I

Offence, Politics and Protest

CHAPTER 2

Political Offensiveness in the Mediated Public Sphere: The Performative Play of Alignments

Martin Montgomery, Michael Higgins and Angela Smith

INTRODUCTION

This chapter explores developing concerns about the rise of offensiveness in the political public sphere and more especially in social media. We argue that current iterations of purposeful political offence should be considered in the context of a number of factors. One is the ascendency of short-form social media such as Twitter and Instagram, which disperse and fragment the discourse of political elites, enabling multi-articulated tactics of address that are subject to processes of remediation. A second factor is the rise of "post-truth" politics (Montgomery 2017), in which

M. Montgomery
University of Macau, Zhuhai, China
e-mail: mmontgomery@umac.mo

M. Higgins (✉)
University of Strathclyde, Glasgow, UK
e-mail: michael.higgins@strath.ac.uk

A. Smith
University of Sunderland, Sunderland, UK
e-mail: angela.smith@sunderland.ac.uk

© The Author(s) 2019
A. Graefer (ed.), *Media and the Politics of Offence*,
https://doi.org/10.1007/978-3-030-17574-0_2

impressions of personal authenticity take the place of facts, and truth becomes less important than "speaking your mind". Finally, however, we suggest that several significant cases of political offence take form and shape along an axis between "authentic" expression (or "speaking your mind") and submission to political correctness.

Offence and offensiveness, of course, just like notions of "fake news" or "impoliteness", are difficult categories to define (see, for example, Wardle 2017; Culpeper 2011). In the case of offence, most commentators stress its situated character. Here, for instance, is Culpeper (2011, 23) on impoliteness and the language of offence.

Impoliteness is a negative attitude towards specific behaviours occurring in specific contexts. It is sustained by expectations, desires and/or beliefs about social organisation, including, in particular, how one person's or group's identities are mediated by others in interaction. Situated behaviours are viewed negatively when they conflict with how one expects them to be, how one wants them to be and/or how one thinks they ought to be. Such behaviours always have or are presumed to have emotional consequences for at least one participant, that is, they cause or are presumed to cause offence.

In order to recognise the situated character of impoliteness and offence, Culpeper's definition is obliged to work at a high level of abstraction. We choose a different route—to build up an account of offence in specific contexts at a specific historical juncture by considering a series of incidents or cases. In so doing, we suggest that the production of offensive discourse in the political domain is routinely enacted within what Goffman (1981) refers to as "participation frameworks". We wish to argue, indeed, that there is a structure to offence in the public sphere—but that this is modulated in the subtle contrasts between publicly oriented offensiveness, particularly using media, and private or face-to-face offensiveness between connected individuals, stemming from important differences between their associated participation frameworks.

Offence, Insult and Participation Frameworks

As a starting point for considering the anatomy of verbal offence it is useful to return to Labov's seminal account of "Rules for Ritual Insults" (1972). In brief, Labov showed how members of a teenage group could say gratuitously offensive things to one other, but if what was said conformed to the rules of the game—thereby observing its ritual qualities—group members avoided outright conflict and its consequential violence.

One element of the ritual required that the insult—the offence—ought to be untrue, even fanciful: indeed, the nearer it got to mundane reality the more likely it was to be judged lame. This creative elaboration would be further mitigated by the use of standard formats for the insult itself, as well as by recurring types of contextual reference. Thus the insulter would commonly comment (in an ostensibly misogynistic fashion) on the insulted's mother and her sexual history, sometimes even claiming to have engaged in sexual relations with her. Insults would be exchanged in rounds with as many as 30 in a 35-minute session, hence alternative titles such as "sounding", "signifying" and "playing the dozens". Within this arrangement, a skilful perpetrator of the art would gain a strong position within the group.

Success would be a matter of assessment, of course, and judgment was externalised and vocalised in the context through the role of the audience, comprising other members of the group. The assessment therefore takes place within what Goffman (1981, 3) calls a "participation framework" in which we can identify at least three participants: (i) the insulter; (ii) the insulted; and (iii) the immediately present audience—or evaluators. As members of the same "participation framework", those occupying these participant roles assent to the rules of the "interactional environment" (Goffman 1981, 153) of the exchange: viz. that the insults are to be ornate and incredible, and that no sincere face threat is intended to the "insulted" party.

The kind of offensiveness in which we are interested differs, of course, from those in Labov's account in various significant ways. For one thing we are primarily interested in offensiveness in the mediated public sphere involving large (though potentially fragmented) audiences with the more complex participation framework that this inevitably entails. Following from this, most of our examples are written rather than spoken. And in the context of social media, at least, this may allow a degree of anonymity in the production and delivery of offence. Unlike Labov we are interested ultimately in utterances which really give offence rather than utterances which are designed to simulate characteristics of offensiveness but where the apparent offensiveness is mitigated by the rules of the game (hence, "rules for ritual insults"). In this way, we are mostly interested in what might be designated deliberate rather than inadvertent offence. A further complication here lies in the possibility, through writing and digital recording, of the re-tweeting (for example) and the recontextualisation and indeed what Iedema (2003) refers to as the resemiotisation of messages. What might have begun as an example of inadvertent offence can be deliberately recontextualised or resemiotised to foreground its potential for offence.

In order, therefore, to clarify the structure of offence in the public sphere, it is possible—building on Goffman (1981) and Labov (1972)—to situate it within a participatory framework in the following terms. At the heart of an act of verbal offence (rather than a ritual insult) we may find the following components:

a. An Offence Giver (one who issues offence);
b. An Offence Taker (which may be an individual or a group);

We should note, immediately, that "Giving Offence" and "Taking Offence" are potentially fuzzy categories that are in any case sensitive to situation and subject to resemiotisation, in ways that we explore later. Nor are the categories of giving and taking offence strictly symmetrical: for instance, offence can be taken where none was intended. The Deputy Governor of the Bank of England, Ben Broadbent, for example, was quoted in an interview in May 2018 in the *Daily Telegraph*, describing the rather lacklustre state of the British economy as "menopausal" —"past its productive peak": "The word 'climacteric' is, according to Mr Broadbent," as reported in the *Daily Telegraph*, "a term that economists have borrowed from biology and means "you've passed your productive peak". It has the same Latin roots as "climax" and means "menopausal" but it applies to both genders", he said. The Deputy Governor was very soon forced to issue a public apology for his poor choice of words saying "how sorry I am for the offence my interview this morning has caused to Bank colleagues", not to mention the general public. Clearly, he had not anticipated the effect of his original choice of words, and so—we may reasonably surmise—had not intended to give offence. The offence, as it were, was discovered in the act rather than intended.

By the same token, just as offence can be taken when none was intended, so also, in theory, can offence be intended, only for none to be taken, though documentary cases of the latter are more difficult to retrieve.

c. A Target of Offence

The *Target* may be implicit or explicit; it may comprise an individual object of the offence—one who may or may not take offence; but most importantly it may include within its focus an abstract set of attitudes or values representative of a way of thinking belonging to, or identified with, a social group (as we shall see later in the in relation to "political correctness").

d. An Audience, or Public

The *Audience* (Audiences or Publics) in practice will be likely to include differing alignments to the offence, divided principally between those that align alongside the Target against the offence and those who align with the *Offence Giver* against the *Target*. This division is most likely where the context or situation is already agonistic—for instance in the context of political campaigning. Segments of the *Audience* may, alternatively, be simply indifferent. Audiences, therefore, may occupy any of at least three positions: A1 (align with the Target against the Offence); A2 (align with the *Offence Giver* against the *Target*); A3 (non-aligned ambient affiliation).

This provides us with the rudimentary outline of the components of a structural or participation framework for understanding the dynamics of offence. We must note immediately, however, that the structural composition of the framework for offence needs to allow for the negotiation or contestation of positions within it. For instance, Mark Meechan—a person with an emerging reputation as a stand-up comic—was prosecuted under Scots law for the crime of hate speech, having posted on YouTube a video (viewed more than 3 million times) of his girlfriend's pet dog, Buddha, responding to the command, "Hey Buddha, gas the Jews" by giving a Nazi salute with its paw. In Meechan's defence he claimed no intention to give offence, and that it was a joke merely to annoy his girlfriend. In sentencing, the Sheriff declared otherwise: "The fact that you claim in the video, and elsewhere, that the video was intended only to annoy your girlfriend and as a joke and that you did not intend to be racist is of little assistance to you. A joke can be grossly offensive. A racist joke or a grossly offensive video does not lose its racist or grossly offensive quality merely because the maker asserts he only wanted to get a laugh". Thus, Meechan was claiming one kind of position for his act, which the Sheriff emphatically rejected.

It is, in passing, worthy of note that an alternative line of defence, offered on Meechan's behalf by other comedians such as Ricky Gervais, claimed rights of free speech for the video: "If you don't believe in a person's right to say things that you might find "grossly offensive", then you don't believe in Freedom of Speech." Or as Rowan Atkinson had put it earlier in the context of jokes about religion (specifically Islam): "the right to offend is far more important than any right not to be offended"—a claim he was to revive subsequently in defence of former UK Foreign Secretary, Boris Johnson. "All jokes about religion cause offence, so it's pointless apologising for them".

Offence and Political Correctness

We can see, therefore, the basic components through which offensiveness is performed and offence may be taken. In this section, we begin to look at this broader cultural context of political offence in media, and in particular how judgements over offence are claimed and contested, by looking at the development and use of political correctness. One significant feature of Trump's presidential campaign and his subsequent presidency has been his predeliction for offence (Montgomery 2017), and this quite deliberately set off in counterpoint to norms of political correctness.

"I think the big problem this country has is being politically correct", said Trump in 2015.

Or as Ivanka Trump observed when introducing her father at the event when he announced his run for the presidency:

"My father is the opposite of politically correct. He says what he means and he means what he says," Ivanka Trump 2015.

Political correctness (or "PC", to give it its popular acronym) has, however, a convoluted history. Perry traces the first printed citation of the term to a 1970 article by Toni Cade on sexism in black politics, in which it is asserted that "a man cannot be politically correct and chauvinist too" (cited in Perry 1992, 73). While this presents political correctness as a positive attribute, Perry (1992, 77) writes that "no sooner was [PC] invoked as a genuine standard for socio-political practice […] than it was mocked as purist, ideologically rigid, and authoritarian". And it was on the basis of this reactionary reinterpretation that PC came to embody the struggle between representation and political and cultural power. Suhr and Johnson comment that:

'Political correctness' was blamed for all the ills perceived in British society: for some it was the hegemony of politically correct thinking, which had rung in a new era of 'mock' politeness and led to a generation paralysed by a fear of denting the all too fragile egos of anyone who might belong to a so-called minority group. For others, 'PC' was to blame for stifling the 'real' debates and conflicts which must be allowed to surface if we are to have any hope of progressing towards a more truly egalitarian society. (Suhr and Johnson 2003, 5)

Fairclough (2003, 21) claims that this labelling is in itself "a form of cultural politics, an intervention to change representations, values and identities" in the way they pursue or confound social development. Although PC has had implications for a variety of political positions, from the perspective of the reactionary right in particular it "has been held responsible for every imaginable form of restriction, well beyond concerns about racism and sexism" (Talbot 2007, 756). Cameron (1994, 127) describes a "discursive drift", in which PC moves beyond its specialist meaning to become a catch-all phrase for the restriction of expression by the mainly bureaucratic forces of aggressive social liberalism. As a consequence, Talbot (2007, 759) argues, PC became a "snarl word" cloaked in negativity or irony and associated with the politics of restriction and exaggeration.

The history of how hostility to political correctness developed in Britain in particular is complex—a subtle interweaving of cultural politics with struggles over the form and shape of governance. In the early 1980s, at the height of Margaret Thatcher's push to dismantle and decentralise larger urban authorities, the Greater London Council (GLC, the largest and wealthiest local government in the UK at the time) was run by mayor "Red" Ken Livingstone. Livingstone's GLC was characterised by a strong socialist agenda which embraced issues of gender and race equality. Many policies directly challenged the agenda of Thatcher's Conservative government, and in a Tory-friendly media, were branded as irrational or detrimental to national values. The GLC was eventually disbanded by the Thatcher government of 1986, but the legacy of their popular press characterisation as the "loony left" continues to this day in terms of the tropes it throws up. Among the "urban legends", for instance, propagated by the right-wing print media in the 1980s include those such as the over-enthusiastic, anti-racist primary school teachers who were reported to have banned the nursery rhyme Baa, Baa, Black

Sheep (Cameron 1994, 117). As Stuart Hall comments, such vexatious reports were difficult to counter because "there was just enough truth in the stories in a few instances to sustain media amplification" (1994, 173), a feature still recurrent in anti-PC stories today.

Beyond the UK too, in its 1980s manifestation, political correctness became a part of a political struggle against political dominance of the reactionary right wing, and hostility towards and ridicule of political correctness became part of the right-wing armoury.

With America in the grip of a sustained period of right-wing government, preaching aggressive free market economics and reduced government welfare, issues of race and gender (issues always associated with the left) had been more or less knocked off the political agenda. PC, both on and off campus, has helped to put them back on (Dunant 1994).

In 2018, we can see this right-wing political thinking once again coming to the fore, in a context in which Dunant links political correctness with an excessive concentration of the effect of language on the sensitivities of minority groups, rather than on the "real" important issues at hand. In a manner that we will examine in more detail below, these correlations with the regulation of language links political correctness with the elevation of "face work" and value good manners over spontaneity and sincerity of expression. In this regard, political correctness has parallels with the forms of civility and courtliness identified by Higgins and Smith (2017) as emblematic of an overly tactical approach to public discourse, and that provide a foil for a less polished and more relatable mode of public talk. It also, however, has come to stand in contrast not just with authenticity and sincerity but also with free speech. Against the stultifying mores of political correctness, the right to speak one's mind and say what one means becomes a badge of honour. What begins and takes shape as a move to champion the rights of minorities, of the marginalised, or of those excluded from power, ends up being regarded as a repressive tool of the elites. One way in which to challenge the rubrics of PC is precisely through acts of offence in which the offence giver speaks his or her mind and reclaims the ancestral rights to free speech.

OFFENCE AS A COLLECTIVE ACTIVITY

In this way, acts of offence, especially those that flout political correctness, readily articulate with countervailing discourses of collectivity and mutual belonging. Indeed, the association between truculent spontaneity and authentic speech ranges from the "righteous indignation" of populist performance (Higgins 2013) to Trump's misogynist language of the "locker room". These forms of authenticity carry claims to certain kinds of group solidarity, so that in the very act of alienating the progressive left, as well as those minorities that political correctness was intended to protect, an appeal to like-minded associates is simultaneously projected. Thus, offence as a collective activity produces a double alignment.

SITUATIONAL SENSITIVITIES AND THE PUBLIC VERSUS THE PRIVATE

In terms of the major distinctions in context of situation relating to the performance of offence, perhaps the most critical but unstable distinction in late modernity lies between the public and the private. Feminism may have justifiably declared that the personal is political but examples of mediated, politically charged, offensiveness typically depend upon the eruption in the public domain of discourses that might have circulated in semi-private contexts relatively unchallenged—or even endorsed by micro-collectivities. This is especially so in the age of digital media which has enhanced what Thompson (2005) identifies as transformations in the character of media visibility, and its implications for the uneven boundary between public and private. Thompson (2005, 121) argues that the late modern period saw an association between public life and a state-centred subjectivity. In a manner that contrasts with the more recent developments described above, this lent itself to what Peters (1995) describes as a set of performative expectations around public conduct, dedicated to the display of responsible citizenship and respectability. Entailed is what Weintraub (1997) describes as a complementary notion of privacy, where localised, personal activities are insulated from state surveillance and the domain of the domestic and the family remains detached from the public realm. This has been replaced, Thompson suggests, by a new form of "mediated publicness", which extends access to public and political events in a manner that admits the images of public life into the personal sphere. The implications for political figures are clear.

Today the careful presentation of self before the distant others whose allegiance must be constantly nourished, and whose support is vitally required from time to time, is not so much an option as an imperative for actual or aspiring political leaders and their parties. In the social and political conditions of the late twentieth century, politicians in liberal-democratic societies have little choice but to submit to the laws of compulsory visibility (Thompson 1995, 137).

As we approach the end of the second decade of the twenty-first century, the responsibilities and expectations of this "compulsory visibility" in the construction of self have multiplied. Politicians' use of media to introduce the "real", unpolished self of the private domestic sphere can be traced to Franklin D. Roosevelt's "fireside chat" radio broadcasts in the 1930s and 40s (Enli 2015, 109) and have merged with broader discourses of the popular through such staged events as Bill Clinton's use of prime-time chat shows (Drake and Higgins 2006). In looking at how public figures manage these expectations, Enli (2015, 111) alights on the notion of "performed authenticity" as a way of understanding the relationship between these forms of media engagement and the expectation that they will reveal something of the private individual behind the public face. In keeping with recent analysis of the presentation of the personal lives of politicians and their families (Higgins and Smith 2013; Smith 2016), Enli (2015) also notes that the introduction of social and participatory media into political campaigning has elevated this responsibility to project an authentic self from a weapon in the armoury cultural politics to an essential strand of the political campaign (Montgomery 2017).

However, as Thompson (2005, 39) argues, this extension of visibility moves further along a continuum that produces risk as well as opportunity for those in public life. In looking to what he describes as the "new visibility" that characterises an increasingly complex, interactional and democratised media environment, Thompson (2005, 49) argues that events are not just driven by the images and backroom glimpses of visibility, but are often constituted by them. And, as the management of image and notions of authenticity become more prominent components of politics (Lyon 2002; Kreiss and Howard 2010), activities such as "scandal mining" (Trottier 2017b) come into play, so that potentially consequential images and statements by political figures are sought out and released into public discourse in order to generate political outrage. This is particularly so in the first of our illustrative cases to which we now turn.

The "Private Correspondence Made Public" Offence

In this section, we consider an example from the UK where offensive remarks that circulated in the first instance semi-privately are subsequently recontextualised in the public realm in such a way that foregrounds and highlights their offensiveness. This case of "resemiotisation" (Iedema 2003) or "remediation" Trottier (2017b)—taking an item of discourse out of one interpretative context and placing it in one where the meanings derived are likely to be different—bears some comparison in its structural characteristics with the leaked audio tape of then-presidential candidate Donald Trump boasting that his fame enabled him to grab women "by the pussy". And in both cases we can see aspects of those "talk scandals" described by Ekstrom and Johansson (2008), where material is mined and cast into the public eye generating a "digital vigilantism" designed to breach "on-/offline" or front/back stage distinctions for political gain (Trottier 2017a).

The scope for the emergence of such material is far greater now than before since the democratisation of communication platforms widens access to a variety of actors in the political realm. These include those lobbyists and public relations agencies that Habermas (1989) would have considered predatory colonisers of public discourse, who, by means of social media in particular, now share the same platforms as senior politicians and policy-makers. Other actors who enjoy an enhanced place in political discourse range from single-issue advocates to ordinarily disinterested members of the voting public. Extending the dangers to public figures highlighted by Thompson (2005) and Brighenti (2007), all of these are subject to parallel risks around political visibility, where breaches of acceptable conduct can offend the norms of political propriety. To take the example of non-conventional political actors, interventions into the political field by non-elected Twitter users can be characterised as "trolling" if they are seen as antagonistic, overly contentious or designed to cause offence.

The example we consider is that of Jo Marney who at the time was the partner of then-leader of the right-wing United Kingdom Independence Party (UKIP), Henry Bolton. In January 2018, a number of Marney's texts and Facebook posts were made available to the news media. Those to excite most public attention were a series of text messages concerning the then-fiancé of Prince Harry, Meghan Markle, from which this sequence of text messages is taken:

> She's a 'gender equality t***
> She's obsessed with race
> And her seed with [sic] taint our royal family.
> Just a dumb little commoner. Tiny little brain.

> She's black.
> A dumb little 'actress' that no one has heard of.
> This is Britain, not Africa. (quoted in Owen, *Mail Online*, 13 January 2018)

These comments, on their publication in the *Mail Online*, were widely deemed to be offensive in their use of highly charged negative descriptors ("tart", "dumb little commoner", "tiny little brain", "dumb little actress"—note the repeated use of "little") and in their negative references to Markle's ethnic background, with particular attention to her racial characteristics ("she's black"), which might come to "taint the royal family". In subsequent posts, racial prejudice is expressed in terms of a denial of personal animosity and is further combined with a classic trope (in the politics of race and immigration) about "invasion":

> Not wanting other faces and cultures to invade your own culture doesn't mean I hate their race. Just means I don't want their cultures invading mine.
> Just don't like her.

One feature worth noting in the context of these ostensibly racist and sexist remarks is the use of "just" as a minimiser: "just a little commoner"; "just means I don't want their cultures invading mine"; and finally "just don't like her". The combined effect of these choices—the uses of "just", for instance, and "little"—is to present the opinions expressed as unremarkable, ordinary matters of personal opinion, consonant with the private realm and not articulated as weighty and rationally founded public commentary.

However, the point at which the messages from Marney move from the relatively private or semi-private domain of texting to operate in the public realm is when the core components of the structural framework for offence come into play: it remains consistent that Marney is the Offence Giver and Markle is the Target, but the recipient(s) of the messages as the Audience is now much broader and diverse in their interpretative position than originally conceived by Marney as Offence Giver.

Indeed, the Audience, becomes vastly extended and differentiated or fragmented, for it is not just the *Mail Online* that remediates the material: it is in turn further remediated on social media and broadcast news. There are clearly divisions in the kind of response which Marney's comments evoke. In the event, and reflecting the much-expanded

Audience, most public commentary aligned emphatically with the *Target* and against the *Offence Giver*.

Of course, objectionable as these views may be in themselves, the basis for their publication for a wider audience in mainstream newspapers was Marney's association with the leader of a political party, with specific implications for Henry Bolton's own views and personal judgement in maintaining their relationship. Similarly, comments on Marney's Facebook page relating immigration to a fire in a block of flats in London (Bennett, *Huffington Post*, 2018) were intended for and originally available only to those admitted as Facebook friends. However, in relation to the remediation of this correspondence as it makes its way into the broader and more visible public realm, Marney tries to reframe her views as part of a legitimate public discussion, saying:

> The language I used was not good, not good at all. I didn't mean to cause offence but I think in a wider, broader context of the things that I said these are things that we need to be discussing. (quoted in Bennett, *Huffington Post*, 2018)

Her response to criticism, therefore, has two dimensions. Firstly, she regrets her poor choice of language (rather like Deputy Governor of the Bank of England). But, secondly, she claims to be highlighting issues of legitimate public concern ("things that we need to be discussing"). Whether successful or not in ameliorating the offence caused by a series of statements intended to be kept private, Marney's response rests upon the instinctive hostility to immigration characteristic of that right-wing populism to typify the post-truth political environment. But, crucially perhaps, the justification made necessary by the reconfigured participation framework produces a variant of the *Offence Giver* merely "speaking her mind" with echoes of the defence invoking freedom of speech.

Offence and Resemiotisation

This next section looks at a more clear-cut example of where what we have referred to as "scandal mining" (Trottier 2017b) is used in order to expose instances of offensiveness by a figure already in the public eye. Here, it is useful again to draw upon Iedema (2003) and the Scollons's (2003) notion of resemiotisation. According to Iedema and Scollon, discourse can be transferred from one setting or mode to another, sometimes to preserve the meaning, but on other occasions in a way that significantly alters its impact or force.

The example we will look at is that of Toby Young. Young has worked as journalist and reviewer since the early 1990s. He started as co-founder of the Modern Review, and has most recently been associate editor of conservative current and social affairs magazine *The Spectator*. Young also enjoyed public prominence as the author of the autobiographical memoir *How to Lose Friends and Alienate People* in 2001. More recently, he became associated with the campaign for "free schools" to be established and run by parents with minimal state interference. It was on the basis of this experience and his apparent credentials in the philosophy and practice of secondary education that Young was announced as a non-executive member of an Office for Students, set up by the UK Government as a mechanism to oversee the conduct and performance of English and Welsh universities.

Young's appointment to this position occasioned immediate controversy. This was initially motivated by Young's commitment to the free market in the delivery of education at school level, and were therefore directed at the ideological commitments associated with Young's chosen political persona, what we have described as a state-centred subjectivity (Thompson 1995). However, critical commentary soon turned to Young's Twitter account, and a number of tweets were identified that were deemed to be offensive. Among the tweets that most caught the public eye are those reproduced below, including ones which feature a performance of misogyny as a particular form of laddish "banter":

> *Example 1* Top Chef announced. Elegant pub pic, @toadmeister's hand on Padma's bottom, Padma looks surprised but pleased http://tinyurl.com/ndu5dd. (@BarryJl)
> Replying to @BarryJl
> @BarryJL Actually, mate, I had my dick up her arse (@toadmeister)
>
> *Example 2* What happened to [Claudia] Winkleman's breasts? Put on some weight, girlie. (@toadmeister)
>
> *Example 3* Serious cleavage behind Ed Miliband's head. Anyone know who it belongs to? (@toadmeister)

This series of tweets perform a classic sexist manoeuvre of reducing women to their body parts: Padma's bottom or arse; Winkleman's breasts; an unnamed MP's cleavage (presumably a woman rather than a man). In Toby Young's first tweet, the offensiveness is accentuated by building on Isaacson's prior suggestion that a publicity picture seems to show Young's "hand on Padma's bottom" (who, it is claimed, looks "surprised but pleased"). Young, then, "doubles down" on this suggestion by correcting it: "Actually, mate, I had my dick up her arse"—rather in the manner of Labov's ritual insults among teenage boys.

Broadly, the structural framework of offence for these tweets consists of Young as the laddish ('humourous') *Offence Giver* and women, identified in terms of their body parts, as Targets for Offence. The *Audience* for this is layered and complex. In some cases there is a defined addressee—for instance, Barry Isaacson, or even Winkelman herself ("put on some weight, girlie"). And in the case of Isaacson, and other members of the associated in-group, it is noticeable that there is a familiar and conversational mode of address: "mate", "anyone know who it [the cleavage] belongs to?". More generally, the conventional implication of this is that there will be a self-selected group of followers for these tweets who can be expected to align with the tweets as laddish humour as much as acts of offence. But there will also be an *Audience*, not necessarily aligned, who relate to the material in a state of what Zappavignana (2011) describes as "ambient affiliation". And in common with the mediated messages in the example above, this is subject to shift. At the time when the tweets were first made the ambient audience on Twitter may have been much smaller than it subsequently became as Twitter moved from 30 million active participants per week to 370 million per week seven years later.

In the context of Young's proposed elevation to the Office of Students, however, Young's conduct on Twitter—driven again by "scandal mining"—occupied a different interpretative field in which their crude sexism appeared at odds with the decorousness and decency necessary for public office. Thus, their offensiveness became foregrounded in the process of resemiotisation by diffusion through traditional media outlets—press and broadcasting—and the extension of the participation framework to the public at large.

Of course, public discourse around the tweets took place in the context of a decades-long shift against political correctness. Critical discussion of Young's tweets and journalism therefore focused on the validity of his role as contrarian, adopting positions designed to inflame liberal sensibilities and taking great pleasure in offending as many people as possible "while guffawing about political correctness" (Foster, *The Guardian*, 2018). Other criticism focused on the seeming inconsistency deleting those tweets that had previously been celebrated as examples of free speech and authenticity (Cowburn, *The Independent*, 2018).

From a defensive position, Young's regression into old-school masculinity forms part of a more general move against the perceived progressiveness of previous governments, as found in this 2012 article for *The Spectator*:

> Inclusive. It's one of those ghastly, politically correct words that have survived the demise of New Labour. Schools have got to be 'inclusive' these days. That means wheelchair ramps, the complete works of Alice Walker in the school library (though no Mark Twain) and a Special Educational Needs Department that can cope with everything from dyslexia to Münchausen syndrome by proxy. If [then education secretary, Michael] Gove is serious about wanting to bring back O-levels, the government will have to repeal the Equalities Act because any exam that isn't 'accessible' to a functionally illiterate troglodyte with a mental age of six will be judged to be 'elitist' and therefore forbidden by Harman's Law. (Young 2014)

The strategy of using single quotation marks for isolated words or phrases in a way quite distinct from the representation of reported speech is one that is available on the printed page and allows the writer to open up an ironic distance between these expressions and their own words. In her research into the language of newspapers, Tuchman (1972) refers to these as a signalling device to distance the authorial voice from the sentiment expressed and thus to question its legitimacy. Systematically, Young's article uses this to highlight lexis (inclusive, accessible) that link to the main features of the move towards equality that the particular education policy in question is engaging with. In this way, we are invited to see the validity of such terms in a questionable light. Instead, Young conflates educational reform in terms of examinations with wider issues of equality and attacks those of lower academic achievement in hyperbolic terms that range from the extremely rare psychological disorder of Munchausen Syndrome, to the dehumanising reference to "troglodytes" rather than teenagers. His reference to "wheelchair ramps and the complete works of Alice Walker" also draw upon shared prejudices to produce an indirect attack on issues of equality, although to many liberal readers the idea of greater physical accessibility and a wider range of literary works available to children would seem to be common sense.

As the participatory framework widens to encompass the general media audience, the rights to engage offensively are therefore distributed on the basis of role and power (Higgins and Smith 2017). Toby Young claims warrant to engage offensively on the basis of his self-styled role as "journalistic provocateur", thus positioning himself within a tradition in which journalists have permission to engage with whatever is most likely to excite controversy.

However, perhaps the most complex aspect of this Framework for Offence in the public sphere is the notion of Target. In the case of Toby Young, as can be seen, his recontextualised tweets, and other writings, target groups such as women, the disabled and working-class students. While these remain the ostensible targets of offence, it is not necessarily the case for various reasons that members of those groups actually take offence or respond to it. Those who did respond held other kinds of position within the public sphere—as journalists, for instance, or politicians—exhibiting a kind of taking offence by proxy on behalf of the ostensible Targets (rather like the Scottish Sheriff in the case of Meechan's pet dog).

In this respect, we can see more clearly how the giving of offence is played out to more than one kind of audience. A tweet such as Toby Young's "Actually, mate, I had my dick up her arse" is designed to elicit one kind of response on its production as part of man-to-man, male banter but meets a radically different kind of response on its subsequent recontextualisation when its offensiveness is discovered and made manifest to a different kind of audience on a spectrum ranging from those who might align with it enthusiastically, to those that see the tweets as empty discursive acts in line with Labov's (1972) ritual insults, to those who take the most grave of offence. In terms of our structural framework for Offence it moves from A2 (align with the *Offence Giver* against the Target) to A1 (align with the *Target* against the Offence).

On the face of it, Toby Young's offensiveness is apparently targeted at groups with a fairly strictly defined membership, such as women (and their body parts—Claudia Winkelman's breasts or Padma Lakshmi's arse, or someone's anonymous cleavage), low-income parents with below average IQs, teachers, functionally illiterate troglodytes with a mental age of six or working-class students at Oxford. Taken as a whole they can be seen collectively as a group whose common membership is normally protected by the protocols of political correctness: in other words, membership of these groups has one overarching requirement—that they should be addressed or referred to by preferred, or at least respectful terms. Young's offensive comments are thus not just an attack on women, or the poor or teachers, but an attack on the protocols of political correctness. His own later reflections on the problematic nature of his tweets—or his journalism, more generally—make this clear. He described his tweets posted between 2009 and 2012 as "sophomoric and politically incorrect". In an attack on the term "inclusive", he dismissed it as "one of those ghastly, politically correct words that have survived the demise of New Labour". Thus, behind the manifest and individuated *Targets* of his offensiveness lies the larger and more abstract *Target* of political correctness—or progressive identity politics more generally.

It is worth emphasising that roles within any participation framework tend to be founded upon various identity claims, ranging from interpersonal (the position of a friend and confidant, for example), and draw upon performative claims from the professional to the unpolished and authentic. While Young's style of engagement might be sustained as a journalist, it was a discursive form found to be inconsistent with a proposed role in government. The Chairman of the Board of the Office of Students welcomed Young's withdrawal from consideration in the following terms:

> "Many of his previous tweets and articles were offensive, and not in line with the values of the Office for Students. Mr. Young was right to offer an unreserved apology for these comments and he was correct to say that his continuation in the role would have distracted from our important work."

In terms described by Iedema (2003) and Scollon and Scollon (2003), the resemiotisation of the tweets saw the intended contrarian frame evaporate, to be replaced by a frame informed by the norms of government and regulatory discourse.

Conclusion

To sum up: we have argued that the production of offensive discourse in the political domain is enacted within what Goffman (1981) refers to as "participation frameworks". We have suggested, indeed, that there is a structure to the performance of offence in the public sphere, whereby it is constituted by key components such as *Offence Giver, Offence Taker, Target of Offence* and *Audience*. These are modulated in late modern societies, especially where digitalisation and social media platforms allow many possibilities for resemiotisation, to allow subtle differences to develop in the way the structural framework is activated between initial utterances and their subsequent reiterations especially in the transition between private or face-to-face offensiveness between connected individuals and publicly oriented offensiveness. Most importantly, however, we suggest that at the present time there is clearly a political stake to offensiveness; and we reviewed in some detail cases where despite the particularity of *Targets* such as Meghan Markle, Padma Lakshmi, Claudia Winkelman—or, more generally, working-class students or the disabled—the ultimate underlying Target seems to be political correctness and its priorities. This seems effectively a move overtly to politicise the cultural terrain itself. And, by and large, wherever this move is resisted—where offensiveness is noted and called out—the defensive riposte takes the form of a claim to the rights of freedom of speech, sometimes quite simply in terms of the supposed authenticity of "speaking one's mind". Inasmuch as the more individuated and concrete Targets of this manoeuvre (rather than PC in general) tend to lack economic, political or cultural power, it could be argued that political offensiveness is more often than not structured in dominance. The attack by members of a dominant majority against members of a minority works to dismantle at a symbolic level some of the kinds of symbolic protections that PC was designed to offer. Boris Johnson's remarks in the *Daily Telegraph* (August 2018) about the burka (sic) looking like a letter box would provide yet another case in point.

On reflection, however, the situation may be more complex. As we noted, the roots of political correctness can be traced to the emergence in the latter decades of the twentieth century of identity politics, particularly around questions of feminism and ethnicity—so neatly captured in the feminist dictum of "The personal is the political". For those on the Left, language, and more particularly the question of how things should be named, became a stake in the political struggle (Dunant 1994; Hall 1994, 167). Although the basic principles and protocols of political correctness may have remained more or less unchanged, the role of political correctness within culture and society over time has undergone significant transformations. In some ways PC was at its most vigorous (some might say strident) around the time of the high point of the Reagan–Thatcher consensus, now summed up as neo-liberalism. At the present moment when the political centre cannot hold but when the basic tenets of neo-liberalism no longer sit easily with the phantasmagorical visions of the right and when on the other hand social movements do seem increasingly capable of mobilising popular support, the working out of political struggle seems increasingly to operate in the sphere of the symbolic imaginary, especially on the Right. "Brexit", for instance, for the Right consists of a politics that lacks any referent but itself ('Brexit means Brexit'). In this climate, it is hardly surprising that voices on the Right should seek to reclaim language for itself through claims to be the authentic voice of the people (hence Trump's claim to his own supporters "I will be your voice"). One kind of claim for authenticity is precisely through pushing back—offensively—against the niceties of political correctness and its restrictions on ordinary speech.

As Stuart Hall commented: "Paradoxically, though PC is its sworn adversary, the New Right shares with PC an understanding that the political game is often won or lost on the terrain of … moral and political issues, apparently far removed from the Westminster … conception of 'politics'" (1994, 169).

However, two decades after Hall's comments it seems that the New Right may be less confident than its occasional electoral success might indicate. Indeed, despite the partial electoral successes of Trump and Brexit, the Right still lacks a coherent political project but is fed rather on xenophobic fantasies of Empire 2.0, "making America great again", "taking back control", white ascendancy and the oxymoron of frictionless trade across stringent border controls. But just as the political contours of neo-liberalism—with its growing fissures and unevenness—has become unsustainable, floating free of points in anchorage in the real world, the resistance of the Right to the Left has come to be fought out with renewed intensity in the symbolic imaginary, with PC providing a kind of totemic Target or shibboleth for those on the right, used mainly to mark out the distance and the dividing line between them and the Left.

Indeed, for Britain the post-war consensus, which rested primarily on the question of how best to manage capitalism through forms of social welfarism, seems finally and irretrievably to have broken down. For Britain—and elsewhere—this has inevitably led to a fracturing of the body-politic and the rise of social antagonisms of all kinds, intensified by the further mediatisation of the public sphere through developments in the internet and digital social media (Smith 2018; Higgins and

Smith 2017). Into this highly charged semiotic space, the offensiveness of Marney, Young, as well of course as that of Trump or Boris Johnson, can be seen not only as a stake in the political (and cultural) struggle but as a defensive and ultimately bankrupt reaction to the incoherence and inconsistencies of their position.

In the discursive confusions of symbolic charge and counter-charge (from which Labour in its internal clashes over anti-semitism is by no means immune), Toby Young and Jo Marney may well prove to be bit players, minor actors in a far larger drama. They are, however, symptomatic figures, epiphenomena of larger currents and patterns. Young himself while attempting to downplay his offence by passing it off as "sophomoric and politically incorrect", could also try and dignify it as the actions of a "journalistic provocateur".

To some it might seem simply, in Matthew Arnold's phrase, as if "we are…on a darkling plane…where ignorant armies clash by night". Indeed, it is perhaps too easy to invoke the language of crisis to try and understand these complex processes of cultural and political change. Nonetheless it seems clear in retrospect that the financial collapse of 2008 marked a turning point in the durability of neo-liberalism as a project. The inevitable economic crisis that followed, with national state and supra-national interventions designed to try and halt the unravelling of the financial system, where the burdens of "austerity" fell most unequally on the poor rather than the rich, has not surprisingly provoked the widespread political crisis in the midst of which we find ourselves. Offensiveness, however, is no substitute for a politics of change. Perhaps Gramsci's words, rather than Matthew Arnold's, can better sum up the present condition: "The crisis consists precisely in the fact that the old is dying and the new cannot be born; in this interregnum a great variety of morbid symptoms appear" (1971, 276).

Toby Young, Jo Marney and, more generally, the publicly mediated language of offence, are best understood as morbid symptoms of the interregnum.

REFERENCES

Bennett, Owen. 2018. "Jo Marney Confronted with Racist Comments in Car-Crash 'This Morning' Interview." *Huffington Post*, February 22. https://www.huffingtonpost.co.uk/entry/jo-marney-this-morning-henry-bolton_uk_5a8ea964e4b077f5bfeba7a2.

Brighenti, Andrea. 2007. "Visibility: A Category for the Social Sciences." *Current Sociology* 55 (3): 323–342.
Cameron, Deborah. 1994. *Verbal Hygiene*. London: Routledge.
Cowburn, Ashley. 2018. "Toby Young Deletes Thousands of Tweets Amid Row Over His Universities Regulator Appointment." *The Independent*, January 3. https://www.independent.co.uk/news/uk/politics/toby-young-twitter-delete-tweets-universities-regulator-appointment-ofs-office-for-students-a8139841.html.
Culpeper, Jonathan. 2011. *Impoliteness: Using Language to Cause Offence*. Cambridge: Cambridge University Press.
Drake, Philip, and Michael Higgins. 2006. "'I'm a Celebrity, Get Me into Politics': The Political Celebrity and the Celebrity Politician." In *Framing Celebrity: New Directions in Celebrity Culture*, edited by Su Holmes and Sean Redmond, 87–100. London: Routledge.
Dunant, Sarah, ed. 1994. *The War of the Words: The Political Correctness Debate*. London: Virago.
Ekstrom, Mats, and Bengt Johansson. 2008. "Talk Scandals." *Media, Culture & Society* 30 (1): 61–79.
Enli, Gunner. 2015. *Mediated Authenticity*. New York: Peter Lang.
Fairclough, Norman. 2003. "'Political Correctness': The Politics of Culture and Language." *Discourse & Society* 14 (1): 17–28.
Foster, Dawn. 2018. "Free Speech Works Both Ways, as Toby Young Is Finding Out." *The Guardian*, January 4. https://www.theguardian.com/commentisfree/2018/jan/04/free-speech-toby-young-office-for-students.
Goffman, Erving. 1981. *Forms of Talk*. Oxford: Blackwell.
Gramsci, Antonio. 1930/1971. *Selections from the Prison Notebooks*. Edited and translated by Quintin Hoare and Geoffrey Nowell Smith, 276. London: Lawrence and Wishart.
Habermas, Jurgen. 1989. *The Structural Transformation of the Public Sphere*. Cambridge: Polity Press.
Hall, Stuart. 1994. "Some 'Politically Incorrect' Pathways Through PC." In *The War of the Words: The Political Correctness Debate*, edited by Sarah Dunant. London: Virago.
Higgins, Michael. 2013. "Governmentality, Populism and Empowerment: David Cameron's Rhetoric of the Big Society." In *The Media, Political Participation and Empowerment*, edited by Richard Scullion, Roman Gerodimos, Dan Jackson, and Darren Lilleker, 58–70. Abingdon: Routledge.
Higgins, Michael, and Angela Smith. 2013. "My Husband; My Hero: Selling the Political Spouses in the 2010 General Election." *Journal of Political Marketing* 12 (2/3): 197–210.
Higgins, Michael, and Angela Smith. 2017. *Belligerent Broadcasting*. London: Routledge.
Iedema, Rick. 2003. "Multimodality, Resemiotization: Extending the Analysis of Discourse as a Multi-semiotic Practice." *Visual Communication* 2 (1): 29–57.

Kreiss, Daniel, and Philip N. Howard. 2010. "New Challenges for Political Privacy: Lessons from the First US Presidential Race in the Web 2.0 Era." *International Journal of Communication* 4: 1032–1050.

Labov, William. 1972. "Rules for Ritual Insults." In *Language in the Inner City: Studies in the Black English Vernacular*, 297–353. Philadelphia: University of Pennsylvania Press.

Lyon, David. 2002. "Surveillance Studies: Understanding Visibility, Mobility and the Phenetic Fix." *Surveillance & Society* 1 (1): 1–7.

Montgomery, Martin. 2017. "Post-truth Politics? Authenticity, Populism and the Political Discourses of Donald Trump." *Journal of Language and Politics* 16 (4): 619–639.

Owen, Glen. 2018. "'Meghan's Seed Will Taint Our Royal Family': UKIP Chief's Glamour Model Lover, 25, Is Suspended from the Party Over Racist Texts About Prince Harry's Wife-to-Be." *Daily Mail*, January 13. http://www.dailymail.co.uk/news/article-5266657/Ukip-leaders-girlfriends-racist-Meghan-Markle-messages.html.

Perry, Ruth. 1992. "A Short History of the Term Political Correct." In *Beyond PC: Toward a Politics of Understanding*, edited by Patricia Aufderheide, 71–79. St. Paul, MN: Graywolf Press.

Peters, John Durham. 1995. "Historical Tensions in the Concept of Public Opinion." In *Public Opinion and the Communication of Consent*, edited by Theodore L. Glasser and Charles T. Salmon, 3–32. New York: Guilford.

Scollon, Ron, and Suzy Wong Scollon. 2003. *Discourses in Place: Language in the Material World*. London: Routledge.

Smith, Angela. 2016. "Mediated Political Masculinities: The Commander-In-Chief vs The New Man." *Social Semiotics* 26 (1): 94–110.

Smith, Angela. 2018. "Gender in 'Crisis', Everyday Sexism and the Twittersphere." In *Crisis and the Media*, edited by Marianna Patrona, 231–260. Amsterdam: John Benjamins.

Suhr, Stephanie, and Sally Johnson. 2003. "Revisiting PC: Introduction to Special Issue on Political Correctness." *Discourse and Society* 14 (1): 5–16.

Talbot, Mary. 2007. "Political Correctness and Freedom of Speech." In *Handbook of Language and Communication: Diversity and Change*, edited by M. Hellinger and A. Pauwels, 751–764. New York: Mouton de Gruyter.

Thompson, John B. 1995. *The Media and Modernity*. Cambridge: Polity.

Thompson, John B. 2005. "The New Visibility." *Theory, Culture & Society* 22 (6): 31–51.

Trottier, Daniel. 2017a. "Digital Vigilantism as Weaponisation of Visibility." *Philosophy & Technology* 30: 55–72.

Trottier, Daniel. 2017b. "Scandal Mining: Political Nobodies and Remediated Visibility." *Media, Culture & Society*. http://journals.sagepub.com/doi/full/10.1177/0163443717734408.

Tuchman, Gaye. 1972. "Objectivity as Strategic Ritual: An Examination of Newsmen's Notions of Objectivity." *American Journal of Sociology* 77 (4): 660–679.

Wardle, Claire. 2017. "Fake News: It's Complicated." Accessed August 30, 2018. https://medium.com/1st-draft/fake-news-its-complicated-d0f773766c79.

Weintraub, Jeff. 1997. "The Theory and Politics of the Public/Private Distinction." In *Public and Private in Thought and Practice*, edited by Jeff Weintraub and Krishan Kumar, 1–42. Chicago: Chicago University Press.

Young, Toby. 2014. "I Am Living Proof That 'Two-tier' Exams Work." *The Spectator*, June 30. https://www.spectator.co.uk/2012/06/i-am-living-proof-that-two-tier-exams-work/.

Zappavignana, Michelle. 2011. Ambient Affiliation: A Linguistic Perspective on Twitter. *New Media & Society* 13 (5): 788–806.

CHAPTER 3

Creating an Emotional Community: The Negotiation of Anger and Resistance to Donald Trump

Karin Wahl-Jorgensen

INTRODUCTION

This chapter takes as its vantage point the notion that emotion is a key resource in mediated politics (Wahl-Jorgensen 2019), and focuses on how anger at Donald Trump is discursively negotiated. In doing so, it takes a particular interest in anger as a mobilising political emotion. It thus engages with this volume's preoccupation with the complexities of offence, seeing it as 'an umbrella term that can encompass such diverse and contradictory emotions and feelings as anger, pain, hurt and shock, but also joy, titillation and glee' (Graefer in this volume). The chapter suggests that an examination of anger helps to uncover its political productivity in the context of the circulation of offence.

The chapter analyses the debate resulting from a tweet posted on 19 June 2018, at the height of the controversy surrounding the Trump administration's family separation policy. The tweet was written by Tim

K. Wahl-Jorgensen (✉)
Cardiff University, Cardiff, UK
e-mail: wahl-jorgensenk@cardiff.ac.uk

© The Author(s) 2019
A. Graefer (ed.), *Media and the Politics of Offence*,
https://doi.org/10.1007/978-3-030-17574-0_3

Grierson, a prominent film critic, and simply stated: 'Being angry all the time is exhausting and corrosive. Not being angry feels morally irresponsible'. This chapter looks at how this tweet created and cemented an emotional community that allowed for the negotiation of a broader set of political emotions. At the same time, the anger central to the emotional community examined here is discursively linked to agency and political action. However, anger is also subject to discursive contestation and attempts at channelling and redefinition. The contestation of anger as a valid response to the actions and speech of the Trump administration signals the importance of the management of emotion. It shows that the expression and interpretation of emotion in public provides a vital framework for political action. By developing the idea of an emotional community in this context, this chapter proposes a new way of approaching political emotions—particularly anger—as a mobilising resource.

Theorising Anger as a Political Emotion

Anger, like offence, has been maligned in political thinking as a negative emotion. It has been seen as an emotion that potentially gives rise to aggression and violence, and therefore requires management (e.g. Hochschild 1983). Philosophers since the Stoics have viewed the 'civilized life as one that avoids anger' (Holmes 2004, 127). Anger is recognised in social theory as a reaction to injustice (Holmes 2004; Aristotle 1968, 1382–1383). Scholars in disciplines such as psychology and philosophy have typically viewed anger as an *individual* emotion which is unavoidable and difficult to control, and ultimately destructive to social relations. For example, the legal philosopher Martha Nussbaum (2016) has provided a compelling articulation of the dangers of anger in her book, *Anger and Forgiveness: Resentment, Generosity, Justice*. Here, she argues that anger is never normatively justifiable. She makes the case that 'anger is not only not necessary for the pursuit of justice, but also a large impediment to the generosity and empathy that help to construct a future of justice' (Nussbaum 2016, 8). This is because individual anger is usually accompanied by a desire for payback or retribution, which is never normatively justified and is socially counterproductive. There is, in Nussbaum's view, one 'borderline case of genuinely rational and normatively appropriate anger that I call *Transition-Anger*, whose entire content is: "How outrageous. Something should be done about that"' (2016, 6). Transition-Anger is appropriate because it entails moving beyond the pure emotion of anger to think about possible ways out of it, towards the resolution of injustices. However, even if anger is rarely normatively justifiable—or rational—it has three roles that are valuable in *instrumental* terms:

> First, it is seen as a valuable signal that the oppressed recognize the wrong done to them. It also seems to be a necessary motivation for them to protest and struggle against injustice and to communicate to the wider world the nature of their grievances. Finally, anger seems, quite simply, to be justified: outrage at terrible wrongs is right, and anger thus expresses something true. (Nussbaum 2016, 211)

While Nussbaum's (2016) detailed excursus into individual anger shows its moral and social inadequacy, her recognition of the *usefulness* of anger occurs in the context of collective anger, or anger expressed by groups of individuals, directed at a shared injustice.

As I have argued elsewhere (Wahl-Jorgensen 2018a, 2019), mediated emotions—or emotions that circulate in public through platforms including social media—are distinctive from emotions circulating in individual bodies. I have proposed that mediated anger is distinctive because it is *performative, discursively constructed* and usually *collective* and *political* (see also Graefer, Bore, and Kilby in this volume for a similar conception). Through these features, some forms of mediated anger are discursively legitimated and come to stand as exemplars of what Nussbaum (2016) referred to as *Transition-Anger* insofar as they are oriented towards claims to justice and social change.

First of all, mediated anger is *performative* in the sense that it is based on the performance of actors in the public sphere. As social movements scholars and anthropologists have noted, emotions are, in the first instance, culturally constructed (Katriel 2015), but the ways in which these cultural constructions take on meaning through their public articulation matter greatly, and are frequently highly strategic. When we speak of mediated anger as performative, this also reflects the fact that the authenticity of the emotions that circulate in mediated public discourse is impossible to ascertain, and that it is both more relevant and more interesting to consider *which* emotions do gain purchase in the public sphere, *why*, and *with what consequence*. The ways in which we speak about anger in public matter hugely, precisely *because* they are performative. And this performative construction of emotion that springs to life through mediated discourses also has significant ideological consequences. It provides an emotional compass that we—as audience members, co-creators of public discourse and citizens—can use to orient ourselves and distinguish between more or less legitimate and rational forms of anger.

Secondly, mediated anger is *discursively constructed* through the narratives of actors in the public sphere. That is to say, when we speak of anger as it appears in public debate, it represents not the emotion as felt by an individual, but rather the narration of these emotions (see also Wettergren 2005). But, if the media are one of the key vehicles used for both establishing and perpetuating particular emotional regimes (Reddy 2001), they also facilitate the sharing of particular legitimate ways of talking about our feelings and hence the conditions of possibility for shared action. As Eksner (2015, 193) has suggested, emotional 'displays in language may be employed as tools of hegemony by dominant groups and state institutions, and as vehicles of resistance by non-dominant groups'. That is to say, the ways in which mediated emotions circulate in public cannot be understood outside the context of power relations.

It is therefore also important to consider how groups that seek to contest dominant power formations, including social movements, draw on emotions. The role of anger in social movements has become a matter of interest over the past few decades, as scholars studying oppositional and marginalised groups have begun to recognise anger as an important resource of collective empowerment (e.g. Goodwin et al. 2001; Jasper 2011). This work shares a recognition that collective anger can be a particularly useful resource for oppositional political life (see also Holmes 2004), and that anger is readily recognised as an expression of shared injustice. As Lyman (2004, 133) puts it, 'anger is an indispensable political emotion—for without angry speech the body politic would lack the voice of the powerless questioning the justice of the dominant order'.

Deborah Gould (2010, 2012) has studied the role of anger in queer and feminist movements. She takes a particular interest in the potential of political empowerment through the labelling of emotions—as when lesbians who are collectively 'feeling bad' relabel their emotion as anger (Gould 2012). By naming and articulating the negative affect of 'feeling bad' about the consequences of patriarchy as 'anger', it becomes a public and collective emotion which empowers the angry group to take action. Similarly, in work on the AIDS activist group Act Up (Gould 2010), she examines how anger, as a collective emotion, has been encouraged as a positive resource, while despair has been discouraged. Frances Shaw (2014), in work on Australian feminist blogging, demonstrates that the affordances of the genre have allowed activists to give 'form and shape to the dissonance they felt in their own lives, and to share the discourses that enabled them to turn it into political claims'. The expression of feelings of anger has then contributed to the creation of an emotional community, coalescing around a shared political agenda. As this chapter argues, such a dynamic is also at work in public debate over the actions of the Trump administration.

The Emotional Politics of Donald Trump: Anger as an Interpretive Framework

Elsewhere, I have developed the argument that Donald Trump's ascent is powered by the emergence of 'angry populism' (Wahl-Jorgensen 2018b). Angry populism—as embodied by Trump—is based on a rhetoric which seeks broad appeal through the deliberate expression of anger. Adopted as an interpretive framework in public debate, it suggests that the anger of Trump, his supporters *and* his opponents is both salient and relevant to political life. For the historian William Reddy (2001), we need to see practices of governance as driven in part by the way we speak in public about emotions. He introduces the term 'emotional regime' to refer to the 'set of normative emotions and the official rituals, practices, and "emotives" that express and inculcate them; a necessary underpinning of any stable political regime' (Reddy 2001, 129). Along similar lines, Michael Delli Carpini (2018, 18) has suggested that the rise of Donald Trump is linked to a broader set of transformations in the 'media regime' associated with political, economic, cultural and technological changes. These transformations in the media regime result in the normalisation of a 'new set of rules, norms, institutions, and expectations'. We can see a change in the media regime as intricately linked to, and making possible, a transformation of the emotional regime. If emotional regimes coalesce through the public expression of emotives, the media play a key role in facilitating their emergence and their change (see also Pantti and Wahl-Jorgensen 2011). The shifting media regime heralds a broader change in public discourse and in the terms of public life, spurred on in part through the affordances of the hybrid media system, including the rise of social media. In the context of understanding responses to Trump, it is clear that social media facilitate the expression and validation of anger.

Affective News Streams and Resistance

The expression of emotions and the creation of an emotional community take a particular form premised on the affordances of Twitter. The platform's facilitation of expression and interaction that may foster a resistance based on emotional resistance is well established in the literature. Zizi Papacharissi has compellingly developed the notion of 'affective publics', which helps us to theorise how 'performative architecture presented through Twitter is an everyday space where dominant narratives are reproduced and can be challenged through performances that are both personal and political' (Papacharissi 2014, 113). These processes of the reproduction and challenge of dominant narratives occur through the collaborative construction of what Papacharissi and de Fatima Oliveira (2012) have referred to as 'affective news streams'. In a study of story-telling on Twitter during the Arab Spring events in Egypt, they emphasise 'the need to consider affect in explanations of the role of media use during mobilization':

> We characterized the news streams we studied as affective, because they blended opinion, fact, and emotion into expressions uttered in anticipation of events that had not yet attained recognition through mainstream media. Combined with the networked and "always on" character of social media, the affective aspects of messages nurture and sustain involvement, connection, and cohesion. We [advance] the concept of *affective news streams*, to describe how news is collaboratively constructed out of subjective experience, opinion, and emotion within an ambient news environment. (Papacharissi and de Fatima Oliveira 2012, 279)

Expanding on this body of work in examining the affective tone of Twitter discussions in the Occupy Wall Street movement, Papacharissi (2014) has likened the role of Twitter to that of music:

> In some ways, Twitter plays a part similar to the role music used to play for movements—by enabling affective attunement with the movement itself. Songs that reflect the general aspirations of a movement allow publics and crowds to feel, with greater intensity, the meaning of the movement for themselves. Affective attunement permits people to feel and thus locate their own place in politics. Antagonistic content injections interrupted the affective harmony of #ows [#Occupy Wall Street], creating an effect similar to that of noise interrupting a song. (Papacharissi 2014, 93)

The metaphor of music evokes both the ambient and the sensual. It suggests that a plethora of forms of discourse may make themselves heard at any moment, but that, just as emotion may play a positive role in bolstering the aims of a movement, it may also interrupt harmonies; it may contribute to challenging dominant narratives and call consensus into question. This insight calls to mind the ideas of radical democrats, who have long been interested in agonistic forms of public discourse (e.g. Mouffe 2005), arguing that the ability to make dissenting voices heard is central to democratic practice. Further, it reminds us of the importance of understanding negative emotions—including anger and offence—as central to motivating and shaping political action (e.g. Gould 2010).

Here, the idea of 'affective news streams' is particularly helpful in highlighting the complexity of political debate and mobilisation on Twitter. The chapter builds on this framework to investigate the dynamics of the emotional community that coalesced around Tim Grierson's tweet.

Background: Resisting Trump

The tweet analysed here was posted on 19 June 2018, amid public outrage over the Trump administration's policy of separating families detained at the US border, which intensified after harrowing images and recordings of young children held in cages and crying for their parents were made public (Moore 2018). While the Trump administration defended the policy, suggesting that it was a necessary response to federal law, the policy was eventually overturned on 21 June 2018, following widespread condemnation and protests.

The tweet was posted by Tim Grierson, who is a senior US critic for *Screen Daily* and vice president of the Los Angeles Film Critics Association. Although he is a prominent writer, he has not generally been associated with anti-Trump activism. The tweet stated: 'Being angry all the time is exhausting and corrosive. Not being angry feels morally irresponsible'. The tweet gives voice to the challenges of negotiating emotional responses to the Trump administration: on the one hand, it references the role of anger as a political emotion, but also suggests that such anger is generative of further—and different—emotional responses, being both 'exhausting' and 'corrosive'. At the same time, it suggests that 'not being angry feels morally irresponsible', and therefore implies that anger is in fact a normatively desirable response to the extraordinary events unfolding at the time. According to such a conception, being a good citizen requires taking offence and, in turn, the performance of anger. As such, it is located within a broader public discourse associated with the emotional regime of 'angry populism' (Wahl-Jorgensen 2018b) which understands anger as salient and relevant to political life. It therefore contrasts with historically dominant conceptions of anger as an emotion that should be avoided, controlled or carefully managed in order to render a civilised society possible (e.g. Elias 2000; see also Wahl-Jorgensen 2019, Chapter 1).

This is an unusual viral tweet in several respects. First of all, it is radically decontextualised and makes no use of the 'socio-informatic backbone of Twitter' (Papacharissi 2014, 36). It makes no reference to particular unfolding news events and stories, and uses no hashtags, images, links or GIFs. It simply makes a general statement about how the author *feels*. In doing so, it therefore relies on the assumption that everyone knows what his or her feelings are *about*. As such, it relies upon and mobilises an already-existing community of like-minded people—those who are part of the affective community offended by the conduct of the Trump administration in a broader sense and angry about the injustice of the family separation policy. But its resonance is also made possible by the fact that discussion of the Trump administration's family separation policy was so dominant on Twitter and elsewhere at the time of the tweet that this context could be inferred. At the same time, because of its openness, it also invites responses oriented towards the broader political environment, as evidenced in the numerous responses that referenced Brexit and experiences of racism and sexual assault.

This particular tweet has not been selected for analysis because it is representative of broader discussions around the family separation policy. Rather, the tweet, with its associated replies has been selected because it represents an excellent example of how the affordances of Twitter facilitate the creation of an emotional community. This emotional community is distinctive insofar as it was premised on the articulation and elaboration of emotions and their political pitfalls and potentials, as well as the negotiation and contestation of these emotions.

To date, the tweet has received 352 replies, been retweeted by more than 14,000 Twitter users and liked more than 43,000 times. Of all replies to the tweet, 241 were accessible on Twitter at the time of the study. These were analysed using inductive coding, informed by the analytical approach of Papacharissi, which focused on investigating how 'the expressive affordances of [Twitter] support identity formation and affinity among like-minded individuals' (2014, 67). In line with Papacharissi's (2014) and Papacharissi and de Fatima Oliveira's (2012) observations on the mechanisms of 'affective news streams', analysis of the replies focused on detecting patterns of agreement, elaboration and contestation in relation to the original tweet. In addition to the categories of agreement, elaboration and contestation, a small number of tweets were coded as irrelevant, because they either contained only the handles of particular Twitter users, or included content (such as an image with phrase 'Moooo') which could not be seen as contributing meaningfully to the discussion. The chapter next discusses each of these categories in turn, with particular attention to how they contribute to the creation of an 'emotional community'. In doing so, the analysis demonstrates how the affirmation and contestation of anger plays a vital role in shaping the mobilisation of opposition to Trump.

Agreement: Supportive Anger

The most frequent type of reply to the original tweet, accounting for just over one-third of all replies, or 34.1% ($n=83$), represented a simple expression of agreement with the original tweet. These included brief exclamations such as 'Yes', 'BIG mood', 'ICanFeelThisShit', 'perfectly said', and 'This. All damn day'. Such statements of agreement provided a basic means of bolstering the emotional community created by the tweet, while demonstrating civic engagement through taking offence and feeling angry (see also Papacharissi 2014, 28). They typified the use of Twitter for 'calls for solidarity among publics, imagined or actual, that share a common set of goals' (Papacharissi 2014, 37). In addition to the replies that expressed agreement, a small number of posts (11.2%, $n=27$) constituted replies to other replies that moved beyond the sentiment and topic expressed in Grierson's tweet. These frequently enforced the solidarity of the emotional community by expressing support for and endorsement of particular replies, and reflecting engagement with other members of the community. Such posts encompassed the social media mainstay of posts of cute animals, including cats, beavers and dogs, as well as statements such as 'Thanks for introducing me to my new favorite word!' (@n8works), and 'Hang in. We all need each other to fight back' (@middlechild).

Some statements of agreement provided more detailed affirmations that contextualised the original tweet, frequently with explicit reference to Trump:

> The defining mood of the tRump era. (@Potterchik)
> I know right. I am so sick about this. I feel like I am on the very [sic] of tears all the time. (@annadodson1959)
> Nailed it. Life in the Trump era. (@Sowses_n_fixins)
> Exactafuckinglactly. Thank you for putting my feelings into the proper sentence. (@GoMissAmyClaire)
> Yes! I am the worst spin-off of a @vindiesel movie right now: "So tired. So furious!" (@teachergorman)

These replies, while endorsing the original tweet, also in some cases expressed other negative emotional and bodily responses reflective of offence and anger, including feeling 'sick', 'on the verge of tears', 'tired' and furious'. The replies thus acknowledged the premise that strong negative emotions—for so long vilified in political thought—in response to the Trump era are not only widespread, but also normatively appropriate.

ELABORATION: HOW TO USE ANGER

The second most prominent category of replies, accounting for just under one-third of the sample (33.1%, $n=80$), provided more extensive elaboration and reflection on the emotions captured in the original tweet, and related these to the lived experience of the posters. These replies contributed to further cementing the emotional community by enhancing solidarity and creating a shared and nuanced discourse on political anger and its consequences. For example, one poster described how the experience of extreme anger seeped into the ordinary, routine and widely recognisable everyday ritual of taking her dog for a walk:

> Walking my dog this morning and listening to the news on YouTube – I became so angry I cussed out a house that always has Republican crap in the front yard. As I had my headphones on, I'm sure I was quite loud. I don't like being this angry all the time. (@anne_mohri)

For other posters, the recognition of the complex constellation of emotions described by Grierson occasioned reflection on the long-term sustainability of such intense anger:

Will I eventually lose my ability to be outraged because it's easier to view the world as some sort of reality show from the comfort of an armchair? (@LukeWhisto)

I am exhausted & trying to find a path forward. It is harder when the man spewing lies is ultimately my boss, yet I serve the country & not the man. This conundrum blunts much of my words and fills me w/greater rage for the words I cannot speak. I need help. (@psycocat)

This is very hard to watch happening. Our democracy is slipping away and too many remain indifferent or paralyzed by the sheer enormity of this relentless fight. (@debthompson1021)

Within this category, many replies were focused on translating anger into political agency and action to bring about social change. Replies of this type tended to underscore the significance of anger as a mobilising, 'fuelling' or 'inspiring' emotion:

I find a cold steely anger bracing enough to fuel me without burning me out. (@HeidiLiFeldman)

[...] I use my anger as fuel. Looking away is a privilege I refuse to indulge in. (@TheCheekyGinger)

Treat anger as a form of inspiration. Recognize anger as legitimate when feelinging [sic] it, then allow it to fade or change, but continue the work of acting on what caused it. (@CharlesFVincent)

You have a choice today. You can sit and stew and let the anxiety build, or you can do something. You know what I chose. (@yesthatabbywood)

Humans have a profound ability to feel anger, joy, sadness, relief, and any other emotion you can think of at the same time. In fact, we do it all the time. It's our superpower. We will get through this. (@ThinkITThruUSA)

The theme of harnessing anger for the productive purposes of action, so central to much theorising by social movements scholars, was a prominent one in the debate. As Deborah Gould (2012) has documented, collective action, however constituted, is frequently premised on the active management of emotions. Groups seeking social change carry out careful 'emotional labour' (Hochschild 1983) designed to channel emotions in constructive directions. Along these lines, inward-looking and passive emotions such as despair and offence tend to be discouraged because they are seen as immobilising and hence disruptive to the goals of social change. As one of the posters noted, 'despair is not an option' (@agunn). By contrast, anger is widely understood as potentially mobilising, even if it is also seen as difficult to control (Gould 2012). Along those lines, the posts calling for the anger to be translated into political action were careful to emphasise the strategic uses of this negative emotion, and the need to rein it in when it proved counterproductive to individual's mental health and collective political projects:

> Find the middle road. Recognize the emotion and feel it, then turn the anger into activism. In the process you will feel better and become a part of the solution. We got this! Have faith in US. #FamiliesBelongTogether #RoadToChange #TheYoungPeopleWillWin. (@Kliggettoni)
>
> Acts count, your feelings don't so much (in the great reckoning). There is no requirement that you are angry, just that you act. (@boodreck)
>
> I have learned to try and pivot my anger into positive action. So when I get angry I clean up, I exercise, I write or read, I support those in need, I find a way to be productive with a vengeance. (@Chocklight_Shama)
>
> Anger is useful if it fuels productive effort, otherwise it is better to train our minds to look elsewhere. (@xueshang)

Replies which foregrounded the constructive harnessing of political anger at the actions of the Trump administration included a range of practical suggestions for what to *do* with the anger. These included voting, registering others to vote, protesting against detention facilities, tweeting, and donating to politicians and activist groups campaigning to change the policy. Several of the replies encouraging specific action also included links to external sites associated with these actions. This demonstrates how the affordances of Twitter facilitate the linkage of emotional expression with a call to specific and easily achievable forms of action. As such, even if the emotional community created by Grierson's tweet was a fleeting and temporary one, representative of the nature of affective news streams and the forms of 'connective action' they encourage (Bennett and Segerberg 2013), it was also one which foregrounded the relationship between shared and narrated emotion and concrete forms of political agency.

CONTESTING ANGER

A final category of replies to Grierson's tweet, accounting for just under one-fifth of the total sample (18.7%, $n=45$), took issue with the fundamental premises of the post. While engaging with the emotional community, they also challenged the normative and practical value of anger and, in some cases, the validity of taking offence in the first place. These replies contributed to disrupting any emerging consensus, thus highlighting the agonistic and conflictual potential inherent in the community (Mouffe 2000; McCosker 2014). At the same time, the contestation embedded within this category took for granted the fundamentally emotional nature of responses to political life—and the legitimacy of discussing emotions in public. The fundamental disagreements, then, were over *which* emotions should take centre stage in the performance of resistance and *how* these should be understood. This included attempts at fine-tuning definitions of anger, as when @gm_wggames argued:

> Don't think of it as corrosive anger. What you are feeling is righteous fury. I.E. "morally right or justifiable; virtuous". The ONLY morally right way to feel right now is "fucking furious".

The distinction between 'righteous fury' and 'corrosive anger' seeks to renegotiate the meaning of anger. As scholars (Higgins 2008; Higgins and Smith 2016) have observed, the notion of righteous indignation (closely related to anger and fury) has a time-honoured place in assessments of public discourse, understood as legitimate anger which is often performed by or on behalf of neglected groups.

However, other participants took issue with the emotion of anger itself. For example, @fredstg replied: 'I prefer being indifferent', while @zoomiewoop rejected the premise of anger as a normatively desirable emotional response:

> You can work to correct bad behavior and right/fight injustice without anger. People do this all the time. Anger isn't sustainable, so if you think that's the only way to be morally responsible, you're in trouble.

For others, the emphasis on anger reflected a denial of underlying emotions which may be more difficult and immobilising, but which nonetheless also required attention and visibility to sustain the normative 'righteousness':

> Anger is often a cover for anguish, grief, fear, and other negative emotions that are painful to feel and tempting to avoid. Important to let yourself feel those feelings too. It helps ease the corrosion, and allows a focus on the righteousness part of the rage. (@myknownalias)

This reply hinted at the need for careful interrogation of a range of political emotions, implying that, while anger is an easy shortcut emotion, the turmoil occasioned by unfolding events may be far more complex.

Some responses did not contest the emotions themselves, but rather the overwhelming sense—implicit in Grierson's original tweet as well as in the vast majority of replies—that the current historical moment is a particularly traumatic and difficult one. Such an approach is evident in the following set of replies:

> It seems almost twee to say this but fewer people are dying from war, famine and disease then [sic] at any point in recorded history. Fwer [sic] people are dying in natural disasters, more people are vaccinated against disease and globally life expectancy is growing unabated [Tweet 1 of 2]. Other things might seem slow but drug legalisation, same sex marriage & minority rights would have seemed outrageous only 25 years ago. These things are now concrete. Social media magnifies our chasms and glorifies the negative. Some things are horrendous but on the whole.... [Tweet 2 of 2] (@Tommybix)
>
> You are right. People who are only feeling anger & outrage in the past 2 years are taking a narrow view IMO. It's not that our political dysfunction isn't horrific. It's that it needs to be seen in the wider context of history (which is full of horrific things). Progress is slow. (@zoomiewoop)

Such replies, which sought to historicise and contextualise understandings of the political situation, tended to challenge the implicit focus on the Trump administration and the controversy over the family separation policy, pointing to global contexts and developments that opened up spaces for more positive assessments and emotions, including hope.

Many other participants in the discussion made pleas for translating the anger into other, more constructive emotions, frequently engaging in therapeutic discourse that incorporated emotional support and redefinition:

> Pace yourself, try acting in compassion, rather than the adrenaline jolt of rage. (@OMissPearl)
>
> Absolutely need to take breaks and pace ourselves. Fighting tyranny is a marathon not a sprint. We don't have to stay angry to stay motivated. Peace. (@rdlaing)
>
> With so much pain and suffering in this country and in the world right now, maybe take a few moments for some #joy. (@relishyourstory)

These and similar tweets reflected attempts at emotion management towards the goals of maintaining individual mental health and a collective momentum directed at social change.

Taken together, the tweets in this category reflect the fundamentally agonistic nature of networked publics, characterised by productive forms of conflict (Mouffe 2000, 126–127). As McCosker (2014) has noted, the appearance of online passion and conflict should be understood as meaningful acts of digital citizenship which may both affect and extend forms of public life and participation in it. At the same time, many of these replies do not constitute trolling or the personal attacks usually associated with agonistic behaviour (e.g. McCosker 2014). Instead, they drew on therapeutic discourses by reframing emotional responses to the Trump administration in more positive directions, seeking to locate and channel energies to sustain political resistance.

Conclusion: Anger, Emotional Community and Networked Publics

This analysis has demonstrated that Tim Grierson's tweet, and replies to it, contributed to cultivating a distinctive emotional community. This community was premised on the explicit articulation, affirmation, negotiation and contestation of anger, as well as related emotions. The majority of replies found resonance with the emotions of constant anger and the resulting fatigue captured in the original tweet, and elaborated on the experience of anger. However, much of the discussion also sought to *manage* and *direct* the anger towards concrete forms of political action, or to *contest* the emotion with respect to its political usefulness. As such, those who weighed in on the discussion carried out political emotional labour (Hochschild 1983). Such discursive work had, as the analysis establishes, several purposes. First, it was designed to mobilise the emotional community in the direction of concrete resistance to the Trump administration. Second, it had a therapeutic aim in providing support for those who take offence and are struggling to deal with their emotional responses. Finally, it served to articulate normative emotions appropriate for dealing with the extraordinary political situation, contributing to an emerging emotional regime (Reddy 2001) which foregrounds the role of anger.

This tweet and the replies it occasioned are atypical: it is rare to see such extensive and explicit discussion of emotional responses to political life. The example studied here therefore represents an exceptional, rather than representative, example of how political emotions are performed, negotiated and contested. At the same time, it highlights the important ways in which the affordances of Twitter facilitate the creation of communities bound together by a shared emotional orientation (see also Graefer, Bore, and Kilby in this volume). In this case, anger formed the basis for the emotional community. Although numerous posters viewed it as a potentially dangerous emotion—one to be managed, channelled and controlled—it was also widely understood as a mobilising and empowering one, as well as normatively desirable: in responding to the Trump administration's family separation policy, the 'good citizen' was an offended and angry citizen who used these emotions to bring about social change. This insight, in turn, calls for a reappraisal of the role of anger as a political emotion in networked publics under the conditions of a changing emotional regime.

REFERENCES

Aristotle. 1968. *The Rhetoric*. Translated by W. Rhys Roberts. New York: Random House.
Bennett, Lance W., and Alexandra Segerberg. 2013. *The Logic of Connective Action: Digital Media and the Personalization of Contentious Politics*. Cambridge: Cambridge University Press.
Delli Carpini, Michael X. 2018. "Alternative Facts: Donald Trump and the Emergence of a New U.S. Media Regime." In *Trump and the Media*, edited by Pablo Boczkowski and Zizi Papacharissi, 17–24. Cambridge, MA: MIT Press.
Elias, Norbert. 2000. *The Civilizing Process*. Rev. ed. Malden, MA: Blackwell.
Eksner, Julia. 2015. "Indexing Anger and Aggression: From Language Ideologies to Linguistic Affect." In *Methods of Exploring Emotions*, edited by Helena Flam and Jochen Kleres, 193–205. New York: Routledge.
Goodwin, Jeff, James M. Jasper, and Francesca Polletta, eds. 2001. *Passionate Politics: Emotions and Social Movements*. Chicago: University of Chicago Press.
Gould, Deborah B. 2010. "On Affect and Protest." In *Political Emotions*, edited by Janet Staiger, Ann Cvetkovich, and Ann Reynolds, 18–45. London: Routledge.
Gould, Deborah B. 2012. "Political Despair." In *Politics and Emotions: The Affective Turn in Contemporary Political Studies*, edited by Paul Hoggett and Simon Thompson, 95–111. New York: Continuum.
Higgins, Michael. 2008. *Media and Their Publics*. Maidenhead: Open University Press.
Higgins, Michael, and Angela Smith. 2016. *Belligerent Broadcasting: Synthetic Argument in Broadcast Talk*. London: Routledge.
Hochschild, Arlie R. 1983. *The Managed Heart*. Berkeley, CA: University of California Press.

Holmes, Mary. 2004. "Introduction: The Importance of Being Angry: Anger in Political Life." *European Journal of Social Theory* 7 (2): 123–132.
Jasper, James M. 2011. "Emotions and Social Movements: Twenty Years of Theory and Research." *Annual Review of Sociology* 37: 285–303.
Katriel, Tamar. 2015. "Exploring Emotion Discourse." In *Methods of Exploring Emotions*, edited by Helena Flam and Jochen Kleres, 57–67. New York: Routledge.
Lyman, Peter. 2004. "The Domestication of Anger: The Use and Abuse of Anger in Politics." *European Journal of Social Theory* 7 (2): 133–147.
McCosker, Anthony. 2014. "Trolling as Provocation: YouTube's Agonistic Publics." *Convergence* 20 (2): 201–217.
Moore, Robert. 2018. "Donald Trump Signs Order Overturning Family Separation Policy." *ITV News Report*, June 20. http://www.itv.com/news/2018-06-20/donald-trump-signs-order-overturning-family-separation-policy/.
Mouffe, Chantal. 2000. "For an Agonistic Model of Democracy." In *Political Theory in Transition*, edited by Noel O'Sullivan, 113–130. London: Routledge.
Mouffe, Chantal. 2005. *The Return of the Political*. London: Verso.
Nussbaum, Martha C. 2016. *Anger and Forgiveness: Resentment, Generosity, Justice*. Oxford: Oxford University Press.
Pantti, Mervi K., and Karin Wahl-Jorgensen. 2011. "'Not an Act of God': Anger and Citizenship in Press Coverage of British Man-Made Disasters." *Media, Culture & Society* 33 (1): 105–122.
Papacharissi, Zizi. 2014. *Affective Publics: Sentiment, Technology, and Politics*. Oxford: Oxford University Press.
Papacharissi, Zizi, and Maria de Fatima Oliveira. 2012. "Affective News and Networked Publics: The Rhythms of News Storytelling on #Egypt." *Journal of Communication* 62 (2): 266–282.
Reddy, William M. 2001. *The Navigation of Feeling: A Framework for the History of Emotions*. Cambridge: Cambridge University Press.
Shaw, Frances. 2014. "Emotional Investments: Australian Feminist Blogging and Affective Networks." In *Internet and Emotions*, edited by Tova Benski and Eran Fisher, 211–224. London and New York: Routledge.
Wahl-Jorgensen, Karin. 2018a. "Towards a Typology of Mediated Anger: Routine Coverage of Protest and Political Emotion." *International Journal of Communication* 12: 2071–2087.
Wahl-Jorgensen, Karin. 2018b. "The Angry Populism of Donald Trump." *Media, Culture & Society* 40 (5): 766–778.
Wahl-Jorgensen, Karin. 2019. *Emotions, Media and Politics*. Cambridge: Polity.
Wettergren, Åsa. 2005. "Mobilization and the Moral Shock: Adbusters Media Foundation." In *Emotions and Social Movements*, edited by Helena Flam and Debra King, 99–118. London: Routledge.

CHAPTER 4

Unruly Women and Carnivalesque Counter-Control: Offensive Humor in Mediated Social Protest

Anne Graefer, Allaina Kilby and Inger-Lise Kalviknes Bore

INTRODUCTION

The Women's March in January 2018 was a worldwide protest to advocate legislation and policies regarding human rights and other issues, including women's rights, immigration reform, health-care reform, racial

---

A version of this chapter has been previously published in:
Journal of Communication Inquiry, Online First, https://doi.org/10.1177/0196859918800485.

A. Graefer (✉)
Birmingham Centre for Media and Cultural Research,
Birmingham City University, Birmingham, UK
e-mail: anne.graefer@bcu.ac.uk

A. Kilby
Lecturer in Media & Communication, Swansea University, Swansea, UK
e-mail: a.c.kilby@swansea.ac.uk

I.-L. K. Bore
Independent Researcher, Oslo, Norway
e-mail: ikbore@gmail.com

equality, freedom of religion, and workers' rights. Most of the rallies were aimed at Donald Trump, largely due to statements he had made and positions that he had taken which were regarded as racist, anti-women, or otherwise offensive. To vent this anger, many protest posters featured offensive jokes at the expense of Trump's body, mocking his "comb over" hairstyle, his small hands, his orange taint, and so on. Such posters were often spotted at protests and shared widely online, much to the amusement of the movement's supporters. While some people suggest that such charged political online humor can mobilize people and serve as "a pre-political gateway to future civic engagement" (Reilly and Boler 2014, 442), there is also concern that it remains inefficient or even antithetical to meaningful sociopolitical change (Thorogood 2016). Thus, in the context of social media, offensive political humor advances the so-called echo chambers where people only speak to like-minded individuals (Bore et al. 2018). Others argue that routine online searches for pleasure and entertainment "entrap[s] us within the circuits of neoliberal communicative capitalism—a process that continuously replaces political action with political feeling, forever turning activity into passivity" (Pedwell 2017).

By drawing on the literature that explores and adapts Bakhtin's (1984) concept of the carnivalesque (e.g., Rowe 1995; Stallybrass and White 1986), this article argues for a more nuanced understanding of offensive political humor as a flexible affective resource that is complexly intertwined with social change (Pedwell 2017). Based on our analysis of 400 social media posts from Instagram and Twitter, we argue that the online circulation of humorous (yet offensive) protest posters creates forms of "polysemic undertow" (Waisanen and Becker 2015, 261) that both contest and confirm normative assumptions about White masculinity and the political public sphere. For this reason, the meanings of these protest posters are not so coherent as to reflect either transgression or backlash politics exclusively. Rather, the contradictory nature of offensive humor holds these circulating online images in tension, thereby enabling what Reilly and Boler (2014) call "prepolitization"—a novel form of civic participation that can mobilize citizens who would not otherwise explicitly participate in civic life, thereby creating new political sensibilities and desires.

We argue that the Women's March provides unique insight into how offensive humor can function as a mobilizing force, without glossing over its limitations in the realm of civic engagement. Offending those in power does not replace rational political debate. Nonetheless, it can be an effective tool for drawing attention to situations of injustice, for binding people together against formal power structures of authority, and for carving out a space for empowering feelings of counter control, which are necessary ingredients for social and political change (Day 2011; Mouffe 2005). In this sense, this article contributes to the work of contemporary scholars of social movements and media who rethink traditional understandings of politics and participatory democracy.

Literature Review: Offence, Online Humor, and Mediated Protest

The cheerful vulgarity of the powerless is used as a weapon against the pretence and hypocrisy of the powerful. (Stamm 1982, 47)

Giving and taking offence on social networking sites is a contested topic. While some celebrate the interactive architecture of social media as a democratizing and diversifying force, others warn that these seemingly antihierarchical affordances invite offensive behavior, such as cyberbullying or the production and circulation of offensive material that more traditional media outlets would have censored or regulated. Thus, social media and other user content hosting companies are increasingly under the ethical and legal responsibility to make their network a "positive" and "safe" space where offence is avoided.

Offence, however, is an affectively charged, slippery subject that escapes clear definitions. As Sonia Livingstone and Andrea Millwood Hargrave note, "offensive material is, in principle, distinguished from that which is illegal (obscenity, child abuse images, incitement to racial hatred, etc.), [and yet] it remains difficult to define the boundaries in a robust and consensual fashion" (2009, 25). Generally, media content is judged to be offensive when it is too graphic or explicit in style and content (Attwood et al. 2012). Intrusive images of suffering, or racist, classist, or sexist depictions that contribute to stereotyping, or bias and inaccuracy in the media are often reported as offending audiences (Livingstone and Hargrave 2009). In public discussions, "offensive" media content is often equated with "harmful" content. This equation is based on simplistic theories of media effects that conceive offence as a monolithic "bad" thing that can be pinned to certain media representations and eliminated through censorship. Such understandings fail to see the contextual, relational nature of offence (offensive to whom? in what situation?) as well as the affective messiness of offence. Offence is far from a monolithic, clear-cut emotion but contains a wide range of contradictory feelings and emotions, such as pain, anger, and frustration, alongside joy and titillation (Das and Graefer 2017). Furthermore, these approaches overlook the potential for the so-called negative emotions to push us into new critical directions, as it has long been theorized by feminist scholars such as Audre Lorde (1984), Sara Ahmed (2007), and Sianne Ngai (2005). Taking offence and "getting angry" is here often conceived as an affective mobilizing force for social and political transformation.

Offensive joking, in particular, has been theorized as offering temporary relief from oppressive social norms and conventions (Freud 1960). Pickering and Littlewood (1998) argue that what remains crucial in this context is whether the humor kicks socially upwards or downwards; whether comic aggression is directed "at those who are in positions of power and authority, or at those who are relatively powerless and subordinated" (p. 295). Such an understanding implies that offence is not in and of itself wrong and that, depending on its direction, it can have a positive or negative impact.

The affirmative and liberating possibilities of grotesque, offensive humorous transgressions are often associated with "the carnivalesque": A general mood of liberation, mocking of hierarchies, and temporary suspension of rules (Bakhtin 1984). For Mikhail Bakhtin (1984), the popular tradition of carnival has the potential to suspend social hierarchies through mostly bodily and bawdy humor, which finds expression in the celebration of bodily grotesqueness and excessiveness, fooling around, and profanities. These markers of indecorum are strictly policed during "normal" times, but during carnival, they can be animated and enable comic reversals. For instance, a jester might be crowned in place of a king, and, as a result, the authoritative voice of the dominant discourse momentarily loses its privilege. Bakhtinian carnival theory has been criticized for its neglect of carnival violence against women and Jews, its failure to consider social relations of gender, and its failure to deal with the consistence of dominant culture (e.g., Russo 1994). We nevertheless see Bakhtin's concept as a valuable starting point and draw on the productive ways in which it has been extended through the work of Stallybrass and White (1986) and Rowe (1995). First, Stallybrass and White (1986) argue that the carnivalesque should be situated within a wider pattern of transgression, in order to "move beyond Bakhtin's problematic folkloric approach to a political anthropology of binary extremism in class society" (p. 28). They maintain that this broader focus on "transgressive symbolic domains" enables us not only to examine cultural hierarchies and binary social structures that underlie the carnival but also to "operate far beyond the strict confines of popular festivities." Second, Kathleen Rowe (1990, 1995) builds on Mary Russo's (1994) work on the female grotesque to adapt Bakhtin's concept for thinking about female unruliness. As Rowe (1995) argues, the transgressive figure of the "unruly woman" can help "sanction political disobedience" but is also associated with dirt and pollution (p. 83). She threatens "the conceptual categories which organize our lives," and this liminality evokes intense, contradictory feelings: "Her ambivalence, which is the source of her oppositional power, is usually contained within the licence accorded to the comic and the carnivalesque. But not always." Our study, then, draws on these two key extensions of Bakhtin's work to examine how transgression spills over the confines of the temporary, local contexts of the Women's March through the online circulation of offensive protest humor. Here, the carnivalesque functions as a malleable resource that can provide spaces for disruption and rebellion, without glossing over cultural differences.

However, while some scholars in critical humor studies have argued that offensive humor can operate as a powerful social corrective as well as a strategic and effective commentator on political issues (Bivens and Cole 2018; Thorogood 2016), others highlight that its uniting-and-dividing function draws a sharp boundary between those who laugh and those who are not "in on the joke" (Kuipers 2011; Lockyer and Pickering 2001). From such a perspective, bawdy political humor that predominantly works by deriding and offending those in power is merely:

> further convincing those who agree with it while alienating those who don't agree. Thus, the satirical mission to "make laugh, not war" only serves to polemicise the gap between those who agree and disagree with its political message, suggesting its transformative worth is limited. (Thorogood 2016, 217)

This so-called echo chamber phenomenon is often discussed in the context of social media. Critics argue that, rather than enabling debate and deliberative compromise essential for creating political change, our social media practices of "posting," "liking" and "sharing," along with algorithms, generate filter bubbles and echo chambers with restrictive partisan sentiments, where only like-minded people speak to each other (Bore et al. 2018; Jamieson and Capella 2008; Pariser 2012). Nevertheless, Bivens and Cole (2018, 6) maintain that "the prevalence of social media use, like Instagram, Facebook, and Twitter, provides a method through which individuals can push back against the legislative structures in the United States." They illustrate in their work on "grotesque protest" that social media provides individuals with opportunities to resist attempts to control bodies and to reinsert individuals' voices in political discourse that is aimed to exclude those bodies (Enli and Skogerbø 2013). In a similar vein, Tufekci and Wilson (2012) found that social media use greatly increased the odds of being involved in a protest, and that it "represent[s] crosscutting networking mechanisms in a protest ecology" (Segerberg and Bennett 2011, 197). Thus, although commonly understood as like minds speaking to like minds, social media can also be seen to diversify protest networks and encourage debate.

Methodology

This article builds on our previous study (Bore et al. 2018), which examined the social media circulation of images from the 2017 Women's March. One of the key themes we identified was the prevalence of images featuring placards that mocked Trump's body. We want to explore this tendency further within the context of the 2018 Women's March, to consider how offensive humor posts of images that were shared on Instagram and Twitter between January 20 and 21, 2018. We chose these two platforms because they are associated with different affordances and cultures. Twitter is reportedly used by 24% of the U.S. adults (Smith and Anderson 2018), and, although it facilitates the sharing of imagery, it is primarily associated with text content (Sulleyman 2018) and has often been used for political communication and activism (Enli and Skogerbø 2013). Instagram is reportedly used by 35% of the U.S. adults (Smith and Anderson 2018). This platform foregrounds imagery and is often considered a feminized online space that is preoccupied with celebrity, beauty, and style (Seligson 2016). We are interested in images of protest signs as a form of visual and affective political communication, and about how protesters and social media users can grab our attention and encourage circulation through the use of offensive humor and spectacle might function as an affective protest strategy. We collected our sample by using the #WomensMarch2018 and #WomensMarchNYC hashtags to search for public posts of images that were shared on Instagram and Twitter between January 20 and 21, 2018. We chose these two platforms because they are associated with different affordances and cultures. Twitter is reportedly used by 24% of the U.S. adults (Smith and Anderson 2018), and, although it facilitates the sharing of imagery, it is primarily associated with text content (Sulleyman 2018) and has often been used for political communication and activism (Enli and Skogerbø 2013). Instagram is reportedly used by 35% of the U.S. adults (Smith and Anderson 2018). This platform foregrounds imagery and is often considered a feminized online space that is preoccupied with celebrity, beauty, and style (Seligson 2016). We are interested in images of protest signs as a form of visual and affective political communication, and about how protesters and social media users can grab our attention and encourage circulation through the use of offensive humor and spectacle.

Our data collection followed a three-step process. On the day of the march, we followed the #WomensMarch2018 and #WomensMarchNYC hashtags on Twitter and Instagram and observed recurring images of individuals and groups of protesters holding protest signs, many of which were designed to offend Donald Trump through bawdy and bodily humor. This trend confirmed that offensive humor was once again a prevalent protest strategy. On January 22, we then used the platform tools to collect the 200 "top" posts from each of the two platforms for thematic analysis. We identified three recurring themes: The ridicule of Trump's body, the association of Trump with excrement, and name-calling and violence targeting Trump. Finally, we selected one illustrative post from each of these three themes for close analysis. We include screengrabs of the images here but have removed social media usernames and profile pictures. The three-case study images were all widely shared on social media. This approach facilitates reflection on how the reiteration and circulation of images "invite polysemic undertow" (Waisanen and Becker 2015, 264) that can unsettle Trump's intended personae as a serious public official and thereby animate political engagement and social change. Having outlined our theoretical framework and our methodological approach, we will now move on to our three-part analysis. We begin by exploring the tendency to mock Trump's skin color.

ORANGE SKIN, WHITE MASCULINITY, AND CARNIVALESQUE COUNTERCONTROL

Trump's body is often the target of ridicule. His "orange" skin tone has inspired large numbers of Internet memes where the president is mocked as "Agent Orange" or "Cheeto Trump." Equally popular targets are his supposedly "tiny" hands. Merchandise includes t-shirts that read "Keep your tiny hands off my rights" and coffee cups with extra small handles, just two of the many physical and digital artifacts through which Trump's opponents publicly ridicule his masculinity. Here, we focus on the recurring degradation of Trump as failed White masculinity and use Bakhtin's (1984) concept of the carnivalesque to consider the ambiguous workings of this offensive humor in political protest (Fig. 4.1).

Figure 4.1 draws attention to the Deferred Action for Childhood Arrivals (DACA) act that the Trump administration has tried to rescind since September 2017. DACA, an Obama-era protection scheme, allows those who entered the United States illegally as children to receive a renewable, 2-year period of deferred action from deportation and to be eligible for a work permit. The scheme is now closed to new entrants and puts 800,000 registered recipients in danger of deportation. Trump's attack on DACA offended not only many DREAMERS (recipients of DACA) but also protesters at the Women's March. Thus, numerous protest posters in the 2018 March focused on DACA and Fig. 4.1 is one such example.

Fig. 4.1 Poster from Women's March 2018 New York, Central Park (*Source* Instagram)

Under the pink headline "DACA DACA TINY COCK-A," we see a cartoon-like drawing of Trump. He is naked, showing off his "orange" skin, and wearing only a blue jacket and a red tie. His signature comb-over hair-do is exaggerated and his arms are wide open. The lines around his small hands make it look as if he is "flashing" the onlooker, showing off his small penis, or his "tiny cock-a," as the poster reads. The poster criticizes the imminent changes in DACA policy and aims to provoke laughter by offending and shaming Trump's body through the use of "carnivalesque" humor. Drawing on Bakhtin's (1984) work, we employ the concept of the carnivalesque to think about vulgar, grotesque, bodily humor that is commonly intended or experienced as offensive, and that is used to challenge privileged positions and reframe public and political discourse.

The rhyme "DACA DACA TINY COCK-A" mimics the ways in which small children try to offend each other in the playground. It relies on the shared understanding that there is a comic incongruity between our expectations for "presidential" behavior and the "childish" and unconsidered ways in which Trump presents himself publicly and politically. Trump's child-like behavior violates dominant assumptions about the rational, male agent in the political public sphere, and it can be argued that it is exactly these kinds of transgressions that Trump's opponents experience as offensive, and which in turn mobilize them to protest and give offence back.

The poster also makes reference to the running joke of Trump's "tiny hands," and the popular myth that a man's hand size is indicative of his penis size. Small hands here suggest a lack of masculinity and a lack of gendered attributes, such as strength and leadership. The link between hands and gender performance is underlined by Janice Winship's (1981) influential work about the relationship between the positioning of hands and sexuality in advertising. According to her analysis, male and female hands are part of an entire message system of representation signifying appropriate gender behavior. In other words, hands allow us to tap into familiar ideologies of masculinity and femininity because the big and strong hand of the "leader" is "naturally" the hand of a man, whereas the small and delicate hand of the homemaker and caretaker is "naturally" the hand of a woman. By repeatedly mocking Trump for his "small" hands, opponents do not only offend his masculinity on a personal level, but they undermine his presidency by insinuating that he is not a "real" man, he is not a "leader" and therefore not someone we should fear, trust, or follow.

Furthermore, the poster constructs the naked, overly tanned Trump as the butt of the joke because orange skin is commonly perceived as a funny tanning "accident" rather than a desired skin hue. As Graefer (2014) argues, "orange" skin invites ridicule and offence giving as it symbolizes excessiveness, lack of taste, and the pollution of "proper" whiteness. Regarded as "ugly" and "tasteless," this skin tone stands in stark contrast to the White hue that the proper White, middle-class subject should embody. The White, middle-class subject is controlled and rational in its desire to darken its skin, making tanning in this case an acceptable and positive habit. Orange skin, on the other hand, is taken as visible evidence of a subject's inner out-of-controlness and illustrates that Trump does not have the supposedly innate cultural tastes and decorum that wealthy White people should have. His highly visible over- and misuse of tanning products also marks him as vain and overly concerned with his appearance, characteristics that are commonly associated with femininity rather than masculinity.

The DACA DACA protest poster then uses offensive, bodily humor to produce Trump as a figure of ridicule, but this kind of humor is riddled with both transgressive and conservative tendencies: One could, for instance, argue that offensive humor works here to undermine the powerful White man via emasculation. Yet it ironically also works to restore dominant assumptions of an idealized White masculinity that is free from feminine traces, such as tiny hands or vanity, and immaculately White, rather than orange. Furthermore, the vulgar ridiculing of Trump's body can also be interpreted as conservative because women have historically been silenced and policed through these same mechanisms of body shaming.

However, we should not reject offensive humor as a tool in mediated social protest altogether. Rather, we suggest that this online sharing of offensive humor aimed at the powerful can be seen as a contemporary expression of Bakhtin's (1984) carnivalesque. Despite the fact that online practices in the context of Instagram and Twitter defy the circumscribed spatial and temporal specificity of "carnival," it still provides a useful tool for understanding the transformative potential of offensive, vulgar humor because it illustrates how the transgression of social boundaries (i.e., being offensive) can be a productive act of resistance. This potential is grounded in the collective experience of transgression:

> Carnival is not a spectacle seen by people; they live in it, and everyone participates because its very idea embraces all the people … It has a universal spirit; it is a special condition of the entire world, of the world's revival and renewal, in which all take part. (Bakhtin 1984, 7)

Notwithstanding the inherent problems of Bakhtin's celebratory universalism, it can be argued that posting offensive placards against Trump generates new forms of collectivity because it serves as a public act of stance-taking (Du Bois 2007), where people align (and disalign) with others through the stances they take toward a particular idea, object, or person. Offending Trump through humor works, then, not only to vent the protesters' anger and frustration but to create a sense of superiority and belonging, through the affective experience of shared laughter:

> Laughing at faulty behaviour [and bodies] can also reinforce unity among group members, as a feeling of superiority over those being ridiculed can coexist with a feeling of belonging. (Duncan 1982 cited in J. C. Meyer 2000, 351)

These acts of online offence giving, then, are performances designed to appeal to like-minded others, thereby aligning bodies with antiracist counterpolitics and drawing boundaries between "us" and "them." Some of the comments in Fig. 4.2 highlight this uniting power of offensive humor.

Expressions such as "Love it" or the powerful arm emoji illustrate that sharing "great signs" beyond the marches enables new forms of collectivity, temporary zones in which feminists are able to take a stance and make their anger visible while enjoying themselves in the process. The glee and pleasure that users experienced when engaging with these offensive online images can be seen as producing carnivalesque moments of countercontrol where activists no longer feel helpless in the face of patriarchy and racism, but where they feel powerful and impactful. Our premise, then, is that offensive humor, as communicated through these images, is affective and, as such, drives online exchanges and attaches people to particular platforms, threads, or groups. A direct, tangible and measurable "effect" of activism might not be easy to locate, yet it would be wrong to ignore results like the production of feeling, which, we argue, is necessary for social change.

Fig. 4.2 Users commenting on the circulated image from the protest (*Source* Instagram)

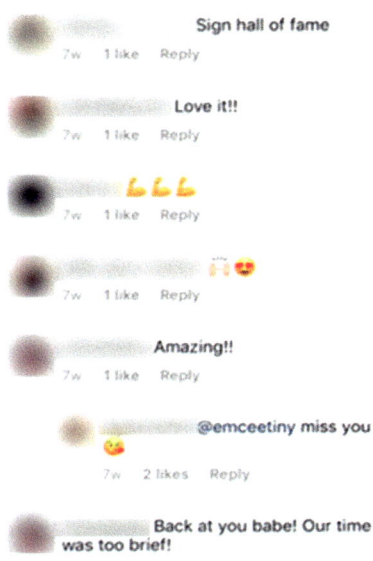

FILTH, CULTURAL TRANSGRESSION, AND IMMIGRANT BODIES

We now turn to the second recurring theme in the circulated images from the 2018 Women's March, which was the degradation of Trump through the semiotic resource of filth. Combining the concept of the carnivalesque with Stallybrass and White's (1986) notion of cultural transgression, we examine a sign shared on Twitter and consider how it responded to Trump's offensive behavior by shifting the shame and otherness he inscribes on immigrant bodies onto the president himself (Fig. 4.3).

This image was posted by a private Twitter user, who photographed and shared his "favorite" signs from the Women's March in New York City. At the time of our data collection, the tweet had been shared 625 times, favorited 1.7K times and had received 70 comments. The sign depicts Trump's face as a bottom that emits a brown puddle. Across his yellow hair, the text reads "F*ING MORON," while text within the brown puddle reads "LIAR." The discursive association between Trump and feces work in two key ways here. First, the sign is a critique of Trump's use of the term "shithole countries" to refer to the nations of

Fig. 4.3 Photo of protest poster depicting Trump's face as a bottom (*Source* Twitter)

origin of immigrants he considered undesirable (Dawsey 2018). Second, the sign uses comic inversion and grotesque imagery to construct Trump as abject. We explore how these strategies work together and reflect on how they invite onlookers to feel both offence and pleasure.

Trump's "shithole" remarks were made in a meeting with the U.S. senators on January 11, 2018, and received extensive international media coverage. The president of Senegal said he was "shocked," the government of Botswana said the remarks were "irresponsible, reprehensible and racist," while an African group of ambassadors at the United Nations described them as "outrageous, racist and xenophobic" (Taylor 2018). The remarks, then, were widely constructed as offensive.

The protest sign shifts the "shithole" label from these nations onto Trump himself, repositioning the offender as the target of offence. Here, Trump becomes the "shithole," reduced to an abject body part and dismissed as a "moron." As in the grotesque imagery described by Bakhtin (1984), we see a decentered body that is ruptured by bulges and orifices. The close-up image fills the entire sign. The buttocks are comically round and disproportionately large. The anus protrudes and leaks filth.

The vulgarity of the picture is echoed by the crudeness of the written language: Trump's debased body contaminates the world with its "shit." Such rhetorical strategies work "to mock, destabilize, and publicize private parts and activities we are socialized to hide" (Bivens and Cole 2018, 20). Situated within protest culture, the sign employed this carnivalesque language and imagery to contribute an affective critique of Trump to public sphere debates around his presidency. By shifting the "shithole" label from developing nations onto Trump himself, it reverted the cultural hierarchy of Trump's racist immigration policy, simultaneously articulating offence at his racism, and giving back offence by degrading and insulting the president.

The reach of the sign was extended beyond the moment and geographical context of the march through the circulation of the image on social media. The Twitter user who shared it used the platform's comment function to share a number of other photographs of protest signs, while other users responded by expressing excitement, laughter, calling for Trump to be impeached, and sharing photographs of other signs that resonated with them. One, held up by a woman with sunglasses, for example, repeats the offensive comparison between rejecting DACA and thereby becoming CACA (Fig. 4.4).

We can locate these photographed protest signs within a wider symbolic practice that degrades Trump by associating him with the lower stratum of the body (Bakhtin 1984). Trump's buttocks and feces were recurring themes in circulating images from the 2018 Women's March, while other social media users have also adopted the hashtags #PEEOTUS and #SCROTUS to avoid mentioning Trump's name and

Fig. 4.4 "If you don't support DACA you're [caca]". Woman with protest poster, Women's March 2018 New York (*Source* Instagram)

title, thereby denying the legitimacy of his presidency (Bivens and Cole 2018). This refusal indicates that he is seen as a transgressive figure. He is both president and other, both insider and outsider. Drawing on Stallybrass and White (1986), we argue that the widespread use of grotesque representations signals a dual sense of disgust and fascination with Trump. His offensive behavior represents base impulses that should have been repressed from the rational public sphere, a notion that is also evident in Hillary Clinton's labeling of some Trump supporters as "deplorables" with "racist, sexist, homophobic, xenophobic, Islamaphobic" views (Reilly 2016). Trump-as-president is a hybrid of high and low discourse, a transgression of established cultural boundaries that creates a "powerful symbolic dissonance" (Stallybrass and White 1986, 25). The recurring use of filth as a semiotic resource in protest signs can be seen as an attempt to reaffirm the classification of him as other, suggesting the coexistence of a desire "to degrade the high and mighty" and "a paradoxical reverence for tradition and hierarchy" (Gilmore 1998, 6). Through this mingling of transgressive and conservative tendencies, the target of laughter and offence is not the presidency as an institution, but Trump as an illegitimate president.

Challenging the universalism that undermines Bakhtin's work on the carnival, Stallybrass and White (1986) were interested in examining the cultural transgressions of class binaries. Our study, in turn, underscores that class structures intersect with those of race, nationality, and gender. In each case, "discourses about the body have a privileged role, for transcoding between different levels and sectors of social and psychic reality are effected through the intensifying grid of the body" (Stallybrass and White 1986, 26). Trump attempts to classify, legislate, and control the bodies of immigrants by associating them with excrement, while protesters use the same semiotic resource to degrade his body and delegitimize his presidency. As Stallybrass and White (1986) note, "somatic symbols … are ultimate elements of social classification itself" (p. 26).

Thorogood (2016) suggests that crude, ambiguous humor can help fight disengagement from formal politics. By "reducing politics to the excretions of the human body," protesters negotiate and challenge geopolitical discourse by connecting contemporary debates to our shared bodily vulnerability. As Grant-Smith (2010) writes, "we all shit," and so defecation can be mobilized to demonstrate our "common humanity and animality" (para. 29). However, we would argue that this sign does not work to position Trump within a human collective but instead positions him as a repulsive other. Its strategy resembles that of the "DACA DACA" sign, as it employs the playground rhetoric of "no, you're the shithole." However, drawing on Bivens and Cole, we nonetheless argue that "grotesque protest" can still work as "an effective tool for opening space, transgressing boundaries, and demanding attention." The excess of protest signs like this one invites us to take gleeful pleasure in offending Trump, reminding him that he is out of place and illegitimate, and demonstrating resistance to his attempts "to control bodies." In this way, the grotesque is mobilized "to strategically reframe public and political discourse about the body" through street protests and on social media (Bivens and Cole 2018, 7).

Across the protest signs focusing on "orange" Trump and Trump-as-filth, his White, male, heterosexual, and wealthy body is subjected to degrading strategies that have long been used to oppress women and minorities. It here becomes violently appropriated as a site of resistance, used to articulate feelings of offence but also to cause offence. This strategy valorizes anger as a political emotion and invites us to take pleasure in voicing that anger without concern for the decorum imposed on women by patriarchal discourse. The last part of our analysis will focus in on this relationship between gender, anger, and offensive humor.

The Retaliation of the Unruly

In this final theme of circulated protest signs from the 2018 Women's March, we examine how female protestors used the characteristics of unruliness, such as offence (Rowe 1995), to appropriate Trump as the target of carnivalesque humor. To illustrate this trend, we conduct a close analysis of the sign saying "Little bitch, you can't fuck with me," which demonstrates the ambiguity that was evident in some of the offensive Trump placards (Fig. 4.5).

This sign mixes humor, politics, and popular culture to promote the embrace of unruly feminism and to protest an epidemic culture of sexual harassment and the policing of women's bodies. The sign features a quote from music artist Cardi B's song "Bodak Yellow"; a "diss" track that skewers those who have mocked B's rise to fame from Bronx stripper to music history maker. In this track, B uses the pejorative term "little bitch" to lambast those who criticize her achievements, but in the context of the Women's March, the term is used to insult Trump's behavior and body.

Fig. 4.5 "Little bitch you can't fuck with me" (Photo of protest placard posted by Cardi B on Instagram)

According to The Urban Dictionary (2006), "little bitch" is a whiny, petty person, willing to stab people in the back. Thus, the sign's reappropriation of the popular term connects these associations with Trump's actions and behavior, such as his claim that "no politician in history has been treated worse" (Gambino 2017) than him, his childish exchanges with North Korean leader Kim Jong Un, and the Republican Party's cutting of Medicaid, which Trump's working-class supporters are reliant on (Harwood 2017). The gendered nature of the term "bitch" further attacks Trump's "inadequate" masculinity, emphasized by the word "little" and its connection to the long-running joke about his small hands and penis.

The sign combines this insult with a threat through the phrase "you can't fuck with me" and the image of Trump's head pinned down by a pair of Black, high-heeled feet. Together, they act as a warning that the Women's March activists are not to be "messed with." This threat is supported by Cardi B's own clarification of her lyrics: "I can be humble but … if you push me, I can really stamp on your head" (Giulione 2017).

While the song incites violent behavior, its meaning within a humorous placard is much more ambiguous. As Lockyer and Pickering (2005, 13) argue, the line between make-believe and reality is not clear in a joking context. This is because humor can be a form of exaggeration, but it can also be used to express real beliefs (Lockyer and Pickering 2005). Thus, while some may view the sign's message as threatening and offensive, others may defend it as "just a joke" or benign violation humor (McGraw and Warren 2010) that appears immoral but is essentially harmless because the words are "just" borrowed from a song and are not the actual words of the protestors.

This image garnered many affective responses because it was posted by Cardi B and circulated to her 17 million Instagram followers. B's cultural and symbolic capital afforded maximum exposure to the protest sign and this particular Women's March message. According to D. S. Meyer (1995, 182), one of the key benefits of celebrity-endorsed protest is "the increased mobilization of support and publicity". Similarly, scholars have argued that music has the capacity to mobilize political action and collective identity (DeNora 2000; Githens-Mazer 2008). Such ideas are applicable to Cardi B's Instagram post, as it acquired over 1 million likes and nearly 13,000 comments. The comments were varied; some expressed support for Trump, arguing that he was "creating a fuck ton of jobs," while some expressed amusement through the crying laughing emoji. However, the dominant response expressed support for the sign's message and B's accompanying comment about the disrespectful treatment of women: "Yaaas" supported by the hands up in agreement emoji; "This is everything"; and "Yas girl, pussy power."

The sign's divisive humor perhaps resonated with Instagram users because it reflects a shift in feminist tone since the 2017 Women's March. The first event launched as a reaction to Trump's misogynistic behavior and the GOP's attempts to cut female health care. But, since then, we have been confronted with the Weinstein scandal and a myriad of sexual harassment cases highlighted by the #Metoo movement and #Timesup initiative. The shocking extent of abuse, identified across different industries, has accelerated and widened the objectives of the current women's movement, accompanied by widespread expressions of anger and the adoption of a combative tone. That tone is evident in this sign, where it takes the form of "rebellious humor that simultaneously mocks the powerful" (Billing 2005, 207, 208) and creates connective laughter among the unruly women of the March.

Unruly women do not conform to traditional norms of femininity that emphasize women's passivity, compliance, and agreeability (Fox 1977; Tolman et al. 2006). Instead, their unruliness is characterized by aggression, humor, and their will to offend and challenge the patriarchal status quo (Peterson 2017; Rowe 1995). Once again, these characteristics draw our attention to Bakhtin's (1984) work on the "carnivalesque" as a form of grotesque resistance. For Bakhtin, the female body signifies the grotesque body because "woman is related to the material bodily lower stratum" (p. 24) through menstruation, pregnancy, and childbirth. This is a problematic label that highlights the limitations associated with Bakhtin's (1984) claims that the carnival was a liberating event that embraced all people. "The female association with the lower bodily stratum connotes shame and filth, which works in contrast to the cerebral upper body that is associated with higher functions of thought and emotion" (Mizejewski 2014, 100). It suggests that the female body was a victim of the carnival's subversive comedy, rather than an instigator of it. This argument resonates with the work of other scholars (Russo 1994; Stallybrass and White 1986), who argue that women were regularly subjected to physical and verbal abuse at the carnival.

The characteristics of unruliness and the grotesque appear to be grounded in misogyny, as they have been used to attack women who do not conform to traditional standards of femininity. However, Rowe (1995, 91) argues that "transgressing this line of acceptability can be a source of power for women, especially when the characteristics or unruliness are recoded and reframed to expose what they conceal": The oppression of women through the expectation that we stay silent, compliant, and do not make a spectacle of ourselves. The women of the March use the semiotic resources of unruliness as part of affective strategies to claim visibility, voice, and agency and to reposition Trump as the grotesque body. Consequently, the male body that stands accused of mocking, attacking, and attempting to police the female body becomes the protestors' symbolic target of collective, angry, and offensive humor.

While Trump may be the sign's chief target, its humorous political message can also be read as an attack on all those who reinforce the patriarchal status quo. Its circulation on Instagram might be particularly valuable, then, because of the site's preoccupation with conventional beauty and body standards (Seligson 2016). However, while Instagram may bolster traditional notions of femininity, its audience of 800 million active users and its visual-led content make it an attractive platform to challenge these conventions via online activism. Deluca and Peeples stress the power of visual communication in their theorization of the public screen. Their work attempts to expand our understanding of political debate beyond the emphasis on face-to-face rational dialogue of the public sphere (Habermas 1974) by arguing that the use of spectacle across image-led media platforms can expand dialogue and make political issues more accessible (Deluca and Peeples 2002). Consequently, Cardi B's post indicates that the circulation of feminist content within the feminized sphere of Instagram might have the potential to attract new supporters to the Women's March movement and create a space for users to deliberate its messages, beyond the temporal and spatial confinements of the marches themselves.

Conclusion

This article has unpacked some of the ways in which protest signs in the 2018 Women's March used offensive humor to challenge Trump and reflected on how they were recontextualized and circulated on Twitter and Instagram. Through the close analysis of three social media posts, we have explored how Trump was dismissed as an improper White, masculine subject, how he was degraded through an association with feces and the lower bodily stratum, and, finally, how he was repositioned as the infantile, feminized victim of unruly women. Emphasizing the ambiguity of offensive humor, we identified a recurring tension not only between its uniting and dividing functions but also between conservative and radical tendencies: Protesters and social media users attacked Trump's patriarchal and racist policies and practices through the use of gendered and raced insults that simultaneously reinforced established notions of ideal white masculinity. This duality worked in two key ways: First, protesters identified and punished Trump as a transgressive other while redrawing the boundaries of appropriate White masculinity. This discourse articulated offence at his transgressions of established norms for public sphere debate and "presidential" behavior while simultaneously giving offence back through the spectacle of unruly, carnivalesque protest. Second, participants repeatedly appropriated aggressive, humorous strategies of offence giving that have been associated with masculine cultures (Pujolar 2000) and used to oppress female and non-White bodies (Thomas 2015). Here, they reversed that hierarchy by repositioning Trump as the abject body; malformed, leaking, and prostrate.

We argue that the use of offensive humor in feminist protest in online and offline spaces can open up new opportunities for unruly dialogue and civic participation. Online networks are central to this practice, as humorous content grabs our attention and is shared through followers and hashtags (Day 2011). This is "spreadable" (Jenkins et al. 2013) media content, which is privileged by popular platforms because it is entertaining and drives online traffic. As such, it "floats to the top" among representations of the 2018 Women's March and becomes part of the "popular memory" (Newman 2014, 16) of the event. This pattern is evident in the frequent publication of news articles listing the "funniest" protest signs from the march, which promotes the value of humor and spectacle in protest communication.

The signs, at the protests and in their new online contexts, offer the pleasures of creative, transgressive humor and offence giving (Pujolar 2000). This invites us to see the world differently through the carnivalesque lens of affective intensities, reversed hierarchies, and a grotesque aesthetic. Thus, in addition to laugher, offensive humor provides an effective intervention in the dominant regime by allowing unheard voices to be heard and to respond to the issues they face. But offensive humor as spectacle is not a tactic solely used by liberal protestors, it has also been used by right-wing Tea Party activists to draw attention to America's economic issues. Interestingly, bar one study (see Mayer et al. 2016) on the political content of Tea Party protest signs there is a deficit of research on conservative movements and humorous collective action strategies. Therefore, we believe that this would make a worthy topic of further research or comparative analysis of oppositional political movements.

Returning to the subject of the Women's March, we argue that offensive humor is a worthy political tool that readdresses traditional understandings of protest strategy in an attempt to publicize neglected political issues. This is because its attention-grabbing power might introduce citizens who do not see themselves as "political" to relevant issues, thereby "preparing them for civic participation and political engagement" (Dahlgren cited in Reilly and Boler 2014, 437). Furthermore, offensive humor appeals to like-minded others, thereby aligning bodies with feminist and antiracist counterpolitics in communities of resistance that include and transcend the geographically and temporally bound march events. This process can facilitate new insight and energize participants to continue their feminist and antiracist work in other spaces.

References

Ahmed, S. 2007. *Queer Phenomenology: Orientations, Objects, Others*. Durham, NC: Duke University Press.
Attwood, F., V. C. Campbell, and I. Q. Hunter. 2012. *Controversial Images: Media Representations on the Edge*. Basingstoke, England: Palgrave.
Bakhtin, M. 1984. *Rabelais and His World*. New York, NY: Wiley.
Billing, M. 2005. *Laughter & Ridicule: Towards a Social Critique of Humour*. London, England: Sage.
Bivens, K. M., and K. Cole. 2018. "The Grotesque Protest in Social Media as Embodied, Political Rhetoric." *Journal of Communication Enquiry* 42 (1): 5–25.
Bore, I. L. K., A. Graefer, and A. Kilby. 2018. "This Pussy Grabs Back: Humour, Digital Affects and Women's Protest." *Open Cultural Studies* 1: 529–540.
Das, R., and A. Graefer. 2017. *Provocative Screens: Offended Audiences in Britain and Germany*. Cham, Switzerland: Palgrave Pivot.
Dawsey, J. 2018. "Trump Derides Protections for Immigrants from 'Shithole' Countries." *The Washington Post*, January 12. Retrieved from https://www.washingtonpost.com/politics/trump-attacks-protections-for-immigrants-from-shithole-countries-in-oval-office-meeting/2018/01/11/bfc0725c-f711-11e7-91af-31ac729add94_story.html?utm_term=.14d9a68a4cff.
Day, A. 2011. *Satire and Dissent: Interventions in Contemporary Political Debate*. Bloomington: Indiana University Press.
Deluca, K. M., and J. Peeples. 2002. "From the Public Sphere to the Public Screen: Democracy, Activism and the 'Violence' of Seattle." *Critical Studies of Media Communication* 19 (2): 125–151.
DeNora, T. 2000. *Music in Everyday Life*. Cambridge, England: Cambridge University Press.
Du Bois, J. W. 2007. "The Stance Triangle." In *Stancetaking in Discourse: Subjectivity, Evaluation, Interaction*, edited by R. Englebretson, 139–182. Amsterdam, the Netherlands: John Benjamins.
Enli, G. S., and E. Skogerbø. 2013. "Personalized Campaigns in Party-Centred Politics." *Information, Communication and Society* 16: 757–774.
Fox, G. L. 1977. "'Nice Girl': Social Control of Women Through a Value Construct." *Signs: Journal of Women and Culture and Society* 2: 805–817.
Freud, S. 1960. *Jokes and Their Relation to the Unconscious Mind*. New York, NY: W. W. Norton.
Gambino, L. 2017. "Trump: No Politician in History Has Been Treated More Unfairly." *The Guardian*, May 17. Retrieved from https://www.theguardian.com/us-news/2017/may/17/donald-trump-presidency-media-coverage-russia-scandal.
Gilmore, D. D. 1998. *Carnival and Culture: Sex, Symbol, and Status in Spain*. New Haven, CT: Yale University Press.

Githens-Mazer, J. 2008. "Locating Agency in Collective Political Behaviour: Nationalism, Social Movements and Individual Mobilization." *Politics* 28 (1): 41–49.

Giulione, B. 2017. "What Does 'Bodak Yellow' Mean & What's Next for Cardi B?" *High Snobiety*, September 28. Retrieved from https://www.highsnobiety.com/2017/09/28/bodak-yellow-meaning-cardi-b/.

Graefer, A. 2014. "White Stars and Orange Celebrities: The Affective Production of Whiteness in Humorous Celebrity-Gossip Blogs." *Celebrity Studies* 5 (1–2): 107–122.

Grant-Smith, J. 2010. "Constructing the Shitting Citizen: The Promise of Scatological Art as Environmental and Social Activism." *Reconstruction: Studies in Contemporary Culture* 10 (3): 1–11.

Habermas, J. 1974. "The Public Sphere: An Encyclopedia Article." *New German Critique* 3: 49–55.

Harwood, J. 2017. "Trump's Core Voters Could Suffer Under GOP Health Care Bill." *CNBC*, June 23. Retrieved from https://www.cnbc.com/video/2017/06/23/trumps-core-voters-could-suffer-most-under-gop-health-bill-but-they-may-not-punish-him-for-it.html.

Jamieson, K. H., and J. N. Capella. 2008. *Echo Chamber: Rush Limbaugh and the Conservative Media Establishment*. Oxford, England: Oxford University Press.

Jenkins, H., S. Ford, and J. Green. 2013. *Spreadable Media: Creating Value and Meaning in a Networked Culture*. New York: New York University Press.

Kuipers, G. 2011. "The Politics of Humour in the Public Sphere: Cartoons, Power and Modernity in the First Transnational Humour Scandal." *European Journal of Cultural Studies* 14 (1): 63–80.

Livingstone, S., and A. M. Hargrave. 2009. *Harm and Offence in Media Content: A Review of the Evidence* (LSE Research Online). Bristol, England: Intellect.

Lockyer, S., and M. Pickering. 2001. "Dear Shit-Shovellers: Humour, Censure and the Discourse of Complaint." *Discourse & Society* 12 (5): 633–651.

Lockyer, S., and M. Pickering. 2005. *Beyond a Joke: The Limits of Humour*. London, England: Palgrave Macmillan.

Lorde, A. 1984. *Sister Outsider: Essays and Speeches*. Trumansburg, NY: Crossing Press.

Mayer, J. D., X. Cai, A. Patel, R. Kulkarni, V. I. Stanford, and N. Koizumi. 2016. "Reading Tea Leaves: What 1,331 Protest Placards Tell Us About the Tea Party Movement." *Visual Communication Quarterly* 22 (4): 237–250.

McGraw, A. P., and C. Warren. 2010. "Benign Violations: Making Immoral Behaviour Funny." *Psychological Science* 21 (8): 1141–1149.

Meyer, D. S. 1995. "The Challenge of Cultural Elites: Celebrities and Social Movements." *Sociological Inquiry* 65 (2): 181–206.

Meyer, J. C. 2000. "Humor as a Double-Edged Sword: Four Functions of Humor in Communication." *Communication Theory* 10 (3): 310–331.
Mizejewski, L. 2014. *Pretty Funny: Women Comedians & Body Politics*. Austin: University of Texas Press.
Mouffe, C. 2005. *On the Political*. London, England: Routledge.
Newman, M. Z. 2014. "Say 'Pulp Fiction' One More Goddamn Time: Quotation Culture and an Internet-Age Classic." *New Review of Film and Television Studies* 12 (2): 125–142.
Ngai, S. 2005. *Ugly Feelings*. Cambridge, England: Harvard University Press.
Pariser, E. 2012. *The Filter Bubble: What the Internet Is Hiding*. London, England: Penguin.
Pedwell, C. 2017. "Mediated Habits: Images, Networked Affect and Social Change." *Subjectivity* 10 (2): 147–163.
Peterson, A. H. 2017. *Too Fat, Too Slutty, Too Loud: The Rise and Reign of the Unruly Woman*. New York, NY: Plume.
Pickering, M., and J. Littlewood. 1998. "Heard the One About the White Middle Class Heterosexual Father-in-Law? Gender, Ethnicity and Political Correctness in Comedy." In *Because I Tell a Joke or Two: Comedy, Politics and Identity*, edited by S. Wagg, 291–312. London: Routledge.
Pujolar, J. 2000. *Gender, Heteroglossia and Power: A Sociolinguistic Study of Youth Culture*. Berlin, Germany: Mouton de Gruyter.
Reilly, I., and M. Boler. 2014. "The Rally to Restore Sanity, Pre-politicization and the Future of Politics." *Communication, Culture & Critique* 7 (2): 435–452.
Reilly, K. 2016. "Read Hillary Clinton's 'Basket of Deplorables' Remarks About Donald Trump Supporters." *Time*, September 10. Retrieved from http://time.com/4486502/hillary-clinton-basket-of-deplorables-transcript/.
Rowe, K. 1990. "Roseanne: Unruly Woman as Domestic Goddess." *Screen* 31: 408–419.
Rowe, K. 1995. *The Unruly Woman: Gender and the Genres of Laughter*. Austin: University of Texas Press.
Russo, M. 1994. *The Female Grotesque: Risk, Excess, and Modernity*. New York, NY: Routledge.
Segerberg, A., and W. L. Bennett. 2011. "Social Media and the Organization of Collective Action: Using Twitter to Explore the Ecologies of Two Climate Change Protests." *The Communication Review* 14 (3): 197–215.
Seligson, H. 2016. "Why Are More Women Than Men on Instagram?" *The Atlantic*, June 7. Retrieved from https://www.theatlantic.com/technology/archive/2016/06/why-are-more-women-than-men-on-instagram/485993/.
Smith, A., and M. Anderson. 2018. "Social Media Use in 2018," March 1. Retrieved from http://www.pewinternet.org/2018/03/01/social-media-use-2018-appendix-a-detailed-table/.

Stallybrass, P., and A. White. 1986. *The Politics & Poets of Transgression*. New York, NY: Cornell University Press.

Stamm, R. 1982. "On the Carnivalesque." *Wedge* 1: 47–55.

Sulleyman, A. 2018. "Jack Dorsey Says Regular Account Holders and Advertisers Want Him to Simplify the Micro-blogging Platform." *The Independent*, February 14. Retrieved from https://www.independent.co.uk/life-style/gadgets-and-tech/news/twitter-redesign-jack-dorsey-how-to-use-videos-pictures-text-a8211041.html.

Taylor, A. 2018. "Ghanaian President to Trump: We Are Not a 'Shithole Country'." *The Washington Post*, January 13. Retrieved from https://www.washingtonpost.com/news/worldviews/wp/2018/01/13/ghanaian-president-to-trump-we-are-not-a-shithole-country/?utm_term=.274d5ff7ba47.

The Urban Dictionary. 2006. "Little Bitch." Retrieved from https://www.urbandiction-ary.com/define.php?term=Little%20Bitch.

Thomas, J. M. 2015. *Working to Laugh: Assembling Difference in American Stand-Up Comedy Venues*. Lanham, MD: Lexington Books.

Thorogood, J. 2016. "Satire and Geopolitics: Vulgarity, Ambiguity and the Body Grotesque in South Park." *Geopolitics* 21 (1): 215–235.

Tolman, D. L., E. A. Impett, A. J. Tracy, and A. Michael. 2006. "Looking Good, Sounding Good: Femininity, Ideology and Adolescent Girls' Mental Health." *Psychology of Women Quarterly* 30 (1): 85–95.

Tufekci, Z., and C. Wilson. 2012. "Social Media and the Decision to Participate in Political Protest: Observations from Tahrir Square." *Journal of Communication* 62 (2): 363–379.

Waisanen, D. J., and A. B. Becker. 2015. "The Problem with Being Joe Biden: Political Comedy and Circulating Personae." *Critical Studies in Media Communication* 32 (4): 256–271.

Winship, J. 1981. "Handling Sex." *Media, Culture & Society* 3 (1): 25–41.

CHAPTER 5

Changing Visual Politics in South Africa: Old and New Modes of Exclusion, Protest and Offence

Marietta Kesting

What constitutes an *offensive* image lies in the eyes of the viewer. At times the act of photographing itself can be offensive—this may be deduced from the gaze of the photographed back at the viewer. An offensive image could be one that insults or that shows an act that is considered to interrupt a normative code of behaviour or that is against the law. As the editor of this volume has suggested, 'offensive' is a rather slippery category, and—not surprisingly—which images are deemed offensive is highly contested in current South African society.

When attempting a necessarily not exhaustive entry into the genealogy of offensive images in South Africa, it is important to revisit the extensive visual archive of gruesome photographs of black bodies in pain, suffering from the physical consequence of state-sanctioned racism (see Enwezor 2006). These well-known photographs taken by the notorious 'Bang-Bang Club', comprised of Ken Oosterbroek, Greg Marinovich, João Silva and Kevin Carter, and other predominantly

---

M. Kesting (✉)
Academy of Fine Arts Munich, Munich, Germany
e-mail: kesting@adbk.mhn.de

© The Author(s) 2019
A. Graefer (ed.), *Media and the Politics of Offence*,
https://doi.org/10.1007/978-3-030-17574-0_5

white and male photographers, constitute ambivalent documents. They could be considered 'offensive', for depicting the consequences of ongoing police violence and oppression (see Osha 2015). In this regard, and through their affective charge, they may have created outrage in viewers, potentially moving them to action, and could be used strategically as political weapons and evidence of injustice. At the same time the very same photographs were also criticised as sensational 'violence pornography' and as showing the black townships primarily as places of danger and aggression. These photographs circulated globally through news media and some even won Pulitzer Prizes in the 1990s, attesting to a Western, sensationalist demand for these very images.

Compared to the black majority, images of white bodies habitually conveyed secure and 'good' lives. During the struggle against apartheid images of suffering black bodies, for example after evictions, arrests or protests, were frequently composed in ways alluding to Christian iconographies, in order to 'move' people—across the colour line—into political action (Kesting 2017, Newbury 2009). After the official end of apartheid in 1992, these documentary media aesthetics changed—due to the new political dispensation, but also through the proliferation of cell phone cameras and social media—but at the same time they have not completely disappeared. This contribution will concentrate on two examples that use offensive images as a mode of protest, empowerment and provocation in a very different way than during the struggle. The materials to be analysed are the works and media coverage of two socially involved artists, Zanele Muholi and Dean Hutton. While the photographs and images that Muholi and Hutton produce look very different from each other's, they are both 'queering' image production and thus offer a critical commentary on the hegemonic mediascape, since queer artists are producing playful, innovative or experimental approaches in order to shake up the order of representation. This analysis seeks to flesh out the paradox that offensive images may be protested against in one context, while at the same time others strive to defend their right to produce them. Since this volume prominently puts an emphasis on the 'politics of offence', only visual case studies that resulted in public discourse and political actions, albeit in different ways, were selected.

The two selected practitioners, Zanele Muholi and Dean Hutton, had already had long experience of having to negotiate stereotypical and denigrating images and were attempting to turn the gaze around, to expand what is visible, to create new and empowering archives (Muholi), and possibly to provoke or offend 'back' (Hutton). To sum up, this chapter compares different materials from the recent past and the present in order to produce a more nuanced view of the complexity of current media politics in South Africa and of how its offensive images are constructed, disseminated, viewed and responded to. It highlights old and new mechanisms of offence, exclusion and protest, and how these are playing out in the visual sphere.

Offensive Images in Post-apartheid Times

After the first democratic elections in 1994, South Africa entered an ongoing phase of (re-) constructing its national identity, which implied democratisation, and in its wake the introduction of advanced capitalism and neo-liberal reforms. At the same time, there was also a transformation of the audio-visual media sphere, in terms of who has access to cameras and networks of distribution (Thomas 2018). The rise of cell phones with advanced imaging technology has contributed to the proliferation of 'citizen reporters' and amateur images entering the public sphere via YouTube and Twitter. Yet the profession of the commenting photographer or artist has not become obsolete, and probably never will.

In spite of the societal and media-circuit transformations, South African society is to this day still strongly divided along old and new fault lines of socio-economic inequality, race, class and gender. Post-apartheid South Africa is a nation in transition and therefore a place full of contradictions, of inherited and new divisions and ambivalences. This situation is not uncommon for a nation-state in the twenty-first century, characterised by a higher complexity of societal and political divisions—what one could also call 'messiness' (Mbembe 2001). The South African constitution of 1996, however, is one of the most progressive in the world in terms of offering rights to minorities, including LGTBQI people.

Zanele Muholi: *Enraged by a Picture* (2005)

In order to introduce a different angle on the question of what an 'offensive image' may constitute and how precarious the visibility of the black female body is, photographer Zanele Muholi's series entitled *Visual Sexuality: Only Half the Picture* (2004) and the subsequent short film *Enraged by a Picture* (2005) make a bold statement. Muholi, who studied at the renowned Market Photo Workshop in Johannesburg, has been one of the first black photographers in South Africa to give visibility to black women's sexuality, and particularly to black lesbian women. Her photographs often document intimate moments between couples and capture both the strength and the vulnerability of her subjects. Muholi's gaze never seems to be that of an outsider, but rather that of a person closely connected to her subjects. She argues that much of her work aims to ensure that black LGTBQI people exist in the visual archive. 'The key question that I take to bed with me is: "What is my responsibility as a living being, as a South African citizen reading continually about hate crimes in the mainstream media?"' (Muholi 2018). The hate crimes Muholi refers to are most often committed against queer black people, and particularly against black lesbians. In South African society black lesbians have a particularly unwarranted status. They are regarded as 'deviant' and are at the highest risk of being subjected to violence, including the crime of 'corrective rape', which is classified as a hate crime against (alleged) lesbians, committed by men who want to discipline and change these women's sexuality (Gqola 2015). One of the stereotypical arguments brought against them from within black society is that 'same-sex marriages are a disgrace to the nation and God', as then-President Zuma prominently declared on Heritage Day 2006 (quoted in Gunkel 2010, 48).

Consequently, Muholi's black-and-white images break several taboos by focussing on female sexuality and related intimate topics, for example showing a sanitary napkin with menstrual blood on a plate with a fork and knife and titled 'Period', but also a naked torso of a black woman wearing a white dildo belt, simply called 'Dildo', as well as a close-up of a rape survivor's torso, wearing male underpants, titled 'Aftermath'. While photographs of naked or half-naked women are not uncommon in tabloids, advertisements and other media, the type of nudity that Muholi's photographs present informs a completely different perspective of appreciation. However, the photographs have been seen as 'going too far' and met with hostile reactions from some viewers, although there have also been positive responses, as Muholi documents in her short film *Enraged by a Picture*, in which several people comment on the images (Muholi 2005). While some consider the work an outstanding example of creating empowering images of black lesbian women, her photographs have been deemed 'offensive' by homophobic people, or simply made viewers uncomfortable with their open display of sexuality. One example of a negative written comment on her pictures submitted by an anonymous viewer that Muholi cites in *Enraged by a Picture* is: 'It is truly unacceptable for you to undermine our races especially black portraying Nudity and sexual explicit content images…' (Muholi 2005). But Muholi, rather than retreating, has taken these reactions as a point of departure for probing more deeply. At the end of the film she states that '…I capture images of sexuality … because I believe that our experiences as black lesbians add to a history of struggle that has not yet been written or recorded'. Her images and film work are an assertion of presence, as she states, 'But our voices are here now, in this visual "text", and perhaps we will be allowed, for the first time, to speak to all the languages and cultures within our communities' (2005).

Remarkably, it is not the images showing intimate sexual relations, but instead the photograph 'Period' that has been considered the most shocking and offensive by viewers, and many have not understood the subtext (Gunkel 2010, 2). Muholi wanted to emphasise with it that 'the same blood that defines us as women, is the same blood which we shed in the attacks against us, while some make a meal of their hatred of us as women, as lesbians' (Muholi, quoted in Gunkel 2010, 2). In addition, once a girl starts to have her period, she is considered to have entered womanhood and it is therefore also a signifier for female sexuality. The leaking of bodily fluids, especially from the female body during the period, or while nursing, or crying, is often constructed as shameful, dirty and as a visual taboo, in the Western as well as in the South African context. While feminist and queer discourse has always argued against these visual silences, in 2015 Instagram still censored photographs from the Indian-Canadian writer and poet Rupi Kaur in which she showed herself lying in bed, from behind, with a stain of menstrual blood on her pants (Kaur 2016; Sanghani 2015). The censoring on Instagram is proof that the topic of periods can still not be represented and is considered a transgression in the global visual realm as well as in South Africa.

MASCULINITY, WHITE PRIVILEGE AND DECOLONISATION

Despite South Africa's progressive constitution promoting gender equality and women's rights, it also has one of the highest rates of violence against women (Sibanda-Moyo et al. 2017). Being at risk is dependent on real or seeming sexual preferences, since '[n]ormative femininity is, above all, defined through sexuality—and, more precisely through (presumed) heterosexuality and its appearance' (Bartky 1990).

Thereby, a binary value system of good, 'traditional' African culture on the one hand, and bad, 'modern', Western liberal culture on the other is reaffirmed. The need for security and a type of visibility that is appreciatory of the female body thus leaves open many questions that cannot be addressed solely in visual culture. As Maxim Bold and Dinah Rajak (2016) have stated, '…violence in its different forms, continues to define the domestic and working lives of millions of poor South Africans'. Masculinity, but also whiteness and enduring white privilege, remain determining factors that structure South African society and culture, as well as the social reality of institutions and the identities of women and men (Burnett 2018). At the same time, these racist and patriarchal structures are repeatedly challenged, especially during the recent formation of a new student protest movement.

At several large universities, students started massive protests in 2014 in the wake of the Marikana killings of black mine workers in 2012 (Makinana 2012; de Waal 2014). The student movements of the 'born-frees'—the first generation that was born and grew up after apartheid officially ended—criticise the ongoing racism and socio-economic deprivation of black workers and students (Pillay 2016). Some have invoked the memory and writings of, among others, Steve Biko, who was a prominent anti-apartheid activist until he was murdered by the apartheid government in prison in 1977 (Biko 1987). As artist and writer Thenjiwe Niki Nkosi observed about the formation of the student protests tagged #FeesMustFall and #RhodesMustFall: 'There is a palpable sense of "knowing" that is happening on university campuses across the country right now. Students and workers are declaring very clearly, "Know there is something wrong with the system"' (2016, 257). Therefore, the realisation of being constantly offended and outraged by continuing discrimination, and that structures that still privileged whiteness were so strong, translated into direct action and demands. The students persisted in demands for the thorough decolonisation of the higher education system in South Africa, and for study to be made more affordable, ideally 'free'—at no cost to students. South African visual culture researcher Kylie Thomas (2018) argues that a new iconography has emerged in this context that references the past, but also breaks away from the social documentary forms of representation that characterised the struggle against apartheid.

The student movement is not a homogenous entity, but rather consists of several different groupings, sometimes at odds with each other, but they agree on declaring it an offence that black people are continuously discriminated against by police, security forces, and white people, even in post-apartheid society, and that their lives are less secure and their socio-economic status often not secured. Thus they can also be linked globally to other movements like 'Black Lives Matter' in the United States or against the 'Black Genocide' in Brazil (Smith 2017). These protests are directed against corrupt and violent police practices and against the persistence of colonial and apartheid-era ideologies that manifest themselves also in the ongoing upholding of sculptures, images and street-names of white racist men in South Africa, like Cecil Rhodes, as tokens of colonialism, the slave trade and Jim Crow history. Consequently, they propose a fundamental decolonisation of the educational sector, its architecture and structures, implicit and explicit role models and symbols, as well as their environments.

OFFENSIVE IMAGES AS PROVOCATION AND LOOKING BACK

An artistic position that was inspired and provoked by the images of the student protest, and that also uses a queer context as a point of departure, is that of white South African Dean Hutton's work. They (Hutton uses the pronoun they and them) are a gender-fluid, queer artist interested in portraiture as co-authorship, social media as narrative, and technology as self-reflection and provocation. After a long career as a photo-journalist, they have moved into the medium of performance and installation. Their practice explores ways in which to build a 'love revolution' from their personal work and to create relationships and gathering collaborators to make South African public and intimate spaces safer through artist-led creation, mentorship and community organising. Much of Hutton's work is concerned with social issues, such as the rights of women, queers and the dispossessed. Two different works are the *Goldendean* (2015) project and the *F___White People* suit (2017). For *Goldendean*, Hutton's body, which would be considered 'overweight' in a normative setting, is covered completely in gold paint and otherwise naked. Hutton commented frankly: 'So I painted myself gold to become more valuable' (Hutton 2018b). This work points to a paradox, especially in an affluent Western society where 'fat'[1] bodies are

---

[1] The word 'fat' is used by body-positive groups in a non-derogatory, self-empowering way.

Fig. 5.1 *Goldendean* (2015) Artwork by Dean Hutton (© Dean Hutton)

hyper-visible in one sense, but at the same time considered shameful and hidden. There is also a common understanding that if you are fat, you should keep your body covered, since 'nobody wants to see this undesirable view'. Therefore, the fat body, and especially the naked female fat body, stands out and is immediately noticed as not normal, while at the same time there are hardly any respectful, positively connoted images in mainstream visual and popular culture, contemporary art or advertising of bodies that do not fit into contemporary body norms (Hermann 2017, 16). Overweight bodies are supposed to be not only unaesthetic, but also unhealthy, and hence often assumptions are made about a person's character and intelligence based on their physical appearance. Since the late 1960s feminist and other groups have protested about this debasing of fatness, with prominent slogans like 'Riot not diet' (Cooper 2016).

What does the action of covering a naked white body in gold suggest about race, skin colour and the value of queer bodies that do not fit in? This work rather coincides with Renate Lorenz's observation that '…images are increasingly appearing in the field of queer art that undermine the established categories of racialised or gender categories, or that show no bodies at all' (Lorenz 2012, 7). Lorenz has proposed working with the artificial figure of the 'freak', which she imbues with the positive values of challenging norms, reproducing difference without reinstating identity. At the same time the '"freaky" … would point to the history of constraints, violence, and self-assertion that is already tied to the historical freak shows' (2012, 7). This figure of the 'freak' seems appropriate for describing the strategies of the *Goldendean* project, which exposes Hutton's own body as a freak show and at the same time in an upgraded version, covered in gold, which can be read both as adding value to an excluded body and as an ironic gesture. They have challenged the norm through accepting the gazes of onlookers on their body in a purposefully voyeuristic setting and by looking back as a subject (see image above), even smiling. By doing so the work explicitly and intentionally plays with offence, turning it around and using it—almost weaponising it—as a means of self-defence and empowerment. On the surface level, however, the *Goldendean* performances often creates warm reactions from viewers, smiles are exchanged, and requests are made to take selfies together, creating a space of openness, while the more difficult topics may come to people's attention only later. But Hutton have also created another performance that has a much more serious, stark and possibly militant impact, and that pushes viewers directly onto provocative and outspoken terrain.

In their ongoing exploration of performative and political strategies and in response to discussion of white privilege they created the *F___ White People* suit in 2016. This is a piece of clothing in white fabric, onto which the words 'F___', 'WHITE', and 'PEOPLE' are printed all over, but with each word appearing repeatedly in straight lines, going around the garments front and back (see image below and further images at SAHO 2018). The installation consisted of a poster with the same words and a chair covered in the text, as well as a pair of golden boots, evoking the *Goldendean* persona and linking the two works.

The piece was inspired by the aforementioned student protest movements in Cape Town, which Hutton had documented as a photographer. The slogan 'F___ White People' had been written on the back of a T-shirt, while the front of the T-shirt said 'Being black is shit'. The student from the University of the Witwatersrand in Johannesburg, Zama Mthunzi, commented: 'I just took a T-shirt and I wrote how I was feeling at that moment. I was angry because so many black students, who are good students, were facing financial exclusion' (Chernick 2016). Mthunzi was reprimanded and disciplined by his university. The slogan also appeared on walls and signs during marches. Hutton appropriated the slogan for their work, and even though Hutton's piece became known under the slogan 'F____ White People', the text could also be read in the piece in different ways, such as 'White People F___' or 'White People F___ White People', or 'People F___ White', etc.

Fig. 5.2 Fuckwhitepeople at IZIKO Gallery. Sitting in front of the installation that was vandalised and drew hate speech charges from a white separatist party in 2016 (© Dean Hutton)

The work was shown at an exhibition called *Art and Disruption* at the Iziko National Gallery in Cape Town and immediately created outrage. Some white people were deeply offended and the work was accused of being hate speech (Pather 2016). The exhibit was vandalised by a group of white men, who mounted a large sticker onto the piece reading 'Love thy neighbour' (Petersen 2017). This group of white people used the label 'offensive' to protect themselves from engaging with these challenging images and their unsettling political questions about white privilege, and the value of black lives. By saying 'This is offensive' they tried to push back what is brought to light and 'on-scene', but should—according to white privilege—be kept off and 'ob-scene', and therefore should remain invisible and unchallenged.

The perpetrators belonged to the separatist and white-dominated Cape Party, which subsequently filed a case against the gallery that had exhibited Hutton's performative installation. The ruling of Magistrate Daniel Thulare, however, declared that the work was found to be neither racist nor hate speech against white people (Wilford 2017). This protected freedom of expression and art also understood the self-reflective dimension of the piece: as Hutton have noted, 'When I say fuck white people, the first white I fuck is me' (Hutton 2018b).

While the *F___White* people suit seemed to grab all the attention, it was also invoking the previously discussed *Goldendean* project, where Hutton's naked body was covered completely with golden paint and they then put themselves on display in a window, like a living shop-window mannequin. This link, however, was lost on many white viewers who read the slogan only as an 'anti-white' sentiment, assumed it had been executed by a black artist, and reacted in panic and fear. These viewers did not seem to care about the personal connection of Dean Hutton and their experiences with the work, but rather were immediately offended and shut themselves off from further discussion.

For others the slogan 'F____ white people' seemed only to restage an angry response to ongoing racism, discrimination and violence in South Africa's supposedly post-racist society. The painfulness of racism is used here strategically and could be linked to other global movements like Black Lives Matter, but making a negative statement and expressing frustration about a world where black lives matter less.

Social justice scholar Samantha Vice has demanded 'silence' and 'humility' from white people in South African society, since any 'white voice in the public sphere would inevitably be tainted by the vicious features of "whiteliness"' (Vice 2010, 340). This seems a problematic proposal, since 'whiteness' works best in silence, as the unchallenged normative ideal, as Mohammad Shabungu suggests in a critical response (2010, 56). Moreover, queer white bodies like Dean Hutton's are completely excluded from white normative beauty and fitness standards, as has been explored in the discussion of *Goldendean* (see Goldendean 2018).

However, there is also the inherent tension of a white artist still profiting from their connection to the mostly white art institutions and circles of funding and recognition. In some regard this provocative art project could even be seen as—unwillingly?—proving again the asymmetry of power, of what a white artist can get away with as a symbolic gesture, or even as appropriating black people's frustration and anger. Social justice researcher and writer Kwanele Sosibo cautions, in a review of the work, that '…it is as an expression of allyship — a person of privilege showing solidarity with a marginalised group — that the work falls short' (2017). As a thought experiment, one could try to imagine the reactions if a black artist had created the *F___ White People* piece. At the same time, Hutton is aware of these contradictions. A lecture format that accompanies their performance quotes James Baldwin, who wrote prominently about whiteness in the United States and who stated that '[u]ltimately, to be white is a moral choice. It's obviously a very deliberate challenge to people who think they are white to re-examine all their values, to put themselves in our place, to share in our danger' (Baldwin 1979). Hutton's work takes up this very challenge and attempts to re-examine whiteness in South Africa, to render it hyper-visible and to criticise it (Goldendean 2018).

Conclusion

This chapter explored how certain iconic photographs and commenting artworks activate, but also abstract from, the cultural photographic archive in South Africa. What constitutes visual instances of 'offence' depends on who has the power to define offence: For some, the ongoing display of sculptures and images of colonial and apartheid leaders may be offensive, whereas others perceive the exhibition of particular naked bodies as crossing the line. By concentrating on two queer artists' works, this chapter analysed how certain images may be used to provoke and offend, but also to instigate political activism or to challenge societal norms. Nevertheless, what can be shown and talked about in the South African public sphere has profoundly changed in the last decade since the first publications of Zanele Muholi's photographs, and especially with regard to queer and non-binary expressions. One example is the black rapper Mx Blouse (Sandiso Ngubane), who performs at public concerts, and their new single *Is'phukphuku* (2018), in which they rap about women's issues and empowerment and state '…it's a revolution when someone like me has your ears when I speak…'. One can also observe, both in the photographic and in the filmic realm, more projects that use fictionalisation and self-staging rather than documentary aesthetics. Zanele Muholi has in her latest series, *Somnyama Ngonyama—Hail the Dark Lioness* (2017), used only herself as a model in all the photographs, taking on different roles, props and costumes.

The new aesthetics in the visual realm of the last two decades, particularly in the work of Zanele Muholi and in the student protest movement, have pushed the boundaries of what can be shown and how. These changes have also influenced or inspired some white artists, who respond to the protests in their own way, as the example of queer artist Dean Hutton's work has proved. In addition, one can detect a frustration with trying to create more 'just' and empowering images in the documentary realm and therefore new strategies of fictionalising and staging are used. At the same time tensions around asymmetrical power relations and positions of (white) privilege within a dominantly white art world also come to the fore when one looks at who is allowed to offend whom. Therefore, while Zanele Muholi's and Dean Hutton's work shares a queer context as a point of departure for engaging with politics of visibility, and conceivably both exhibit an aesthetic of exposure and bluntness, they are, of course, also completely differently coded by blackness and whiteness, respectively, which constitute both symbolic and material differences regarding access to the Western art market, white privilege, and lived experiences. South Africa in 2018 is not a post-racist society, even though that is what it aspires to be.

Instead of offering a general survey of the state of the visual sphere or how to deal with offensive images, this text has offered two examples and the need to consider these as a mode of intervention, without offering any resolutions, and instead provoking more questions and a grounded analytical gaze. In this reading, offensive images can create instances of probing violence and violations, ethical dilemmas and power relations.

Before looking away or quickly asking for censorship, one needs to access each case in all its complexities. As has been argued in relation to the different visual materials, outrage about offensive images may be justified and considered progressive, or it may be deemed reactionary. To conclude that exclusionary practices still exist in post-apartheid society is the basis for an analysis of the present visual politics of protest and offence, where the categories of difference have diversified, but not disappeared.

Acknowledgements This work was supported by the Austrian Science Fund (FWF) [grant number P 27877-G26].

References

Baldwin, James. 1979. Interview in *New York Times*, September 23.
Bartky, Sandra Lee. 1990. *Femininity and Domination: Studies in the Phenomenology of Oppression*. New York and London: Routledge.
Biko, Steve. 1987. *I Write What I Like: Steve Biko. A Selection of His Writings*, edited by Aelred Stubbs. Oxford: Heinemann.
Bold, Maxim, and Dinah Rajak. 2016. "Introduction: Labour, Insecurity, and Violence in South Africa." *Journal of Southern African Studies,* special issue on Labour, Insecurity and Violence in South Africa, 42 (5): 798.
Burnett, Scott. 2018. "Giving Back the Land: Whiteness and Belonging in Contemporary South Africa." Doctoral thesis, Faculty of Humanities, University of the Witwatersrand, Johannesburg, South Africa.
Chernick, Ilanit. 2016. "The Man Behind THAT Wits Tshirt," February 12. https://www.iol.co.za/news/south-africa/gauteng/the-man-behind-that-wits-t-shirt-1983503.
Cooper, Charlotte. 2016. *Fat Activism: A Radical Social Movement*. Bristol: HammerOn.
de Waal, Shaun. 2014. "Method to Marikana Massacre." *Mail and Guardian*, June 6.
Enwezor, Okwui. 2006. *Snap Judgments: New Positions in Contemporary African Photography*. New York: International Center for Photography.
Goldendean. 2018. *Plan B: A Gathering of Strangers (or) This Is Not Working*. Bayreuth: Iwalewahaus, University of Bayreuth.
Gqola, Pumla. 2015. *Rape: A South African Nightmare*. Auckland Park, SA: Jacana Media Ltd.
Gunkel, Henriette. 2010. *The Cultural Politics of Female Sexuality in South Africa*. New York and London: Routledge.

Hermann, Anja. 2017. "Introduction." *FKW Journal for Gender Studies and Visual Culture* (62), August. https://www.fkw-journal.de/index.php/fkw.
Hutton, Dean. 2018a. *2point8*. http://www.2point8.co.za/. Accessed August 1, 2018.
Hutton, Dean. 2018b. *Goldendean*. https://www.goldendean.art/. Accessed August 1, 2018.
Kaur, Rupi. 2016. *I Am Taking My Body Back*. Ted Talk, published September 2. https://www.youtube.com/watch?v=RlToQQfSlLA.
Kesting, Marietta. 2017. *Affective Images: Postapartheid Documentary Perspectives*. Albany, NY: SUNY.
Lorenz, Renate. 2012. *Queer Art: A Freak Theory*. Bielefeld: Transcript.
Makinana, Andisiwe. 2012. "Marikana Tragedy: Who Authorised the Use of Live Ammunition?" *Mail and Guardian*, August 21.
Mbembe, Achille. 2001. *On the Postcolony*. Berkeley, Los Angeles, and London: University of California Press.
Muholi, Zanele. 2004. *Visual Sexuality: Only Half the Picture*. Exhibition of photographs, first shown in 2004 at Market Photo Workshop, Johannesburg.
Muholi, Zanele. 2005. *Enraged by a Picture* (Short Film). Available on Youtube. https://www.youtube.com/watch?v=JLSMCBWDKSU.
Muholi, Zanele. 2018. *Zanele Muholi on Resistance*. An Interview by Renée Mussai. https://aperture.org/blog/muholi-interview/. Accessed September 11, 2018.
Mussai, Renée. 2017. *Zanele Muholi, Somnyama Ngonyama: Hail the Dark Lioness*. London: Autograph, ABP.
Mx Blouse (Sandiso Ngubane). 2018. *Is'phukphuku*. Single released May 2018, with music video. https://www.youtube.com/watch?v=lt2zRiyzpyY.
Newbury, Darren. 2009. *Defiant Images: Photography and Apartheid South Africa*. Pretoria: Unisa Press.
Nkosi, Thenjiwe Niki. 2016. "Radical Sharing." In *African Futures: Thinking about the Future in Words and Images*, edited by Lien Heidenreich-Selene and Sean O'Toole, 257. Bielefeld and Berlin: Kerber.
Osha, Sanya. 2015. "The Bang-Bang Club." *Bakwa Magazine*, June 16. https://bakwamagazine.com/2015/06/16/the-bang-bang-club/A.
Pather, Ra'eesa. 2016. "Students Continue to March at UKZN, Protesting Against Rape and Police Violence." *Mail and Guardian*, July 9.
Petersen, Tammy. 2017. "'F**k White People' Artwork Vandalised at Cape Museum." *News24*. https://www.news24.com/SouthAfrica/News/fk-white-people-artwork-vandalised-at-cape-museum-20170118.
Pillay, Taschica. 2016. "Student Shot in Crossfire at KwaZulu-Natal Varsity Protest." *Herald Live*, August 9. http://www.heraldlive.co.za/tag/bongeka-mntaka/.
SAHO, South African History Online. "Dean Hutton." http://www.sahistory.org.za/people/dean-hutton. Accessed May 21, 2018.

Sanghani, Rahdika. 2015. "Instagram Deletes Woman's Period Photos—But Her Response Is Amazing." *Daily Telegraph*, March 20. https://www.telegraph.co.uk/women/life/instagram-deletes-womans-period-photos-but-her-response-is-amazing/.

Shabungu, Mohammad. 2010. "Precarious Silence: Decentring the Power of Whiteness in South Africa." *The Salon* 10: 52–61.

Sibanda-Moyo, Nonhlanhla et al. 2017. *Violence Against Women in South Africa: A Country in Crisis*. Johannesburg: Centre for the Study of Violence and Reconciliation.

Smith, Christen A. 2017. "Battling Anti-Black Genocide in Brazil." In *NACLA Report on the Americas* 49 (1): #BlackLivesMatter Across the Hemisphere. https://doi.org/10.1080/10714839.2017.1298243.

Sosibo, Kwanele. 2017. "Is 'Fuck White People' Fucking Itself?" *Mail and Guardian*. https://mg.co.za/article/2017-02-03-00-is-fuck-white-people-fucking-itself. Accessed February 3, 2017.

Thomas, Kylie. 2018. "Decolonisation Is Now: Photography and Student Social Movements in South Africa." *Visual Studies* 33 (1): 98–110. https://doi.org/10.1080/1472586X.2018.1426251.

Vice, Samantha. 2010. "How Do I Live in This Strange Place." *Journal of Social Philosophy* 41 (3): 323–342.

Wilford, Greg. 2017. "Court Rules That 'F**k White People' Posters Are Not Racist." *Independent*, July 8. https://www.independent.co.uk/news/world/africa/fk-white-people-racist-hate-speech-posters-art-south-africa-iziko-south-african-national-gallery-a7830441.html.

PART II

Offence, Representations and Popular Culture

CHAPTER 6

Other Bodies Within Us: Shock, Affect and Reality Television Audiences

Jacob Johanssen

This chapter presents and analyses qualitative interview data from a research project on audiences of *Embarrassing Bodies* (Channel 4, UK 2007–2015).

Embarrassing Bodies (*EB*) was a medical reality programme in which patients were diagnosed and treated by a team of doctors. It often featured graphic and detailed surgical sequences, as well as common, rare or tabooed medical conditions which were shown in front of the camera.

The research project drew on Freudian psychoanalysis, both as a method for qualitative interviews (through the notion of free association) and in its analytical framework, in order to analyse the affective relationships between subjects and their consumption of a television programme. I was interested in why viewers watched the programme and what their thoughts on the patients and doctors were (Johanssen 2019). I pay particular attention here to narratives from interviewees

J. Johanssen (✉)
St. Mary's University, Twickenham, UK
e-mail: johanssenjacob@gmail.com

© The Author(s) 2019
A. Graefer (ed.), *Media and the Politics of Offence*,
https://doi.org/10.1007/978-3-030-17574-0_6

in which they spoke of or alluded to feeling offended, and in particular disgusted and shocked, by some of the *EB* sequences. While the term 'offended' as such was seldom used, other words and expressions were uttered which, I suggest, circled around the feeling of being offended. These narratives often implicitly referred to affective responses to the television programme. Drawing on psychoanalysis, I argue that such feelings, and specifically their articulation, may in some instances function as a defensive act whereby that which offends the speaker is split off from them. In the case of *EB* audiences, the graphic display of so-called 'embarrassing' bodies made viewers who were part of the study think about and reflect on their own bodies and their own fragility.

Eventually, those aspects were often disavowed and dismissed during interviews by being labelled 'shocking' or 'extreme' and attributed to the patients only. For many interviewees, offence thus worked as a defence mechanism in order for them not to engage with functions or aspects of the body that we all share or may all potentially be confronted with one day. This was further shown in some interview narratives in which interviewees were keen to stress that their bodies were fundamentally different from the ones on the show.

I further argue that viewers also took pleasure in feeling shocked, offended and disgusted by what they saw. I conceptualise such modes of engagement as a *perverse form of voyeurism*. The interviewees in the sample were at once drawn to the abject bodies and rejected them through narratives that spoke of offence, shock and affective responses. Many such narratives were coupled with moments of joy, excitement and entertainment. Rather than only figuring as a way of creating boundaries between audiences and content, such modes of engagement also legitimised the viewing of a programme that might otherwise be ethically problematic or 'trashy'. In speaking of their excitement, viewers embraced the offensive material that they had at the same time split off from. This enabled their continued consumption in the light of the inter-subjective dynamics of an interview situation where they were asked questions about the programme. They could articulate being shocked, and different from the 'embarrassing' bodies, while at the same time justifying their continued consumption to me by evoking light-hearted motives around entertainment.

Offence, Disgust, Shock and Embarrassing Bodies

As written in the introduction to this volume

> Generally media content is judged to be offensive when it contains offensive language, violence or depictions of sexual activity. Intrusive images of suffering or racist, classist or sexist depictions that contribute to stereotyping, or bias and inaccuracy in news reports and documentaries, are also often reported as offending audiences. (Livingstone and Millwood Hargrave 2009, 26 cited in Graefer 2019, 13)

Offence and what constitutes being offensive is difficult to define and often lies in the eye of the beholder. Reality TV as a genre has perhaps come to epitomise the category of offensive television with its reliance on stereotypes and graphic scenes of all kinds. In this chapter, I want to approach the 'messy affective fabric' (Graefer 2019, 3) of offence as something that is clustered around other, equally slippery, signifiers and notions: disgust, shock, and the abject (Kristeva 1982). In the case of *EB* and in particular its scenes that depict surgical operations, nudity or graphic medical conditions, many viewers I interviewed articulated a response that grappled with the content and made some references to feeling offended, shocked, or disgusted. The programme itself sets the tone in a particular way by often ridiculing and shaming the *EB* participants. The *EB* presenters and doctors themselves often perform shocked and offended reactions to the patients they see. For example:

> *Trina*: Yeah, I had surgery done. I had part of my bowel removed, erm, from colitis.
> *Dr. Dawn*: What where the symptoms that you were experiencing?
> *Trina*: Erm, just, erm, being able to control, erm, toilet, having accidents, daily, erm.
> *Dr. Dawn*: Oh my word! So you were actually leaking faeces, were you?
> *Trina*: Basically.
> *Dr. Dawn*: And was there a lot of blood and so on?
> *Trina*: Yeah.
> (S5, E4: 09.45–10.26)

In response to a patient with tonsil stones, Dr. Dawn responds in another episode:

Now you've got big tonsils and you've got big pits, you've got big craters there, holes, dents, nooks and crannies in which all sorts of food particles are gonna get stuck.
(S5, E3, 13.04–14.21)

Such practices of performativity enable audience responses that articulate feelings of shock and offence that are totally justified on their part, because the presenters act similarly. Many interviewees spoke of their shock when viewing certain scenes:

> Sometimes I am, shocked probably isn't the right word, sometimes I am a little bit surprised that people's almost lack of dignity to completely expose these things to the general public but, but it doesn't stop me watching it, obviously (chuckles). I mean, yeah, the one they did on the face of that chap whose face was completely decomposed from the tumour, I've seen a lot of horrible chopping things and I actually found that quite shocking. That's probably the only one that I've actually thought "Oh, I don't know if I can actually look at that". (I5, 162–168)

> I think it was just quite shocking that people were either willing to come on TV and show everyone they had this thing that could be deemed embarrassing, erm, but also illnesses or disease that you didn't even know exist and some of the treatments for them, where you didn't realise that things were so invasive or shocking. (I3, 201–205)

The two quotes above express feelings both of shock and possibly of offence at some of the bodies and body parts that are put on graphic display by the programme, but also the individual patients who go on the show are being labelled as lacking in dignity or shame. Their willingness to expose themselves to the cameras was met with shock by the two interviewees. As one said, 'Really? They're on the telly with that? Go to the chemist and get x or y! But I suppose for them it's an opportunity to get on telly, the whole Andy Warhol fifteen minutes of fame, isn't it?' (I5, 233–235).

In relation to initial feelings of shock, two interviewees spoke about the first time they had ever seen *EB*:

> Oh my god, erm, it was a really long time ago now. I think, I think I was quite shocked, I think, 'cos there were some bits where it was, like, okay, full-on boobs and vaginas and penises on TV and, like, I think back then maybe we weren't, erm, desensitised to it, but I think we've become

desensitised to seeing that kind of thing on TV now. Erm, it's almost, like, as long as it's a medical problem and it is a penis then it's ok to show it on TV. It is just the way it seems, but at the time I was a bit, like, "Oh, that's a bit gruesome showing that on TV", but then I don't know... we have, I certainly have, become desensitised to it. I don't know if other people have. Again, it might be because I'm used to seeing that kind of horrible stuff now, but I'm not as affected by it, but I did think it was a bit shocking at first, but then I also thought it was quite good that people who had these kinds of problems could, well, could go somewhere. But then I was a bit confused 'cos I was thinking if you're so embarrassed, again, why are you going on TV? Yeah, erm, that was my initial reaction. (I7, 213–226)

I think, it was more, don't know, maybe a grotesque interest, a morbid interest in it, 'cos to begin with, I think, the first episode, everything was quite extreme. It wasn't, it wasn't some of the things that you see now. Especially if you have the *Embarrassing Bodies* live clinic now, people show you what [inaudible] or whatever they've got. Erm, I think it was just quite shocking that people were either willing to come on TV and show everyone they had, this thing that could be deemed embarrassing, erm, but also illnesses or, or diseases that you didn't even know exist and some of the treatments for them, where you didn't realise that things were so invasive or shocking or... I think it definitely was a shock factor, but in a good sense. (I2, 195–206)

Feelings of shock were presented here in relation to beginning to view the programme. With more and more episodes consumed, the impact of its extreme and graphic nature subsided for the two viewers and they became somewhat used to, or numb to, the extraordinary scenes. Feelings of shock and disbelief about 'gruesome' and 'horrible' images later gave rise to 'morbid fascination' and a 'desensitised' way of viewing. Such initial responses thus eventually gave way to strong attachments and attractions to the show, as all interviewees emphasised to me that they watched it regularly whenever they could. Shock and offence may thus have functioned for Channel 4 as a calculated mechanism to lure audiences in, so that they tuned in every week. But what were the viewers really shocked about? Was it naked or somehow 'other' bodies such as one normally does not see, unless one is a doctor? Was it the implicit shamelessness of the patients in exposing their bodies to the viewers, as some interviewees remarked? Was it the graphic detail of operations and bodily conditions? As I go on to argue, the set of narratives presented above indicates reactions on the surface, while there are also deeper motives and reasons for feelings of offence, shock and disgust. Before addressing these, it is useful to reflect on the social nature of the strong reactions to the show that were voiced by the interviewees. Such reactions are specifically and socially coded. What is offensive may vary according to different societies and belief systems. Nothing is offensive in its own right. We learn to be offended by various situations. In the first instance, viewers may have felt an (unconscious) need to respond to a call to be offended and to stress such sentiments during the interviews. They were being questioned by a university researcher on their motives for watching the programme and rather than talk about commonly articulated motives for watching reality television—escapism, *Schadenfreude*, entertainment (Hall 2006; Sender 2012; Skeggs and Wood 2012)—notions of shock, or disbelief were stressed early on in each interview. This may have occurred because the articulated narratives were very much what one would expect given *EB*'s status as a unique media text that broke with conventions, even by Channel 4 standards at the time. Motives such as escapism or entertainment may have been perceived by the viewers as misplaced if articulated to me. The illusive state of being shocked was thus first evoked, in order to conform to social expectations that the interviewees believed I held. In reality, I had not told them what I thought of the show. According to widely held beliefs, and as articulated by the programme itself, the scenes on display simply *must* be shocking, embarrassing, extreme, even offensive to some. This seemed, perhaps, like common sense. Why was this the case? As the interviews went on and narratives flowed, the specific notion of disgust was mobilised in more detail by some and the viewers' positions were more specifically articulated:

> I don't watch *One Born Every Minute* because I don't particularly like it. I don't wanna watch it. It's not very… I find that disgusting, so I think it all depends, some people like to watch operations and disgusting conditions. Essentially they are not nice, it's not something you'd want to look at if you want to relax. But then some of us I reckon, are just interested and we're not all gonna be doctors, we don't all want to see, I don't know, cysts and things like that. It's just, yeah…. (I6, 159–166)

> I was shocked last week with the chap, the chap who had his eye removed that was that was [inaudible]… I guess almost I wanted to look away.

Part of me does that and part of me always wants to look so that I think that's probably the most shocked I've ever been, to be honest. And the fact that he's still sort of talking so normally, I've never seen anything you know quite as extreme, so that was, that was really interesting. So, yeah, I mean obviously some of the other things… I suppose the sort of, erm, erm you know, there's the usual kind of gross-out things, I guess, and, and stuff to do with sexual things, I suppose. I suppose they have to put a full range of the things. Again, it ultimately has to entertain, hasn't it? But I suppose really I'm just really interested in things that can happen to all our bodies. So, you know, it can range from "Oh my god" to back to just "Oh that's quite interesting". (I7, 118–127)

Yeah, yeah, yeah, definitely there's something like, you know, when there's, like, really gross infections, when you kind of think that is quite disgusting, like, when things are, like, septic or whatever, or just generally, like, people go on there with all manner of things, don't they? Erm, and like, erm, you never really know what you're gonna get, but there's a few times I've kind of gone "Eurgh". It makes me feel really squeamish, but I think 'cos they also kind of do, like, a lot of… they'll show, like, operations and stuff, they're not afraid to show the really gory stuff. I think that helps. I think it helps. It wouldn't be right if that show kind of didn't show you stuff, You know, it's important that it does. (I10, 207–215)

Writing on the affective power of disgust, Sara Ahmed (2004) argues: 'Disgust pulls us away from the object, a pulling that feels almost involuntary, as if our bodies were thinking for us, on behalf of us' (Ahmed 2004, 85). This image of the body that suddenly pulls away was also present in many of the interview narratives, as they spoke of moments of turning away from the television screen when they were too shocked and disgusted to look. We could interpret feelings of disgust as mere biological responses that we have been trained to execute. A close-up of a gaping wound is disgusting and our gut feeling affirms this—we may feel our stomach churn or sensations of nausea. However, there is a political dimension to disgust and shock. Disgust reinforces and secures a border between the one who is (made to be) disgusting and the one who is disgusted (Ahmed 2004, 87), between the patient who was leaking faeces and the clean, proper doctor who has reinforced the border between them by asking the question. Such forms of separation are relayed to audiences. Perceiving something as disgusting entails morality, as Winfried Menninghaus (2003) writes: the body before us 'should *not be,* at least not for *us* and in *our* presence. It should *go away*' (Menninghaus 2003, 53; italics in original). What is interesting about the above narratives is that bodies are *made* to be disgusting through speech acts. They *are* disgusting, or gross, according to the viewers. Bodies, conditions and things have a negative quality. They are made to acquire and become disgust/ing as an overpowering quality that overshadows everything else about them. Some scenes in *EB* (and related programmes) were thus termed 'disgusting' by viewers, but what lies behind the act of casting something or someone as disgusting?

Julia Kristeva (1982) has coined the notion of 'the abject', an affective response to someone or something that is similar to disgust. She argues that the abject puts one 'at the border of my condition as a living being' (Kristeva 1982, 4). One is affected by an experience that is unfamiliar and reacts in defence and fascination. One looks and looks away at the same time.

I suggest that such speech acts by viewers were manifestations of an unconscious desire to create a border between patients and themselves, to draw a line between 'embarrassing' and not-embarrassing bodies. The great detail and passion used by the interviewees to talk about their shock, offence and disgust thus serves a defensive purpose. They split themselves off from the patients and from fears of becoming *EB* themselves. This will be illuminated further in the next section.

Feeling Offended as a Defensive Act

Many viewers were keen to stress how *different* they were from the patients. I suggest that feelings of offence, shock and disgust were particularly emphasised to me during the interviews so that the interviewees could differentiate themselves from people on *EB*. Many of the conditions presented on the programme are conditions that each and every one of us could have, be it as a result of an accident, ageing, a botched surgery, etc. 'There's no shame, we're all the same', as the show's slogan states. In that sense, there is nothing extraordinary about the programme. This sensation may have occurred during the interviews and offended the individuals' narcissistic fantasies of their own ideal and perfect bodies.

Kristeva argues that seeing the abject results in 'a narcissistic crisis' (1982, 14) for the ego, because we are reminded that we are in fact not perfect or forever young. In moments of abjection, we are reminded of our finitude and bodily limits. Some of the scenes of *EB* touch something that is always already lost in the ego (according to psychoanalysis): a coherent sense of a whole and unified subjectivity. Thus, scenes of such a nature are offending to the ideal fantasy of the ego's coherence and invulnerability and must be (unconsciously) split off. Viewers spoke about some of their responses to and thoughts on the programme in specifically *affective* terms that showed a difficulty with speaking about them: '"Eeeurgh." You are imagining the pain, but that's what it is, you are imagining the pain, you don't know what it is like' (I9, 409–410), as one remarked. Another woman said:

> Just the surprise, I mean, I have never seen something so magnified. I mean, we all have an idea of how, especially women, we have an idea of how it is, but this kind of… it was so magnified, erm, I might say, probably for a few seconds I might felt a bit, like, "eurgh" […]. (I1, 647–650)

> I mean, yeah, you do get those sort of, "eeeh", squirmy moments where, you know, you can't even look at the screen. (I2, 367–368)

Attempts to describe affective responses, such as 'eurgh' or 'eeeh', point to difficulties on the part of the viewers to speak about their embodied reactions to the programme. The narcissistic crisis that comes about as a result of viewing certain scenes is met with such strong reactions that viewers have difficulty in rendering these into discourse. The body speaks itself in such responses (Johanssen 2016).

By rendering scenes as shocking or disgusting, viewers made use of strong terminology in order to dis-identify with them. They imagined what it might be like to have the bodies that are put on display in front of the cameras, and this created a fear of becoming like them. There is almost an affective contagion through the television screen that needs to be combated: 'Yeah if it's all too real then, I do…, don't know, it could be me, it can still be me, I can catch anything and be affected' (I6, 203–204), as one person said. Another man said that he could not look at other men having surgery:

> I didn't wanna look because, especially if it was a guy and he had a… because I couldn't look… oh, if I had that, erm, that… they went into surgery, and if they were doing something and I can't watch that, you know. (I9, 215–217)

A female interviewee gave a very detailed account of a body she did not want to end up having:

> You know, thinking what life must be like to be, to have that impact on your body and how sometimes that's a choice as well! How can you choose to allow yourself to become quite so big? Some people don't mind if they're a certain size, but when you get so big that you can't even wipe your own bum after going to the loo that's something else! I don't think we really learn much from those problems, but it's perhaps more of a shock factor to people, or if you're thinking that you're getting a bit big and you wanna lose a bit of weight that might inspire you, thinking "You know what, I don't wanna end up like that, so I've got a choice to do something about it". (I2, 390–400)

We can see how disgust, shock, offence and affective responses serve as defence mechanisms for viewers, stressing the difference between the viewers bodies and the patients' bodies. Many viewers were keen to point out to me how healthy they were and that they were thankful for their bodies. I asked them if they would consider going on the programme, and all declined:

> I: *And would you yourself go on Embarrassing Bodies?*
>
> I10: No. Erm, erm, no, I… I mean, I'm thankful that I've never had to see anyone about anything embarrassing, erm, which is… I'm really thankful for. But, you know, I don't think I'd go on it unless… no, no I can't, I can't see a reason why. (I10, 265–268)

The almost performative utterances of disgust, shock and offence during the interviews thus serve a defensive purpose of splitting off (Klein 1988) fantasies of mortality, changing bodies or sudden medical conditions that result in bodies that are out of control. They may have also been uttered in relation to the interview dynamics, with interviewees not wishing to appear to be 'weak' or 'embarrassing' if they had told me that they had fears of becoming like the bodies on the programme who were in need of, sometimes urgent, medical help. Instead, interviewees emphasised how different their bodies were. For instance, one interviewee said:

Yeah, fine, I am pretty happy and healthy, you know, and haven't really got any hang-ups. Erm, yeah... [inaudible]. I think shows like this do make you appreciate... You know, everyone is, like, critical of themselves, but shows like this, they put a perspective on people. People go through a lot worse, like, scary stuff [...]. (I10, 323–326)

A young woman I spoke to remarked:

Erm, I'm very lucky. I don't... I think stretch marks are the one, like... when people come on and they say 'I have really bad stretch marks' and you get to see their body... and I feel better because I know I'm not the only one. Erm, I, I also don't like the weight I am, I'd like to lose weight, so when chubby people come on, like: "Yeah, you go", I feel better. But, erm, I tend to be, I'm quite lucky to be honest, I think, compared to people who go on it. It makes me feel normal, like the small mistakes I have, it's not the end of the world. (I6, 250–255)

One female said:

Erm, on the whole, I'd say fairly okay. I mean, I suppose I have, like, some irrational problems, like, I've got a bit of a belly on me, like, the other day someone actually thought I was pregnant on the tube, which I was quite shocked about [...]. (I8, 437–439)

These narratives further distance the interviewees from the patients. Their bodies are healthy, happy, lucky, okay. Not embarrassing. Indeed, this woman was shocked when mistakenly perceived as pregnant. One may understand how *EB* as a media text may have served an (unconscious) function of defending against fears of becoming out of shape, or out of control. These fears were not really spoken about in the interviews, but expressed themselves in the passionate rejection of the patient bodies and in the emphasis on the healthy bodies of the interviewees. I do not mean to discredit such feelings: we all have them. It is, however, problematic to render certain bodies as shocking, disgusting or offensive, and not others. As I have discussed, such words were used by the interviewees for two reasons: to conform to social expectations in an interview situation, and to (unconsciously) defend against fears of becoming a body in need of medical help.

The reader may ask at this point: if viewers were so shocked, offended and (unconsciously) fearful of the programme, why did they continue to consume it week after week? Psychoanalysis can help in answering this question: ultimately, there was a degree of perverse pleasure in viewers' consumption of the show.

A Perverse Form of Voyeurism: Embracing and Rejecting *Embarrassing Bodies*

In addition to narratives of shock, offence or disgust, many viewers also spoke of feelings of excitement and of how entertaining the programme was for them. Such narratives were arguably less socially acceptable, given the 'trashy' and shocking nature of most reality television formats, but they were uttered nonetheless.

> I: *And when you watch a recorded episode, 'cos then you can sort of rewind, do you sometimes do that?*
>
> I2: Yeah, if they have said something particularly shocking or if I have missed it, erm, or my boyfriend said "Oh my god, did you catch that bit?" (I2, 311–314)

> I, like, I really like parasites, so parasitology, so if they do… I think at some point, James, or whatever his name is, had to swallow tape worms and they went off and saw how they lived in his gut, essentially. I thought that was really cool. I quite like malaria or something, like when they pick up on pretty exciting things rather than just boring… Like, I don't mean to be harsh, but, like, dermatitis and acne… yeah, it is, when it's really bad it's really bad, but it's quite common so I prefer to see a bit [inaudible] especially from people who travel and catch things there. I don't particularly like…, I like it when, like, people have something wrong with their genitalia, I think it's quite interesting, but, erm, like, STIs are a bit boring now 'cos you heard it everywhere. When they go on the beach and they talk to people, like, what they do over the weekend when they're drunk, you're just, like, "Yeah, we all know this". (I6, 175–184)

> I'm always excited to watch it, 'cos I wanna see what's on next! (laughs) Erm, I just find it really interesting. (I3, 222–223)

> Excited… erm, yeah, quite. That's why I like to record it 'cos I hate the adverts. I need to be on it! Like, I kinda, like, stop because I want to see what happens next and I don't like when they talk too much. I'm just, like, "no, no, show me, show me everything". Erm, yeah, excited is the word. It's quite sad. (I6, 77–80)

In speaking of their excitement about the show, more light-hearted motives came to the fore, perhaps associated with entertaining qualities. Viewers were able at the same time to embrace and reject *EB*. They had rejected and othered the patients' bodies, but in speaking of their excitement they were able to embrace them again. This suggests that experiencing the affective states of disgust, shock and offence was oddly pleasurable for the viewers. I call such forms of engagement a *perverse form of voyeurism*. '[C]ausing offence is always tinged with a certain *jouissance*, and being offensive in public is a political act brimming with psychic investments' (Baraitser 2008, 424). Perhaps the same is true to a degree of being or feeling offended. While such feelings may be perceived as deeply unpleasant and negative, a psychoanalytic angle suggests that they can be oddly pleasant and satisfying at the same time. I suggest that this was the case for the interviewees. Two psychoanalytic concepts allow us to think about this further: perversion and voyeurism. As a concept which originates from psychoanalysis, voyeurism primarily refers to sexual gratification from looking at other people without being seen (Fenichel 1995). For Freud (1981), voyeurism has a distinctly sexual component. He describes it as an act of looking without being seen by the other so that sexual pleasure can be achieved. Fenichel (1995) argues that in looking at a scene (for instance of sexual intercourse), voyeurs are (unconsciously) reminded of childhood experiences such as seeing a parent's genitals. These experiences arouse an anxiety in them. Such scenes, resembling the early experiences of voyeurs, are repeated again and again in order to achieve mastery over them. However, there can also be a voyeuristic dimension to viewing practices which are not aimed at sexual arousal or pleasure (Metzl 2004).

Viewers of *EB* perhaps exhibited such voyeuristic viewing practices because audiences are able to see bodies they would normally never see, unless they were working in the medical sector. The programme may thus have a highly voyeuristic appeal. Rather than speaking about such a voyeuristic appeal, the viewers in the study turned it around by stressing their feelings of offence, shock and disgust.

I argue that the viewing practices and the narratives about them that are discussed in this chapter also go beyond mere voyeurism. They are explicitly coupled with perverse tendencies. Post-Freudian psychoanalysts have defined perversion as a particular psychodynamic relationship. The pervert's object (be it a real person, or a thing) is (ab)used and handled instrumentally while at the same time being valued and adored.

The pervert attempts to enact mastery over another, and through this act ultimately disavows human fragility, loss and death (Lacan 1994; McDougall 1995; Ogden 1996). While the relationship between the viewers and the programme was of course not exactly the same as a perverse relationship between two human beings in person, some tendencies that characterise the psychodynamics of perversion were apparent nonetheless.

In speaking of their excitement, viewers were able to (unconsciously) reverse defensive reactions to the patients. They were able to *enjoy* their own disgust, shock and offence. After all, they had reminded themselves and me during the interviews of how different they were. Their fears of becoming like the patients were thus completely unreasonable. The patients' suffering and 'otherness' thus enabled a form of agency in the viewers' minds that allowed them to manipulate the patients as objects to be excited by. The patient's bodies could be mentally used for purposes of being offending and entertaining. Viewers could rewind and re-live their shock, and shudder in excitement at naked bodies. They could be excited about and entertained by their own disgust and take perverse pleasure in it, as well as in the patients' miseries.

> I think it's very… it is entertaining. I like the sort of production style of it, you know. It flows very well and, erm, it feels wrong… I must admit it feels wrong sometimes watching it for entertainment, but you know what I mean… it's, erm, I find it very interesting, although I've always been interested in medical stuff like that so… (I2, 357–360)

Another interviewee said: 'I suppose anyone who watches it has got a general [inaudible] in a weird way to be entertained by some of the grossness that can happen to the body' (I7, 76–78). A female remarked: 'I do also think that people watch it for entertainment value and, and I think that I'm probably being guilty of that as well to be honest' (I8, 472–476). Through enjoying and being entertained by the programme, viewers were able to disavow their own (unconscious) fears of fragile human existence. Their initial narratives of shock, offence and disgust acquire another quality when put in relation to their emphasis on how different their bodies were from the patients' and how excited they were by the show. Their narratives thus not only functioned as a way of articulating socially expected responses to the 'extreme' scenes of the programme, but also enabled them to acquire a sense of agency and mastery over their unconscious fears and defence mechanisms. It is this agency that bears perverse tendencies because it disavows the viewers' possible anxieties about their own bodies as well as the patient's real medical problems. The patients undoubtedly appeared on the programme not because they wanted to act as offensive/entertaining bodies, but because they sought genuine medical help.

The interview narratives also served as an additional justification, to the interviewees themselves and to me, of why they kept watching the programme. Rather than ceasing to consume it because they were too shocked or offended, the emphasis on their bodily difference and on the entertaining qualities of the series enabled continued consumption. The paradox of embracing and rejecting the bodies on the programme was thus kept in dynamic motion through the stressing of light-hearted motives.

Conclusion: Loving the Shock

What might the implications of the model of pleasurable shock, disgust and offence that I have put forward in this chapter be for wider cultural analyses of our times?

As a number of contributors to this volume have identified in their chapters, we live in an age where the 'right to offend' is diagnosed by various commentators as being under threat. So-called 'political correctness' has made it more difficult to offend because certain discourses are no longer tolerated in public, university or media spaces. Of course, those who have bemoaned such a fading of free speech are the ones who often were the perpetrators of such discourses: sexist, racist, classist, ableist narratives which are no longer tolerated. Offence, shock and disgust are something societies should tolerate in order to guarantee freedom of expression, some voices say. Being offended that the right to offend is under threat is perhaps an irony that we have to learn to come to terms with. I would suggest that the spectacles of reality television and social media have enabled an acceleration of offence, disgust and shock where the next scandal is just around the corner: it only takes one tweet for another 'shit storm' to erupt. Reality television production houses and social media companies, of course, love offence, disgust and shock, for they attract more audiences, more clicks, and enable the generation of profit through data mining. Audiences have perhaps equally bought into the viral nature of these affective states. Yet another outrageous tweet by Donald Trump, for example, allows us all to be united in collective offence and uproar. But doesn't it also secretly give us a feeling of joy, euphoria and collectivity? Affective states, offence, disgust and shock enable collective movements and allow us to be moved collectively. While one must be careful not to generalise, in the light of the various justified waves of offence that we have witnessed in the last few years in relation to sexualised, racialized and ableist violence, it seems that there is perhaps a perverse tendency in some reactions that are marked by a sense of collective pleasure.

In the light of the then newly formed coalition government of Austria's conservative ÖVP and Jörg Haider's right-wing FPÖ, Slavoj Žižek (2000) wondered 'why we all love to hate Haider' (2000, 37). Haider had become a common denominator that all so-called democratic political parties and citizens could project their hatred on.

> Plain to see, in fact, is the structural role of the populist Right in the legitimation of current liberal-democratic hegemony. For what this Right— Buchanan, Le Pen, Haider—supplies is the negative common denominator of the entire established political spectrum. These are the excluded ones who, by this very exclusion (their 'unacceptability' for governmental office), furnish the proof of the benevolence of the official system. (Žižek 2000, 37)

While Žižek has done plenty to offend people through his provocative and often problematic statements (see e.g. Ahmed 2008 for a critical discussion), he perhaps has a point here. Are we dependent on the *EB* patients, Trump, Weinstein and other contemporary abject phenomena in order to reassure ourselves of our good qualities as citizens? To an extent, both subjects like Trump and the medicalised bodies on *EB* represent bodies that are (made to be) out of control. They need to be inhibited, disciplined and policed by our discourses so that a functioning symbolic order is upheld and so that we can reassure ourselves of how 'good' we are. Our shock is thus not only a 'natural' response in the light of what is deemed good and moral, but leads to a collective force that produces endless commentaries expressing an almost pleasurable shock coupled with (justified) offence.

References

Ahmed, Sara. 2004. *The Cultural Politics of Emotion*. Edinburgh: Edinburgh University Press.
Ahmed, Sara. 2008. "Liberal Multiculturalism is the Hegemony–It's an Empirical Fact: A Response to Slavoj Žižek." *Darkmatter: Post-colonial Futures*, February 17. http://www.darkmatter101.org/site/2008/02/19/%E2%80%98liberal-multiculturalism-is-the-hegemony-%E2%80%93-its-an-empirical-fact%E2%80%99-a-response-to-slavoj-zizek/.
Baraitser, Lisa. 2008. "On Giving and Taking Offence." *Psychoanalysis, Culture & Society* 13 (4): 423–427.
Fenichel, Otto. 1981 [1995]. *The Psychoanalytic Theory of Neurosis*. London: Routledge.
Freud, Sigmund. 1981. "Repression." In *Standard Edition of the Complete Psychological Works of Sigmund Freud. Volume XIV: On the History of the Psycho-Analytic Movement, Papers on Metapsychology and Other Works*. London: Hogarth Press and Institute of Psycho-Analysis.
Graefer, Anne. 2019. "Introduction to Media & the Politics of Offence." In *Media and the Politics of Offence*, edited by Anne Graefer, 1–20. Basingstoke: Palgrave Macmillan.
Hall, Alice. 2006. "Viewers' Perceptions of Reality Programs." *Communication Quarterly* 54 (2): 191–211.
Johanssen, Jacob. 2016. "Not Belonging to One's Self: Affect on Facebook's Site Governance Page." *International Journal of Cultural Studies* 21 (2): 207–222. http://journals.sagepub.com/doi/full/10.1177/1367877916666116.
Johanssen, Jacob. 2019. *Psychoanalysis and Digital Culture: Audiences, Social Media, and Big Data*. London: Routledge.
Klein, Melanie. 1988. *Love, Guilt and Reparation and Other Works, 1921–1945*. London: Virago.
Kristeva, Julia. 1982. *Powers of Horror: An Essay on Abjection*. New York: Columbia University Press.
Lacan, Jacques. 1994. *Le Seminaire. Livre IV: La Relation D'Objet*. Paris: Seuil.
McDougall, Joyce. 1995. *The Many Faces of Eros*. New York: Norton.
Menninghaus, Winfried. 2003. *Disgust: Theory and History of a Strong Sensation*. New York: SUNY Press.
Metzl, Jonathan. 2004. "From Scopophilia to Survivor: A Brief History of Voyeurism." *Textual Practice* 18 (3): 415–434.
Ogden, Thomas. 1996. "The Perverse Subject of Analysis." *Journal of the American Psychoanalytic Association* 44: 1121–1146.
Sender, Katherine. 2012. *The Makeover: Reality Television and Reflexive Audiences*. New York: New York University Press.

Skeggs, Beverly, and Helen Wood. 2012. *Reacting to Reality Television: Performance, Audience and Value.* London: Routledge.
Žižek, Slavoj. 2000. "Why We All Love to Hate Haider." *New Left Review* 2: 37–45.

CHAPTER 7

'Period Sex': *Crazy Ex-Girlfriend* and the Feminist Politics of Offence

Katrin Horn

When cartoon versions of the supporting cast call the main character of The CW's *Crazy Ex-Girlfriend* (2015–) exactly that—a crazy ex-girlfriend—in the opening credits of Season One, the offended Rebecca Bunch (played by co-creator Rachel Bloom) vehemently protests that 'the situation is a lot more nuanced than that!'. TV critics mostly agree, calling the show 'witty, well-acted, brazenly inventive, and a pleasure to watch' (Bastién 2017) or simply 'The Best Show on TV […] that demonstrates the near-total creative freedom of TV's latest evolutionary period better than any other' (Zoller Seitz 2016). A *Slate* review that proclaims it 'one of the most critically acclaimed programs on broadcast television', however, also notes that *Crazy Ex-Girlfriend* (*CXG*) is not '*among* the lowest [rated], but consistently in the absolute last spot, almost as if it's trying to make a point' (Wilson 2018). Headlines like '4 reasons why "Crazy Ex-Girlfriend" is the best show you're not watching' (Fitzpatrick 2015) are therefore a staple of the show's critical reception. The explanation usually given—'Hate the title? Us too […]' (Pandell 2016)—is that the show's title, a 'sexist term', as the credit sequence

K. Horn (✉)
University of Bayreuth, Bayreuth, Germany
e-mail: katrin.horn@uni-bayreuth.de

© The Author(s) 2019
A. Graefer (ed.), *Media and the Politics of Offence*,
https://doi.org/10.1007/978-3-030-17574-0_7

acknowledges, is so offensive that it repels most potential viewers. The embrace of offensiveness in the 'subversive show with the terrible name' (Lenker 2016), however, does not stop there. It instead extends to narrative as well as aesthetic levels. As such, the title is not so much 'terrible' as it is telling: it proclaims the show's reliance on offence, which is used, this article argues, as a tool of feminist critique of contemporary modes of representation of women, romance and mental illness.

LEVELS OF OFFENSIVENESS

For those willing to look past the title and who venture to watch the first episode, the show commits its next offence through the sex of its protagonist, who is narcissistic, vengeful, mentally unstable—and female, in contrast to the narcissistic, vengeful and mentally unstable male anti-heroes who became one of the defining characteristics of 'complex television' (see Mittell 2014, 75). The final offence has nothing to do with sex or sexism, but with form and taste: rather than offering a dark drama (in which offensiveness might be considered part of a show's verisimilitude), *CXG* is a dramedy and a musical—the genre supposedly least suited to television's serial mode of realistic storytelling.[1] The show's premiere accordingly featured CGI-enhanced fantasy sequences and a full production number, a nervous breakdown, and a mention of an earlier suicide attempt—all in the first ten minutes. By the first half-hour mark, viewers were additionally confronted with blood splattered on a bathtub during a song interlude called 'Sexy Getting Ready Song'.

Such gross-out humour and forms of cringe comedy, in which the central character's behaviour is sometimes 'so cringe-worthy that it's hard to watch' (Pandell 2016), are as central to the show's tone as is its reliance on musical interludes, which embrace their own brand of offensiveness by breaking the rules of standard TV narrative. Beyond these structural taboos, the songs also repeatedly serve to transmit sexist sentiments (for example, in 'Let's Generalize about Men', S03 E01) or to enhance the gross-out factor (for example, 'Period Sex', which was deemed 'too dirty' to be included in the broadcast and made available exclusively online). Other songs, in contrast, satirise the sexualised

---

[1] See Plasketes (2004) for an analysis of *Cop Rock* (ABC 1990), whose spectacular failure is often seen as proof of the incompatibility of televisual verisimilitude and musical phantasma.

depiction of female bodies in popular culture. They thus participate in the show's taking of offence at the cultural milieu. Finally, *CXG* is consistently engaging with issues often deemed too offensive or divisive for broadcast television, ranging from abortion to racism and, most crucially, mental illness. Following a recent trend towards dramedies with complex female lead characters, *CXG* similarly offers the signature combination of 'humorous approaches to dark subject matter and/or tragicomic portrayals of characters', inviting audiences reactions 'that alternate between laughter, uneasiness, and frustration' (Havas and Sulimma 2018, 2). The show enhances this frustration by seemingly relying on the tired trope of the hysterical woman, yet making light of it through its musical format.

Refuting such a reading, this article, in contrast, will untangle *CXG*'s several strands of crudity and overall offensiveness to make the case for the show's complex commentary on postfeminism and contemporary media culture. Rather than looking at the musical interludes or comic elements as clashing with the show's exploration of feminist issues, this reading will position these as essential to the biting critique that has made this portmanteau-hyphenated television outlier—a female-led dramedy-cringe-musical series—a critical, if not commercial, success. This article makes this argument by outlining the show's critique of 'abject postfeminism', before tracing its rejection of the romanticising of 'crazy women' in US American popular culture. Exemplary readings of selected scenes detail how the series employs different levels of offence in order to push the limits of female representation in contemporary television.

Bad Feminists

As Das and Graefer summarise, there are a myriad of ways for the media to elicit offence, many of which, such as its reliance on offensive language or its 'raunchy' depiction of sex, *CXG* gleefully employs (2017, 7). Primarily through these aspects, the series positions itself firmly within a postfeminist discourse characterised by, among other features, the mobilisation of offensive images which are sold as edgy and feminist, with a 'knowing wink' to audiences who are in on the joke (McRobbie 2009, 17). Humour in these instances becomes 'a way of "having it both ways," of expressing sexist or homophobic or otherwise unpalatable sentiments in an ironized form, while claiming this was not actually "meant"' (Gill 2007, 159). This 'double address' of postfeminist media serves to undermine contemporary feminist politics at the same time as it claims the success of past efforts (Tasker and Negra 2005, 108).

In many ways, Rebecca Bunch is the quintessential postfeminist woman. As a successful real-estate lawyer with degrees from Harvard and Yale (who lists Mandarin under special skills in her CV), she has reaped the benefits of feminist efforts for equality in the workplace and in education. Yet she starts to doubt her life choices after she is repeatedly confronted with an advertisement for butter which asks 'When was the last time you were truly happy?', reflecting the central role of consumerism in postfeminist discourse (see Tasker and Negra 2005; Gill 2007). She subsequently suffers from a panic attack after an offer to become a partner in her elite New York law firm, during which she runs into her ex from summer camp, Josh Chan (Vincent Rodriguez III). This chance encounter prompts her to eagerly leave her professional success behind to follow her crush to a Californian suburb (S01 E01). There, she takes up a job at a subpar law form in order to keep up appearances and relies on her social and financial capital to get closer to her ex (who, it turns out, has been with his current girlfriend since high school), while continuously insisting that this radical break was just for herself. Rebecca thus follows the cultural script of 'downsizing', in which women's withdrawal from the workforce in favour of the pursuit of romantic fulfilment is perceived as empowering (Tasker and Negra 2005, 108).

The series refuses in at least two ways to further this dismantling of feminism. First, Rebecca is often shown as taking offence at sexist sentiments, however neatly packaged, and thus refutes the 'ironic' reliance on sexist tropes (for example, by calling out the use of 'sexist term[s]', see S01 E01). Despite her many alliances with the above-mentioned postfeminist tropes, Rebecca thus commits the cardinal sin of the contemporary woman: she presents herself as an angry feminist. Fittingly, Rebecca repeatedly recommends Roxane Gay, author of *Bad Feminist*, to her female friends (S02 E05). In her essay collection, Gay contemplates her own failings in living up to a feminist ideal:

> I am failing as a woman, I am failing as a feminist. To freely accept the feminist label would not be fair to good feminists. If I am, indeed, a feminist, I am rather a bad one. I am a mess of contradictions. (314)

Gay lists among such contradictions her joy in being independent, which clashes with her need to feel taken care of, and her awareness of unrealistic beauty standards and of pop culture's role in perpetuating stereotypes—and her inability to reject either. *CXG* builds on similar contradictions, which define Rebecca and the obvious gap—obvious at least to audiences and characters like her friend Heather (Vella Lovell) or her therapist Dr. Akopian (Charlene 'Michael' Hyatt)—between her feminist ambitions and her actual behaviour. More often than not, Rebecca's dismissal of what another character refers to as 'patriarchal bullshit' (S01 E01) is only lip service and a depoliticised version of neoliberal empowerment through individual self-betterment. When Rebecca decries the 'very misogynist myth that women can't get along' (S01 E02), as Paula (Donna Lynne Champlin) questions her sudden interest in befriending Josh's girlfriend Valencia (Gabrielle Ruiz), the set-up is easily recognisable as a ruse to get closer to Josh. Over the course of the series, however, Valencia and Rebecca develop a friendship that survives both of their respective break-ups with Josh. Similarly, Heather, who initially dates Josh's friend Greg (Santino Fontana), while he pines after Rebecca, remains a constant source of support in Rebecca's life, even after Greg has ended his relationship with both women. Together with Paula, the paralegal at Rebecca's new firm who quickly becomes Rebecca's motherly (and enabling) best friend, this group of women gradually becomes the emotional centre of *CXG*. While skewering faux-empowering tropes of girl power through musical interludes (as in the Spice-Girls-meet-*1984* spoof 'Friendtopia' in S02 E06 or Valencia's 'bitchy' *Lilith Fair*-inspired anthem 'Women Gotta Stick Together' in S01 E09), the show's narrative dispels the myth of female incompatibility. Similarly, the only tangible action that follows Rebecca's insistence that she and Valencia should cast off the 'cisgender patriarchal hegemonic hold on our imaginations and our hearts' (S02 E04), is that they pee on their ex-boyfriend Josh's audio equipment. Yet the overall focus of the series on the detrimental effect of this 'hegemonic hold' of an obsession with romance gives weight to Rebecca's statement in a way that Rebecca as a character does not.

Rather, her failings as a 'bad feminist' give the series ample opportunity to employ its second strategy of skewering postfeminist complacency through the exaggeration of tropes to the point of alienation. To borrow from Middleton's discussion of *Inside Amy Schumer*, it depicts 'the condition of postfeminism [as] one of abjection' (2017, 124). Among the most explicitly abject depictions of postfeminism in *CXG* are its gross examples of the 'makeover paradigm' and of subjectification, that is the internalisation of the male gaze (Gill 2007, 147, 156–158). The series pilot's 'Sexy Getting Ready Song' sets the scene for multiple variations on these themes throughout, as Rebecca goes through a gruesome process of perfecting her appearance interspersed with scenes reminiscent of a stylised music video. Contrasting the harshly lit bathroom in which Rebecca is getting ready with the dance sequences on a lush stage bathed in the soft light of numerous candles, the interlude is choreographed to fit the song's R&B melody. Between takes of the music video sequence showing Rebecca and four dancers with perfect hair and make-up, Rebecca—within the series diegesis—plucks her eyebrows and nose hair. While the dance sequence shows the women seductively writhing on the floor, Rebecca is visibly in pain during her bathroom routine. To the almost hushed 'so soft' of the lyrics, Rebecca is shown on a toilet seat vigorously scrubbing her heels ('bye bye skin', the background singers croon). And while 'music-video Rebecca' fantasises about 'a night you'll never forget', 'bathroom Rebecca' yanks a wax strip off her behind and screams in pain, as blood is splattered on her bath tub ('ass blood', the background singers proffer, in perfect harmony yet visibly disgusted). The two parallel scenes overlap when Rebecca relies on one of the dancers to violently pull up her Spanx. After this overlapping of the two 'realities', the dancers are shown still sexily swaying to the R&B song yet with face masks, hair-removal strips, and rollers in their hair. Their choreography is interspersed with images of 'bathroom Rebecca' burning her neck with a curling iron. Nipsey Hussle then enters the bathroom to rap about sexy women, but leaves horrified after observing Rebecca's arsenal of beautifying tools, which prompts his realisation that he has some 'bitches to apologize to'. The episode's tag uses this as an excuse to repeatedly call women by derogatory terms, even in this moment of a feminist awakening—an incongruous combination through which it challenges the normalisation of such language. It also details the offensive requests made of women in the entertainment industry (such as 'It was wrong of me to tell you what to do with that big fat butt. You can wiggle it, or you can keep it in school [...]'). Regardless of this intervention, the scene returns to the music-video scenario, where the song ends on the lyrics 'I'm gonna whisper your dick hard'. Abject postfeminism might scare rappers and make viewers cringe, but it will not deter Rebecca.

Rebecca is less oblivious in another, more explicit, take on the internalisation of the male gaze packaged as female empowerment. In the tenth episode of Season One, she follows Josh to a summer camp for at-risk teenagers and ends up devastated after their romantic trip to 'blowie point' and down memory lane ends with Josh laughing at an old love letter from her. She nonetheless proceeds to give the scheduled female empowerment presentation, where she—still visibly recovering from an allergic reaction to bug bites—is mocked by the attendant teenage girls. When she bursts into tears, however, they offer to 'empower' her. In her second-wave feminism frame of mind, Rebecca assumes this to mean she should read more Gloria Steinem and 'grow [her] pit hair out'. Her teenaged companions are appalled by Rebecca's suggestions—they meant a makeover. Emulating Fifth Harmony's video for 'Bo$$' and its stylised runway-strutting, the song 'Put Yourself First' teaches Rebecca that she should 'Push them boobs up [...] Wear six-inch heels / Just for yourself'—a sentiment that is rendered absurd by the presence of a Terry Richardson lookalike in a T-shirt with 'male gaze' printed on it. When Rebecca interjects 'If it's just for myself, shouldn't I be comfortable?', they answer emphatically 'No! Put yourself first in a sexy way'. The girls proceed to enumerate various version of sexy empowerment, such as 'Wear fake eyelids' (a bizarre exaggeration of fake eyelashes) and 'Put a hole in your earlobe', to which Rebecca reacts first with growing irritation and then with a pained scream when they pierce her ear with a hot needle. Summarising the contradictory entanglement of female agency and desirability, the song poignantly ends on the line: 'put yourself first for him'. While Rebecca has rejected this logic throughout the song, in the end she enthusiastically exclaims that the makeover makes her 'feel so much better' despite the bleeding wound on her ear.

Rebecca's susceptibility to perverted forms of empowerment is at this point in the series well established. Just one episode prior, she has bragged about her feminist pole-dancing classes, because 'Oh my God, who pole-dances for male attention? [...] true pole is about reappropriating the male gaze!' (S01 E09)—right after she pole-dances for Josh's attention (and makes everyone present uncomfortable in the process). The show continues this strategy of emphasising the self-defeating logic of such tropes through Rebecca's uncomfortable lack of self-awareness and a gross exaggeration of their imagery in the second season's makeover. After a recording of an embarrassing 911 call has gone viral (Rebecca is seen emerging from her fire-damaged house complaining 'I've got poo on my shoe'), Rebecca decides to follow the example of a product rebranding which has been pitched to her by a client (S02 E04). The scenario not only spoofs female empowerment by making decidedly un-sexy douches the product of choice to bring about women's liberation, but also stresses the overlap between neoliberal consumerism and idealised postfeminist behaviour, aligning Rebecca herself with a consumer product. To re-invent herself as 'Miss Douche' (to win an Instagram competition), Rebecca undergoes yet another makeover. The accompanying song 'Makey Makeover' (based sonically and visually on Toni Basil's 1982 hit video 'Mickey') points to the formulaic nature of TV makeovers as the lyrics—'process / process / reveal! / reveal!'—are synchronised with the corresponding scenes from Rebecca's own transformation. Furthermore, the song stresses the destructive rationale behind such procedures when its lyrics—'Old you in the garbage [...] old you was a diaper'—clash with the upbeat accompaniment. Reflecting her internalisation of these values, Rebecca is appalled by Paula's suggestion that she simply be herself for a change: in a typical makeover, the (both physically and emotionally) abject 'before' is to be 'dispelled through the disciplinary mechanisms of transformation' (Middleton 2017, 129). Accordingly, Rebecca blurts out 'My authentic self? That's disgusting!'. Yet her 'after' is as emotionally distressed as the 'before': to the public humiliation of the 911 call Rebecca's adds a cringeworthy performance at the 'Miss Douche' contest. Her outer transformation is discarded by the end of the episode, after Josh misreads her 'new look' as a 'funny costume'. Even more strikingly, when a strand of her newly glued-on blonde hair falls into Paula's lap, Rebecca corrects her friend's assumption that it is horse hair by stating that what fell off her head was in fact 'dead people's hair'. This prompts an unnerved Paula to mumble 'disgusting'. Rebecca has come full circle and the futility of her endeavour for once becomes apparent even to herself.

In its attack on postfeminism, *CXG* thus employs both the gross-out—which until the success of *Bridesmaids* (2011) was mostly reserved for male comedians—and the cringe factor of dramedies like *Girls* (HBO 2012–2017). While gross-out humour relies on bodily functions and filth to 'offer a radical challenge to taste and value' (Paul 1994, 20), the cringe results from 'the painful laughs derived from the awkwardness of social interaction and around people's lack of self-awareness' (Susman 2013). Together they create moments of uncomfortable laughter in which pleasure and disgust are productively negotiated in order to denaturalise postfeminism's potency.

Crazy in Love

Rebecca's new-found conviction that she should change her 'inside' instead of her 'outside' and move on from both Greg and Josh is expectedly short-lived. In the very next episode, she stalks Valencia in order to have someone to talk to about Josh. With this focus on the obsessive nature of Rebecca's behaviour, *CXG* goes beyond postfeminism's focus on romantic fulfilment to additionally invoke the history of romantic comedies that thrive on the assumption of ultimate compatibility, even in the face of momentary discord (McDonald 2007, 12–13). 'Embarrassing gesture[s]' are as central to this standardised depiction of love, as is the resulting monogamous, heterosexual union (13). The genre, furthermore, makes 'everything irrelevant besides the search for love' (White and Mundy 2012, 77) and, especially in the screwball sub-genre, celebrates characters who 'act in unpredictable and unconventional ways, as if crazy or drunk' (McDonald 2007, 23). The romantic comedy thus offers the frame in which much of Rebecca's behaviour seems appropriate—and in which she herself makes sense of it. This is explored, among other ways, in the lyrics of the song 'I'm the Villain of My Own Story (S01 E13), where she acknowledges that she is 'the villain in [her] own story / The bad guy in [her] TV show' and, more importantly, 'the bitch in the corner of the poster', whereas Valencia in this fantasy sequence sees herself as Kate Hudson, perpetual protagonist of romantic comedies. An even more overt acknowledgment of Rebecca's attempt to follow a script and the insistence of the series on the unbridgeable distance between fantasy and reality comes courtesy of 'The End of the Movie' (S03 E04). Rebecca realises she has hit rock bottom after Josh has left her at the altar to go to 'priest school', and she has slept with Greg's father. On her walk home from this drunken one-night stand, she is serenaded by Josh Groban, who clarifies that life is 'not some carefully crafted story / It's a mess and we're all gonna die'. Beyond such rather general, if sobering, wisdom, the lyrics offer a very specific commentary on Rebecca's life: 'People aren't characters […] Their choices don't always make sense / That being said / it's really messed up / that you banged your ex-boyfriend's dad'. The scene therefore initiates a turning point by shattering (through the externalised explanation of her regret) the connection between Rebecca's unhealthy coping mechanisms and genre scripts.

Up until this point, *CXG* has continuously employed tropes from the romantic comedy—such as a feigned interest in the love interest's favourite pastimes (ping pong, S02 E02) or rash decisions to commit (Rebecca's acceptance of Josh's proposal, S02 S11)—which traditionally deliver the protagonist into the blissful future towards which the romantic comedy, by definition, develops. Yet through their repetitive enactment over the course of series (rather than as a singular occurrence in a movie), the very same actions tie Rebecca instead to an ongoing, painful present that is uncomfortable to watch. The show thus offers a biting critique of the behaviour otherwise condoned as 'romantic' and counters the concomitant trivialisation of mental illness.[2]

The development of this critique is indicated in the season's different theme songs. While in Season One Rebecca simply insists that 'the situation is a lot more nuanced' than what can be explained by the moniker 'crazy ex-girlfriend', in Season Two she embraces the accusation of madness: 'I'm just a girl in love / I can't be held responsible for my actions'.[3] In Season Three, the theme song comprises a medley of four different musical genres and their different, yet intersecting, clichéd uses of 'crazy' as pertaining to women in love. Season Four introduces "other Rebecca" in its sitcom-like intro as an alternative to "too hard to summarize" post-therapy Rebecca, whose narrative arc does not fit the mold provided by mainstream media anymore. The theme songs thus alert audiences to the different thematic cores of each respective season. Furthermore, they underline how the show's status as a musical, which helps its spoofing of pop cultural expressions of postfeminism, becomes even more relevant in its twofold endeavour to distance itself from mediated clichés of romance and to provide a more nuanced approach to mental illness.[4]

HYSTERICAL WOMEN

In recent years, TV has increasingly embraced central characters with depression, addiction, anxiety, and a range of undiagnosed 'quirks'. Repeatedly, mental illness has been used as a trope to propel the story one

---

[2] The abusive patterns celebrated in romantic comedies made headlines, when a study proofed they normalize stalking (Beck 2016).

[3] In a flashback at the end of season two, this expression is revealed to be a quote from Rebecca's mother, Naomi (Tovah Feldshuh), and originally used in court, when Rebecca was tried for arson—which retrospectively puts a much darker spin on the Busby Berkeley-evoking opening credits (S02 E13).

[4] One of the seminal postfeminist texts, *Ally McBeal* (Fox 1997–2002), not only prefigures *CXG*'s basic premise—a young, bright lawyer pining after an unavailable former

week, only to be dropped the next (for example, PTSD on *Scandal*, ABC 2012–2018). Sometimes, the mental health of television characters provides ground for running jokes (*The Big Bang Theory*, CBS 2007–). Other times—in line with a broader cultural script of the 'mad as genius' (Rohr 2015, 234)—mental illness is taken as a kind of super-power that makes people better at their jobs, especially in criminal procedurals such as *Bones* (Fox 2005–2017) or *Elementary* (CBS 2012–). Neither of these apply to *CXG*, in which the protagonist' mental health issues are a continuous presence that is neither reflected in their professional performance nor played for laughs. The series also distances itself from a Western feminist tradition of reading 'madness' as a metaphor for female resistance (see Gilbert and Gubar 2000). The show instead casts a wider net in order to address the historical connection of women's association with madness, especially through the figure of the hysteric, which 'still packs a punch as a way to silence and discredit women' (Mizejewski and Sturtevant 2017, 1). '[C]razy or "high maintenance" girlfriends' remain a staple among 'hysterical women' (1) whose medical diagnosis has been reincarnated in catchily dismissive phrases: 'no need to ask or try to understand why a woman might be upset. Bitches be crazy' (2). Illuminating this observation, in almost every episode of the first two seasons several characters, including Rebecca herself, use 'crazy' dismissively to describe her. Such comments range from Valencia's reaction to Rebecca's drunken attempt to kiss her—'Are you crazy?! What is wrong with you?!' (S01 E02)—to Greg's dismissal of Rebecca's passionate legal plea—'She's crazy. Who goes into a courtroom and says all of that?' (S01 E13)—and finally Rebecca's father in the Season Two finale, in which Rebecca tells him to leave for good (S02 E13). 'You're crazy', he darkly replies. 'A little bit', she concedes (Paula having barely talked her out of jumping off a cliff). The same Rebecca who is quick to be outspokenly offended by sexism and racism has up to this point almost never engaged with these kinds of comments. The one time she points out that '[c]razy is a pejorative term and it's an over-generalization of a number of disorders', her explanation is directed at a child, and thus someone even more 'certifiably cute'[5]—and therefore more 'subordinate and unthreatening' (Ngai 2010, 949)—than the image she has created for herself (S01 E05).

---

boyfriend—but also anticipates the lead character's withdrawal 'into her inner world delusions', which are usually accompanied by music, yet—in contrast to *CXG*—'ultimately romanticized' (Sandars 2006, 204).

[5] This self-description is taken from opening credits of season two.

In contrast to this 'over-generalization' common among its characters, the series makes Rebecca's diagnosis—Borderline Personality Disorder—the focal point of Season Three, grounding her symptoms in flashbacks to scenes from previous seasons, and thus countering the vagueness which often surrounds depictions of mental illness on television and in film. It also forces audiences to reconsider their own prior readings of these scenes and thus to confront their own susceptibility to the trivialisation of mental illness. At the same time, the series thereby studiously avoids one of the main causes of offence in contemporary media, namely that of racist, homophobic, sexist or—in this particular case—ableist depictions which 'contribute to stereotyping' (Das and Graefer 2017, 7). The series instead relies on its musical elements to offer insights into Rebecca's mind that hint at her repressed pain and suffering, despite the show's raunchy and comedic tone. The musical interludes, usually derided for their incompatibility with serial verisimilitude, thus add to one of the main reasons given for why the show is perceived as 'unwatchable' (Rhee 2018)—which is neither its supposed sexism nor its grossness, but rather, its uncomfortable realism.[6]

Serenading Trauma

CXG follows the example set by musical episodes from earlier TV shows (most prominently *Buffy the Vampire Slayer* (The WB/UPN 1997–2003), *Scrubs* (NBC/ABC 2001–2010) and *Xena: Warrior Princess* (1995–2001), and presents most of its interludes as parodies of films, musicals and music videos (see Kassabian 2013, 54). Nonetheless, the show also strives for the effect of classical film musicals 'in which a heightened sense of reality is enacted through the brazenly artificial' (Knapp 2010, 8). The musical may, in fact, be singularly suited to illuminating Rebecca's state of mind, as it shares her obsession with romantic love: 'Pairing-off is the natural impulse of the musical', Rick Altman argues, contending that the genre 'seems to suggest that the natural state of the adult human being is in the arms of an adult of the opposite sex' (1989, 32). Furthermore, musical interludes in both film and television

---

[6]In this regard, the series most akin to *CXG* is *Unbreakable Kimmy Schmidt*, which 'resembles a Nickelodeon tween show—which is just how its heroine might imagine her own life. Yet, without any contradiction, it's also a sitcom about a rape survivor' (Nussbaum 2015). Not incidentally, *Unbreakable*, offers a similar combination of low humour and complex television (cf. Havas 2016).

have traditionally served to reveal characters' innermost feelings and secrets (Lodge 2007, 301). In *CXG* this 'lack of filter' emboldens the musical interludes to be particularly raunchy (for example, 'Pound away my morals / [...] Let me choke on your cocksuredness' in 'Strip Away My Conscience', S03 E02, and 'Help clear the table / like I drained your scrotum' in 'I Give Good Parent', S01 E06, or gross (for example, 'I Gave You a UTI', S01 E17). Yet it also opens unique insights into the characters' (overwhelming or denied) emotions. This latter effect is intensified through reprises, in which songs are used as a shorthand for a character's emotional state in scenes that might otherwise necessitate a flashback.

The emotional boundary-breaching of the musical interludes extends to the formal level, as the distinction between songs that are fantasy or dream sequences and those that take place within the story world is consistently blurred. Some numbers are sung by several, seemingly aware, characters or introduced by intradiegetic dialogue ('this is gonna be disgusting', an onlooker comments before the song 'My Sperm is Healthy', S03 E08), while other numbers go unnoticed by non-singing characters. Many songs which focus on Rebecca's emotions are clearly marked as fantasy either by dialogue (for example, Dr. Akopian's explanation of 'Dream Ghost') or by stylistic deviations (for example, the use of black and white in 'Maybe She's Not Such a Heinous Bitch After All', S03 E05). Yet even these seemingly clear demarcations may be seen as unreliable after the reveal in Season Three that one of Rebecca's symptoms in rehab was singing to herself (S02 E13). This continuous breaching of boundaries and stylistic messiness add to the show's cringe and gross-out factors, as they open the possibility that some of the issues addressed and expressions used in the songs are not being relegated to pure fantasy.

Often the effects of emotional intensity and lyrical crassness interact, as in Paula's reaction to her chance of attending law school. For the ballad 'Maybe This Dream' (S02 E02), Paula imagines a life in which opportunities are not instantly disappointed, such as, for example, her past attempts at running. In a comically exaggerated escalation of crudity, Paula remembers how she had to initially cut her run short, because she had 'to take a dump', a situation quickly made worse, when she also gets her period. '[M]enstrual cramps plus dump cramps' force her to quicken her pace, yet due to her pregnancy-induced incontinence, she pees her pants. When she finally gets home from what was supposed to be an empowering experience, the only noteworthy results is that her 'undies smell like a sewer rat'.

The lyrics appear even more offensive in the context of the performance, which is modelled on Disney's *Sleeping Beauty* (1959). Frolicking through the office, which is decorated to look like a forest (including the presence of a deer carcass), Paula wears an outfit evocative of Aurora, whose vocal style she also mimics. This stylistic contrast between fairytale setting and filthy imagery enhances the song's comedic effect. It does so, however, without diminishing the emotional impact of Paul's heartfelt wish to finally fulfill her professional goals.[7]

Rebecca's song 'You Stupid Bitch' follows a similar rationale, insofar as its theme of pathological self-loathing clashes with the form of a crowd-pleasing power ballad (S01 E11). Rebecca even imagines fans frenetically applauding and singing the chorus—'You ruined everything, you stupid bitch'—back to her. This song is just one in a succession of musical treatments of Rebecca's symptoms over the course of the series which mimic musical formats associated with love. These songs usually also contain comedic elements that elicit laughter, such as this power ballad's expression 'poopy little slut'. Yet it is an uncomfortable laughter at best. 'Comedy has issues', Berlant and Ngai argue, as it is just as likely to 'dispel anxiety' as it is to produce anxiety, 'risking transgressions, flirting with displeasure, or just confusing things in a way that both intensifies and impedes the pleasure' (2017, 233). Precisely this intertwined intensification and impeding of pleasure is achieved by *CXG*'s framing of uncomfortable or emotionally complex issues through a mix of comedy and musical. This makes the often disturbing themes seemingly more palatable, while the contrast to the presentation simultaneously makes the content more deeply unsettling. Putting the character's innermost (often negative) feelings explicitly into words and music, *CXG* offends and alienates audiences not because of its artificiality, but because the character becomes 'too relatable' (Dionne 2017).

This effect is never more apparent than in Season Three's pivotal narrative and musical moment: Rebecca's euphoric anticipation of her 'diagnosis [...] a new path for her life' after her suicide attempt, which

---

[7] Paula's delivery of sugary sweet songs to package 'too real for comfort'—descriptions of bodily functions is repeated in 'Miracle of Birth' ('explosive diarrhea / Means that labor's drawing nearer'), which nonetheless takes serious both Paula's joy in motherhood and Heather's apprehensiveness before her first birth (S03 E13).

prompts her to burst into the Disney-esque 'I want' song, 'A Diagnosis' (S03 E06). Bathed in warm sunlight (even though she is walking down the hallway of an outpatient care centre) and accompanied by a full orchestra, Rebecca fantasises about her new sense of belonging, as she asks her psychiatrist to 'prescribe [her] tribe'. Her heartfelt rendition makes tangible the elation she feels at the prospect. Yet the series still incorporates comedic elements which serve to lighten the mood, even as they remind audiences of her underlying issues. As Rebecca weighs her different options—'Schizophrenic or bipolar lite / I've never heard voices / but maybe it's time to start'—she promptly starts hearing voices which comment on her 'confusing' choice of words ('Time to blow this joint / and by joint I mean my inner sense of confusion') and thus serve yet again as an externalisation of her inner critic. The musical style and visual parallels (such as Rebecca's walk towards the camera with a man in the background catching something she throws and people dancing in circles around her) furthermore connect 'A Diagnosis' to the very first song in the series, 'West Covina', which introduced the romance plot and whose reprise has repeatedly kept that theme alive. By 'confusing things'—to return to Berlant and Ngai's argument—here by swapping diagnostic certainty for romantic fulfilment in this ode to Rebecca's new future, 'A Diagnosis' may be the harshest indictment in the series of the 'crazy in love' trope. It also presents an affectively intense moment of identification with a lead character, not despite but because of her mental disorder.

Offensively Uncomfortable

Keith Phipps echoes several other critics when he notes that *CXG* is 'so comfortable making viewers uncomfortable that it's hard to watch too much at once' (Phipps 2017). From its premise of a 'mad woman at the centre' *CXG* derives the leeway to employ a variety of offences against form and taste. Its heightened sense of reality helps to ground the musical format, which in turn allows for extended interior monologues in song format that justify moments of gross-out and cringe humour—if people are basically talking to themselves, why would they censor themselves? The show intensifies the uncomfortable laughter resulting from these transgressive forms of humour through often incongruous visual or musical styles, which add, however, their own kind of pleasure through their inter- and metatextual references. Such references, in turn, connect the show to the cultural scripts of postfeminism and romance, whose offensive key characteristics—filtered through music as an expression of deeper truths and vis-à-vis Rebecca's excessive obedience to their demands—are made impossible to ignore. By furthermore treating Rebecca's mental illness as neither a metaphor nor a joke, *CXG* condemns the habitual conflations of love and madness, and the media tropes and formats which support these. At the same time, the cringe/musical/dramedy series format uses its uncomfortable humour to broaden the spectrum of female representation and of feminist comedy as it 'break[s] down the barriers that say women must not speak about scatological, gynecological, or sexual matters in public' and rejects the assumption that women are 'not funny' because of their 'very different attitude towards filth and embarrassment' (Mizejewski and Sturtevant 2017, 3). Basking in the 'messy affective fabric' (Graefer 2019, 3) of humour that is as pleasurable as it is distasteful and of musical interludes that are as catchy as they are darkly disturbing, *CXG*, may not be—to return to the aforementioned *Slate* review—'trying to make a point' through its low ratings, but certainly it aims to do so through the underlying creation of deep discomfort.

References

Ally McBeal. 1997–2002. Created by David E. Kelley. Fox.
Altman, Rick. 1989. *The American Film Musical*. Bloomington: Indiana University Press.
Bastién, Angelica Jade. 2017. "What *Crazy Ex-Girlfriend*'s Depiction of Mental Illness Has Meant to Me This Season." *Vulture*, December 13. http://www.vulture.com/2017/12/crazy-ex-girlfriend-mental-illness-what-it-has-meant-to-me-this-season.html.
Beck, Julie. 2016. "Romantic Comedies: When Stalking Has a Happy Ending." *The Atlantic*, February 5. https://www.theatlantic.com/health/archive/2016/02/romantic-comedies-where-stalking-meets-love/460179/.
Berlant, Lauren, and Sianne Ngai. 2017. "Comedy Has Issues." *Critical Inquiry* 43 (2): 233–249.
Bones. 2005–2017. Created by Hart Hanson. Fox.
"Bo$$." 2014. Performed by Fifth Harmony. Directed by Fatima Robinson.
Bridesmaids. 2011. Directed by Paul Feig. Universal Pictures.
Buffy the Vampire Slayer. 1997–2003. Created by Joss Whedon. The WB, UPN.
Cop Rock. 1990. Created by Steven Bochco and William M. Finkelstein. ABC.

Crazy Ex-Girlfriend. 2015–. Created by Rachel Bloom and Aline Brosh McKenna. The CW.
Das, Ranjana, and Anne Graefer. 2017. *Provocative Screens: Offended Audiences in Britain and Germany.* Cham, Switzerland: Palgrave Macmillan.
Dionne, Evette. 2017. "'Crazy Ex-Girlfriend' Is Talking About Mental Illness in a Way You Never See on TV." *Revelist*, January 17. http://www.revelist.com/ideas/crazy-ex-girlfriend-mental-illness/6562/the-cw-series-follows-rebecca-bunch-rachel-bloom-a-successful-lawyer-who-encounters-her-summer-camp-crush-josh-chan-vincent-rodriguez-iii-in-manhattan-new-york-she-sees-their-unexpected-runin-as-a-sign-its-time-for-a-change/1.
Elementary. 2012–. Created by Robert Doherty. CBS.
Fitzpatrick, Molly. 2015. "4 Reasons Why 'Crazy Ex-Girlfriend' Is the Best Show you're Not Watching." *Splinter*, December 10. https://splinternews.com/4-reasons-why-crazy-ex-girlfriend-is-the-best-show-your-1793853462.
Gay, Roxane. 2014. *Bad Feminist.* New York: Harper Perennial.
Gilbert, Sandra M., and Susan Gubar. 2000. *The Madwoman in the Attic: The Woman Writer and the Nineteenth-Century Literary Imagination*, 2nd ed. New Haven: Yale University Press.
Gill, Rosalind. 2007. "Postfeminist Media Culture: Elements of a Sensibility." *European Journal of Cultural Studies* 10 (2): 147–171.
Girls. 2012–2017. Created by Lena Dunham. HBO.
Graefer, Anne. 2019. "Introduction to Media & the Politics of Offence." In *Media and the Politics of Offence*, ed. Anne Graefer, 1–20. Basingstoke, UK: Palgrave Macmillan.
Havas, Julia. 2016. "What's in a Burp? Therapeutic Gross-Out Humour in *Unbreakable Kimmy Schmidt.*" *CST Online*, June 30. https://cstonline.net/whats-in-a-burp-therapeutic-gross-out-humour-in-unbreakable-kimmy-schmidt-by-julia-havas/.
Havas, Julia, and Maria Sulimma. 2018. "Through the Gaps of My Fingers: Genre, Femininity, and Cringe Aesthetics in Dramedy Television." *Television & New Media* 13 (1): 1–20.
Inside Amy Schumer. 2013–2016. Created by Amy Schumer and Daniel Powell. Comedy Central.
Kassabian, Anahid. 2013. *Ubiquitous Listening: Affect, Attention, and Distributed Subjectivity.* Berkley: University of California Press.
Knapp, Raymond. 2010. *The American Musical and the Performance of Personal Identity.* Princeton: Princeton University Press.
Lenker, Maureen. 2016. "The Subversive Show with the Terrible Name: 'Crazy Ex-Girlfriend' Satirizes Sexist Tropes with Song and Dance." *BitchMedia*, October 12. https://www.bitchmedia.org/article/subversive-show-terrible-name/crazy-ex-girlfriend-satirizes-sexist-tropes-song-and-dance.

Lodge, Mary. 2007. "Beyond Jumping the Shark: The New Television Musical." *Studies in Musical Theatre* 3 (1): 293–305.
McDonald, Tamar Jeffers. 2007. *Romantic Comedy: Boy Meets Girl Meets Genre*. London: Wallflower.
McRobbie, Angela. 2009. *The Aftermath of Feminism: Gender, Culture and Social Change*. London: Sage.
"Mickey." 1982. Performed by Toni Basil. Directed by Toni Basil.
Middleton, Jason. 2017. "A Rather Crude Feminism: Amy Schumer, Postfeminism, and Abjection." *Feminist Media Histories* 3 (2): 121–140.
Mittell, Jason. 2014. "Lengthy Interactions with Hideous Men: Walter White and the Serial Poetics of Television Anti-Heroes." In *Storytelling in the Media Convergence Age: Exploring Screen Narratives*, ed. Roberta Pearson, 74–92. Basingstoke, UK: Palgrave Macmillan.
Mizejewski, Linda, and Victoria Sturtevant. 2017. "Introduction." In *Hysterical! Women in American Comedy*, ed. Linda Mizejewski and Victoria Sturtevant, 1–31. Austin: University of Texas Press.
Ngai, Sianne. 2010. "Our Aesthetic Categories." *PMLA* 125 (4): 948–958. Special Topic: Literary Criticism for the Twenty-First Century, October.
Nussbaum, Emily. 2015. "Candy Girl: The Bright-Pink Resilience of 'Unbreakable Kimmy Schmidt'." *The New Yorker*, March 30. https://www.newyorker.com/magazine/2015/03/30/candy-girl.
Pandell, Lexi. 2016. "WIRED Binge-Watching Guide: *Crazy Ex-Girlfriend*." *Wired*, October 12. https://www.wired.com/2016/10/binge-guide-crazy-ex-girlfriend/.
Paul, William. 1994. *Laughing, Screaming: Modern Hollywood Horror and Comedy*. New York: Columbia University Press.
Phipps, Keith. 2017. "What Are the Best 'Unbingeable' TV Shows?" *Uproxx*, April 21. https://uproxx.com/tv/unbingeable-tv-shows/.
Plasketes, George. 2004. "Cop Rock Revisited: Unsung Series and Musical Hinge in Cross-Genre Evolution." *Journal of Popular Film and Television* 32 (2): 64–73.
Rhee, Margaret. 2018. "The Unexpected Feminism of Crazy Ex-Girlfriend." *The Rumpus*, February 1. http://therumpus.net/2018/02/the-unexpected-feminism-of-crazy-ex-girlfriend/.
Rohr, Susanne. 2015. "Screening Madness in American Culture." *The Journal of Medical Humanities* 36 (3): 231–240.
Sandars, Diana. 2006. "It's More Than Just Another Silly Love Song: Ally McBeal Brings the Hollywood Musical to Television." In *Searching the Soul of Ally McBeal: Critical Essays*, ed. Elwood Watson, 198–218. Jefferson, NC: McFarland.
Scandal. 2012–2018. Created by Shonda Rhimes. ABC.
Scrubs. 2001–2010. Created by Bill Lawrence. NBC, ABC.

Sleeping Beauty. 1959. Directed by Clyde Geronimi. Walt Disney Productions.

Susman, Gary. 2013. "Discomfort Zone: 10 Great Cringe Comedies." *Time*, May 12. http://entertainment.time.com/2013/05/13/discomfort-zone-10-great-cringe-comedies/slide/intro/.

Tasker, Yvonne, and Diane Negra. 2005. "In Focus: Postfeminism and Contemporary Media Studies." *Cinema Journal* 44 (2): 107–110.

The Big Bang Theory. 2007–. Created by Chuck Lorre and Bill Prady. CBS.

Unbreakable Kimmy Schmidt. 2015–2019. Created by Tina Fey and Robert Carlock. Netflix.

White, Glyn, and John Mundy. 2012. *Laughing Matters: Understanding Film, Television and Radio Comedy*. Manchester: Manchester University Press.

Wilson, Carl. 2018. "Crazy Exegesis: On *Crazy Ex-Girlfriend*, Mental Illness and Musical Deconstruction Go Hand in Hand." *Slate*, January 4. https://slate.com/arts/2018/01/crazy-ex-girlfriend-deconstructs-pop-music-and-destigmatizes-mental-illness.html?via=gdpr-consent.

Xena: Warrior Princess. 1995–2001. Created by John Schulian and Robert Tapert.

Zoller Seitz, Matt. 2016. "The Best Show on TV Is *Crazy Ex-Girlfriend*." *Vulture*, n.d. http://www.vulture.com/2016/06/best-show-crazy-ex-girlfriend-c-v-r.html.

CHAPTER 8

Fans at Work: Offence as Motivation for Critical Vidding

Sebastian F. K. Svegaard

To be a fan is to have feelings for an object of fandom, and some fans, often referred to as transformative fans (see, for example, Petersen 2017; Stein 2010) express their fannish affect through creating works of art. Vids, a type of fanwork, are short, remix music videos made by fans in Western media fandom (Jenkins 1992), referred to as vidders. Vids look like music videos, but are a distinct genre. They draw their visual side chiefly from TV and film, and are not meant to promote a song or artist, but rather to present an argument (Coppa 2008) or tell a story with/about their visual source(s). A vid can be understood as a vidder's path through a text (Gray 2010), as a part of a historiography (Stevens 2015) and as a deconstruction of the media out of which they are made. Some vids, called critical vids, are explicitly intended to be critical of the media they are constructed from or speak to. As numerous blogs and niche media (such as *The Daily Dot* or *The Mary Sue*) show, critical fan commentary is hardly exclusive to vidding. However, the process of creating a remix of something in order to criticise it is perhaps particularly

S. F. K. Svegaard (✉)
Birmingham City University, Birmingham, UK
e-mail: Sebastian.Svegaard@mail.bcu.ac.uk

poignant and effective in making such a point. The act of cutting and remixing a work can be seen as deconstructive, and thus it is possible in general to consider vidding a critical art form.

In this chapter, I argue that, for fans, being critical of or offended by a text does not contradict loving it, that offence can be shared through fanworks, and that vids are particularly good at communicating feelings because of their multimedia format. Through producing and consuming fanworks, fans share feelings, meaning that offence can inspire not only creative production but stronger subcultural bonds.

The emotive qualities of fandom have long been documented (see, for example, Grossberg 1992; Hills 2002). However, fan offence has not been much explored, although the idea of the offended fan is one that appears in public debates whenever fan reactions hit the mainstream media, for instance regarding the casting of actors against the racial identity found in the source text—as with the whitewashing of *Ghost in the Shell* (Sanders 2017)—or against expectations, as with John Boyega's black stormtrooper in *Star Wars: The Force Awakens* (Abrams 2015). In this chapter, I am using offence as an umbrella term to denote the messy tangle of feelings of being let down by, angry at, hurt or offended by a text of which one is a fan. I am considering fan offence as a rupture in the unwritten and unspoken—but deeply felt—contract between fan and text, which is built on a foundation of trust and love. When the expectations within the fan-text relationship are not met, hurt is created and fans may vent these feelings.

In the following, I expand on the place of this kind of offence in the spectrum of fannish affect and, via an example, show how the feelings of being hurt, let down or offended by a text may appear in a vid, and how this may create ripples of emotional resonance within its immediate circle of reception in fandom. By 'resonance', I mean here the way in which engagement with screens can, as Susanna Paasonen (2013) writes, create tactile reactions in the viewer. I am, however, mostly speaking of sound—which is where the term 'resonate' originates—and how music can move us emotionally across place and time (Kassabian 2013; Erlmann 2014; Chion 1994). In order to do this, I conduct a textual analysis of an example vid, *Women's Work* (Luminosity and sisabet 2007), drawing on the three elements of the vid—music, image and lyrics—to show how the feelings of both offence and love for the source text are communicated in and around the vid. For the examination of the vid's reception and how feelings are transferred through the medium of vidding, I engage here in online ethnography. Because I am working with an 11-year-old vid—and also with 11-year-old online comments—I have not sought consent from everyone engaged in the debates, as I did from the vidders themselves. To do so would be impossible, since several commenting identities have been abandoned, deleted, or have no contact information. Instead, I have attempted to protect the identity of the people commenting by paraphrasing their words, rather than quoting them outright, and by not linking directly to the debates I am quoting from. Furthermore, all commenters are, like the vidders themselves, using fandom pseudonyms, which also offers some anonymity.

Fan Affect as Fan Culture

Fandom's affective dimension is something that fan studies scholars, have been exploring to various degrees for a long time, from Bacon-Smith (1992) to Hills (2018). That fandom is, among other things, characterised by fans having feelings for and about the objects of their fandom is, then, not a surprise. Louisa Ellen Stein (Stein 2015) refers to fandom as a 'feels culture' (Stein 2015, 156), and points out the dichotomy of feelings inherent in fandom's being intimate yet no longer private, and instead building what she refers to as an 'intimate collective' (ibid.). In this way, fandom can be viewed as a culture which is powered by feelings. Fandom can also be understood as functioning through a gift economy consisting of fanworks and comments/debates surrounding these works (Stanfill 2018; Coppa 2014). These gifts are also shared emotional engagements, something which becomes clear when thinking through Stein's concept of the 'feels culture'. Following this line of thinking, we can understand fanworks as expressions of emotional engagement, shared freely as gifts to the culture of feels in which they are created. The cycle of the gift economy is mirrored by a cycle of affect that comes with the engagement with the work. A fan creator is moved to work through affect, and pours it into her work, while her audience are moved to consume for the same reason and, as they consume, to experience emotions shared by the creator. They can 'share this back' in the feedback sections of a fanwork, debating with the creator and other fans and again sharing feelings. This allows us to see the fandom gift economy as an economy of feelings.

Love is what we most commonly think of when considering fan engagement, perhaps especially with regard to creative fanworks, and, as

Anna Wilson (2016) points out, this can lead us to understand fanfic as a form of reparative reading (Sedgwick 2003), which allows the fan creator and her audience both to experience personal healing and to promote social change. Wilson notes that fanfic, as interpretation, consists of a hermeneutics guided by feelings. As fan critique is also interpretation, this is also true of critical fan readings. Critical vids cannot be understood so easily as reparative readings, with their explicit aim to do what Sedgwick argues with: be critical. However, critical vids also aim to heal and to affect change, so neither are in opposition to reparative reading. Fans know a text intimately, meaning that they are uniquely placed to see and understand its failings and strengths alike. Fannish love and critique coexist, and fandom shows that it is possible to love a text which one also experiences as problematic. Precisely because fans love a text, they are moved to critique it, to want it to be better. This fits with Lauren Berlant's (2012) concept that the pleasure principle and the death wish are two sides of the same coin—to wish at the same time to preserve and to destroy an object is concurrent with what happens in critical fandom. It is not uncommon to see fans expressing love for a text in spite of its failings, in spite of being exasperated or even angered by it— something I have come to think of as the act of critiquing with love. Love and critique constantly exist side by side, and form a mode of engagement in fandom, to the point that there is a guide to 'How to be a Fan of Problematic Things' (Rachael 2011). As the intended audience for a vid is fandom, a critical vid can open discussions within fandom about difficult topics.

The fact that fans are devoted and critical at the same time is often used to dismiss them, especially in the parts of fandom I am concerned with. Centred around LiveJournal (a blogging site), DreamWidth (a fan-run clone of LiveJournal) and Archive of Our Own (one of the largest archives for fanworks, run by The Organisation for Transformative Works), these parts of fandom (also found on the micro-blogging site tumblr), have a majority of women and/or LGBTIQA+people as participants (centrumlumina 2013). Normatively, being emotional is coded as irrational and intimate (and feminine), while being critical is coded as rational and distanced (and masculine). (Sports fans, who are chiefly understood as normatively masculine males, tend to get a pass for the same behaviour. Few seem to find it remarkable that a fan still loves a team which loses, and at the same time voices vocal criticisms of this team.) Seeing media fans perform a mix of these two modes, essentially using emotions as critique, is remarkable. Fandom shows that the two modes are not necessarily in opposition, but can not only coexist but enhance each other when critiquing with love. Intimacy and love lead to intimate knowledge, which leads to a possibility of noticing flaws that a casual audience might not. Fans can then use this knowledge to create critical fanworks.

Fan Offence

Fan affect is complex and messy, and thus it can be difficult to separate out one emotion from the rest. The 'feels' that Stein (2015) and Hills (2018) write about are unspecified. They are simply feelings: jumbled, overwhelming, and the (relatively recent) practice of expressing them as 'feels', rather than being more specific, makes sense for this very reason. Attempting to zoom in on any particular feeling is difficult, but can lead to new ways of considering fan motivation. First, however, it is necessary to address the idea of the offended fan as it currently often appears. Recently, offended fans have showed up in the context of fans addressing issues of representation, either demanding more diversity or protesting about adaptations that provide increased diversity. Such debates have spawned think pieces which problematise fan critique as entitlement, as fans going too far, or as part of a supposed culture of seeking to be offended (see, for example, the debates previously mentioned about *Ghost in the Shell* and *Star Wars*). The offended fan is often produced as a spectre, an antagonist to the creators of texts, particularly noticeably with regard to Hollywood mainstream and other big, studio-driven productions where the power difference is huge. However, offence is a feeling like any other, and experiencing it is equally legitimate. It can also be a productive and constructive feeling, provoking thought and inspiring creation. This latter capacity is what is of most interest to me here.

A good deal of attention has been paid within fan studies to fans as critics and to fan activism. Lawrence Grossberg (1992) points out that fans' emotional investment is what creates fan empowerment and the possibility of resistance. So, following this line of thinking, the feeling of being offended is a way to resist as a fan. Loving the text is what makes one a fan, and being offended by it leads to critical fan love. Several scholars (Jenkins 2012; Brough and Shresthova 2012) have researched fans as activists, showing that fan affect can lead to such activities as charity, social justice efforts and attempts to rescue or change a beloved text. Fanworks can communicate many kinds of feelings: love, protest, critique, offence, and these can coexist within the same culture.

Women's Work: Offence in Practice

At first glance, *Women's Work* (Luminosity and sisabet 2007) is a music video that shows a montage of moments centring on female characters from the American TV show *Supernatural* (Kripke 2005–), showing horror and violence towards women. The show focuses on two brothers solving supernatural mysteries and hunting down and disposing of supernatural beings, but the vid does not showcase them. Instead it shows women who are attacked, injured or killed in the show, with the overall effect of an audiovisual assault on its audience as this montage-like parade of violence happens on the screen. As is perhaps already clear, *Women's Work* is not a conventional music video, nor is it meant to celebrate the song playing along with these clips. It is a vid, and it is intended to speak to and about its visual source. The vid has an argument to make about the problematic treatment of women in the TV show. This is an example of a critical vid, a piece of transformative fanwork, which engages in the act of critiquing with love. Because vids use music to tell their story and to argue their point, they are uniquely placed to engender emotional responses. Music is a carrier of emotions, which gives vids a particular strength in communicating in the feels culture of media fandom. Following the music in a vid, and how it cooperates with the visuals to tell its story, can show us how affect is performed and communicated in this medium.

All of the women in *Women's Work* are minor/supporting characters, as there are no weekly recurring female characters in the show. It is noteworthy that *Women's Work* is not, as is common with vids, named for its song, but instead has a title that ambiguously reflects the argument within. It could refer to the work of the women in the vid, or to the work of the vidders and the fact that most people engaged in this section of media fandom are women, meaning that the vid is about, by and mainly for women. The vid summary is cited by some sources (Flummery 2007) as 'Our Bodies, Our Selves', pointing to the title again. It is as if the vidders are telling us that they are the women in the vid, or that these women stand in for all women.

Music is an essential part of a vid, not just for the vidders but for the audience as well. Vidders like Here's Luck (2011) often mention that the choice of music is the first part of making a vid. The music and lyrics guide the editing and choice of clips, and the mood and tone of the music set the mood of the vid itself. As film music shows, for example in the work of Anahid Kassabian (2013) and her analysis of *The Cell* (Singh 2000), the way music is read by audiences against and with moving images adds a whole interpretive layer, and one that is specifically intended to guide emotional responses. So not only is song choice a factor in production and aesthetics, but it creates half the message for the audience, and takes them on an emotional journey. Music seems capable of going straight to our feelings in order to make us labile and open, and to resonate emotionally within us, in harmony with what we hear (just think of how a song can brighten a day, or how we often adjust our gait to match a song we hear while walking). As Julie Levin Russo (2017) puts it in, expanding on the work of Turk (2015):

> Beyond offering interpretive cues, "music is the throughline of a vid… [and] thus a crucial factor in whether the audience experiences a vid as a coherent whole" (2015, 167). Song choice also carries, in large part, the affective tone and impact of the vid (in Internet vernacular, the "feels"). (Russo 2017, 1.9)

The opening of *Women's Work* gives the audience the initial idea of what this vid is about and what to expect. The first aural impression is a feeling of something dark and unsettling. The harmonies have recurrent dissonance, and there is a screeching sound of the guitar and a jagged rhythm. Visually, the stand-out images in this early part of the vid are of a small girl curling up in bed, then a pre-teen girl doing the same, both clearly terrified. The colour palette is blue-toned and dark, adding to the feeling of danger and in keeping with *Supernatural*'s horror aesthetics. The effect is to build a sense of fear or dread, which stays as the song's lyrics begin to come in. The singer's voice sounds almost depressed at first, starting with the non-sequitur of 'And the sky was made of amethyst'. The song is 'Violet' (Love and Erlandson 1994) by Hole, fronted by Courtney Love. The lyrics as a whole give the impression of a sarcastic, angry parroting of the kind of things women constantly hear regarding sex and rape, about wanting and/or 'asking for it'. Love's normatively female-sounding voice helps the audience focus on women's experiences and construct the narrative from women's point of view throughout the vid. This first section already gives the audience a lot of emotional responses, chiefly related to fear for the women we are guided to identify with. Thus the vid sets up some key premises: it plays on horror, is about women, and the women are the points of identification. This first verse is dedicated to the victims of the 'monster of the week' (a type of episode where the plot solves a supernatural mystery/crime). As the song shifts upwards in intensity and aggression, it is matched by fast-paced cuts between scenes that quickly feel relentless in their violence. Love's voice yells 'you should learn how to say no', underscoring the intimate nature of the violence on screen and linking to victim blaming. In fact, in the moment these words are sung the matching scene looks like a rape. The clips show threats that make the viewer shrink away (such as an unforgettable close-up of the point of a knife millimetres from a widely staring eyeball), and scenes of women alone with the spying/prying camera and hinting at yet-to-be-discovered threats. We see women in the shower, swimming, in bedrooms and in situations that reference rape—being thrown to the floor, held down, forcibly undressed—much of it eroticised by the source. The entirety of the vid is almost overwhelming on an emotional level, and it communicates the offence which moved the vidders to create. We experience what they experienced when watching the show, and the audiovisual format of the vid makes the offending tropes abundantly clear. All this violence functions as plot in the show, and afterwards the women it happens to are no longer of any consequence to the story as people, but become a case for men to solve. We may be offended through sharing in the feelings communicated by the vidders, or by the images themselves as the vid presents them to us, but the emotional impact comes through regardless.

The bridge leading into the chorus has lyrics telling us that 'when they get what they want, they never want it again', to a surprisingly soft, almost resigned part of the melody, different from the rest of the song. Who 'they' are is unsaid, although in the context of the vid it seems to point outwards towards anyone who is not the women on our screens. An undertone of anger rises through the verse to become the main feeling of the chorus, with its torn and jagged sound. By then, Love's voice has moved to an almost screaming anger, crying the words 'go on, take everything, take everything, I want you to', accompanied by an intense beat and more distorted guitars—a dense, noisy soundscape. The music signals anger, but also discomfort; it is not a sound to live in, it is a sound to speak and argue with, one of action. The 'everything' that is taken in the vid is the ultimate thing: life. In this section, lyrics and voice both accuse and make the viewer complicit in the actions on the visual side of the vid. The audience, and by extension the fans of the show, are part and parcel of what happens in it, through watching, supporting and loving it, regardless of what we may think of this type of plot device. We are part of the 'they' who take and take, along with the show's creators, producers, etc. The vid invites us to feel anger and discomfort through the use of music, and enhances these feelings by pairing the music with uncomfortable and offensive images. We are led to share in this way another level of the vidders' offence.

In the second verse, the focus is on women who are mothers, girl-friends, colleagues—recurring characters who are closer to the narrative centre of the show. This matches a shift of pronouns in the lyrics to 'I', adding to the sense of something increasingly personal or intimate. Additionally, this is a verse that has less of the opening softness of the first by virtue of the drums carrying through. The focus in the first part of the verse is on the mother of the two main characters and the girlfriend of one of them. These two are killed in the same way in the show, burning to death stuck to a ceiling, and the vid draws this out for the viewer in all its striking detail. There are other women in this verse, other ritual sacrifices, along with some who are abandoned by the main duo. The consequence of love, the vid seems to say, is to die or to be abandoned—if you are a woman. The men get to walk away, the worse for wear but still alive and in focus for the viewer. Significantly, the lyrics contain the words 'I want it again, but violent, more violence', sung in a voice which signals anger and violence, which is what the vid delivers. When the aggressive chorus kicks in, the clips again become more action-filled, showing struggling women fighting for their lives. All of this is also sexualised, with nightgowns, skimpy costumes and writhing bodies on display, all at the site of conventionally attractive women's bodies. Here, the offence is the corruption of love, the sacrifice of women, so that men can be motivated to act or to show feelings. While the emotional tug of the music is the same, the way it is matched to images means we are understanding the different levels and layers of offensive material drawn from the visual source.

The final part, a coda, opens with a brief moment of softness, and is dedicated to female villains. At first it can feel like a moment of respite, simply due to the shift in the gender balance of the violence. Some of the women are perpetrators here, but the vid does not let the viewer forget that villains are also there to die, and brings this point home with a closing shot of a woman getting her neck broken with one horrible snap. Women can fight too, but only if they are evil, and only for a limited time. This examination of evil as the only way women can fight back is the final aspect of offence shared here by the vidders, and there is a definite shock factor in the ending of the vid. It has a final emotional punch before it fades to black, and a final impact of the felt offence is being shared with the audience. This finale communicates a sense of desperation, at first bordering on resignation, but with that last shot anger is punched through again.

As a whole, the vid is deeply disturbing. Cut off from their context and edited to focus on the issue the vidders are addressing, the clips give a strong impression of the violence in the TV show, literally to the exclusion of any other narrative. The focus on women's bodies as eroticised, even—or especially—when they are also sites of crimes, is emphasised through repetition, and if the vid is seen without any surrounding metatext or introduction it can cause offence in itself. However, one of the vidders mentions in her announcement post that she has a 'crazy, fierce, totally madlove for Supernatural', making this vid an example of critiquing with love. She also writes that: 'Just so it's clear and all – the vid could have been made using *anything* – seriously. Look around, this shit is *everywhere*' (sisabet 2007).

Presumably the 'shit' sisabet refers to is the systematic sexual/ised violence against female characters and the lack of more nuanced female characters who are not victims, villains or various emotional motivation for the male characters. So *Women's Work* is an expression of offence communicated to an insider audience of other fans by two women who are self-declared fans of the TV show they are criticising.

SHARING OFFENCE AS SUBCULTURAL PRACTICE

In the analysis above I point towards examples of communicated emotion, which all coalesce into the concept of fannish offence that I began this chapter with. My claim is that this offence is communicated through the vid and taken in by its audience, which I will now turn to. *Supernatural* had and has a large and active fandom, as evidenced by the number of fanworks (still) produced in its fandom (as per *Archive of Our Own*). The size and activity of the fandom is worth bearing in mind when engaging with the metatext and commentary surrounding the vid. The vid premiered at the vid convention VividCon in 2007 and was shared online afterwards. Posts by the two vidders on LiveJournal and DreamWidth announce the vid and have it embedded. These posts are where I have conducted the bulk of my reception analysis and where I quoted the vidders from. In addition, the fandom history wiki Fanlore has an entry for the vid that contains copies of commentary and links to sites where it was debated.

Despite the comment from sisabet above, stating that the vidders could have easily chosen another source with the same result, most of the commentary surrounding the vid hinges on *Supernatural* itself. The first, and most prolific, debates are from the time of the vid's release in 2007, although the last entry linked on Fanlore is from 2012, and the latest comment I found is from 2016, showing ongoing debates within fandom about both vid and show. While some discussions are now hard to find, several comments on the posts refer to raging debates elsewhere, and to anger and hate directed back at the vidders. Some of these comments mention that this anger relates to other fans' love for the show, leading one commenter to note that the vidders could have chosen another source, but that the fact that they chose this (very popular) one added to the impact of the vid. Fans may critique with love, but to experience critique levelled at something you love can hurt, and it is easy to react with dismissal, anger or offence. A comment from one of the vidders mentions that they have been accused of doing what the show does—eroticising violence towards women—by making it so blatantly obvious. This is reflected in one comment accusing the vid of having a 'medieval' view of women, showing tensions about when and how something offensive can be debated and explored, and when and if such acts are themselves offensive.

There are also positive reactions; in fact, most of the comments I can find applaud the vid and its critique. Some commenters who were not already watching the show mention not wanting to do so after this, while some state that the vid has changed how they experience the show and made the eroticised violence more visible. In some instances, commenters mention not having been conscious of the systematic violence towards women in the show before watching the vid. The sharing of offence here is a mirroring; these commenters are offended with the vidders, not at them. By communicating their offence, the vidders have opened other fans' eyes to a problem they are passionate about. It is in these comments that the vid's potential for critique is most clearly seen.

Another point of interest is the visceral reactions that commenters report feeling when first viewing the vid. Two go so far as to mention that they felt physically ill—and at the same time one of them says that this is their favourite *Supernatural* vid—while yet another mentions their love for vids which cause a physical response. Someone else reports shuddering when watching particular clips, and another that they have been shaken by the vid. Words like gut-punching and visceral come up several times, all pointing to bodily reactions from watching. Other words, in no particular order, are anger, disgust, horror, shock and emotional pain (several 'ow's and 'ouch'es). The bodily responses and the emotional impact of the vid are, as with other fan feelings, mixed and complex, but they can be understood as results of offence. This is how *Women's Work* communicates: by making the audience feel the discomfort and pain that the vidders feel when watching the TV show, showing us an example of the resonance described by Paasonen (2013). Through affect, it is possible to make sense of these varied reactions under one umbrella of offence, and to see them as productive. As a large number of comments express, the vid makes the viewers think and reflect, and at times fundamentally change how they view screen eroticisation of female suffering. Several of the comments also mention having to rewatch the vid to 'get it', that is, to reach a conclusion about the message of the vid. Others mention wanting to watch it again in order to fully receive the impact, showing that fan audiences are interested in the (loving) critique presented in the vid.

Conclusion

The comments show that within fandom itself the vid has sparked strong feelings and debates, and that its impact creates cognitive as well as physical and emotional responses. By understanding these emotions as expressions of shared offence, we can see the vid as a communicator of the feeling of being offended and of media criticism through this affective message. Using Stein, we can see this as circulating 'collective affect' (Stein 2015, 14), while acknowledging that this circulation of affect can have many, even contradictory, effects. For those of the vid's audience members who are in agreement with the critique, this offence is directed at the TV show, while for those who disagree it is directed back at the vid and at the vidders. In both cases, the offence sparks further discussion and is mirrored back and forth between the participants in the debate, providing an example of how affect is transmitted between people through online media. This affect is transmitted through a piece of creative media output, and perhaps especially through the emotive power of music. It is likely that showing a montage sans music would not have the same impact, demonstrating that the affective effect of music is something which demands attention and merits further investigation.

The example of *Women's Work* also shows how affect can be a bearer of culture and a social adhesive by transmitting feelings in an exchange between fan creators and audiences. Offended fans can use their emotions to produce responses, which in turn work to share and communicate these feelings within fandom's 'feels' culture. In the case of fans motivated by offence, we can see that love and offence are not necessarily in opposition, but can coexist and create a productive tension between themselves. Critical fandom demonstrates that the affective relations between fans and texts are complex, and that supposed contradictions can coexist. The fan motivation for creativity is not love alone, but can also be other emotions, even one as seemingly antithetical to love as offence, pointing to a more complex affective relationship between fan and text than the one commonly assumed.

REFERENCES

Bacon-Smith, Camille. 1992. *Enterprising Women: Television Fandom and the Creation of Popular Myth*. Philadelphia: University of Pennsylvania Press.

Berlant, Lauren. 2012. *Desire/Love*. Brooklyn, NY: punctum books.

Brough, Melissa M., and Sangita Shresthova. 2012. "Fandom Meets Activism: Rethinking Civic and Political Participation." In "Transformative Works and Fan Activism," edited by Henry Jenkins and Sangita Shresthova, special issue, *Transformative Works and Cultures* 10. https://doi.org/10.3983/twc.2012.0303.

centrumlumina. 2013. "Heterosexual Female Slash Fans." *The Slow Dance of the Infinite Stars* (Tumblr), October 4. http://centrumlumina.tumblr.com/post/63112902720/heterosexual-female-slash-fans.

Chion, Michel. 1994. *Audio-Vision: Sound on Screen*. New York: Columbia University Press.

Coppa, Francesca. 2008. "Women, *Star Trek*, and the Early Development of Fannish Vidding." *Transformative Works and Cultures* 1. https://doi.org/10.3983/twc.2008.0044.

Coppa, Francesca. 2014. "Fuck Yeah, Fandom is Beautiful." *Journal of Fandom Studies* 2 (1): 73–82.

Erlmann, Veit. 2014. *Reason and Resonance: A History of Modern Aurality.* Brooklyn: Zone Books.
Flummery. 2007. "VVC 2007: Disc Two (Premieres Part 2, also premiering) (3/5)." *Flummery* (blog), November 18.
Ghost in the Shell [feature film] Directed by Rupert Sanders. Paramount Pictures, DreamWorks & Reliance Entertainment, USA, 2017. 107 min.
Gray, Jonathan. 2010. *Show Sold Separately: Promos, Spoilers, and Other Media Paratexts.* New York and London: New York University Press.
Grossberg, Lawrence. 1992. "Is There a Fan in the House? The Affective Sensibility of Fandom." In *The Adoring Audience*, edited by Lisa A. Lewis, 50–65. London: Routledge.
Here's Luck. 2011. *Feminism in Focus Interview* [video] Available at https://www.youtube.com/watch?v=xX_zus0TGeE. Accessed 31st May 2018.
Hills, Matt. 2002. *Fan Cultures.* London and New York: Routledge.
Hills, Matt. 2018. "Always-On Fandom, Waiting and Bingeing: Psychoanalysis as an Engagement with Fans' 'Infra-Ordinary' Experiences." In *The Routledge Companion to Media Fandom*, edited by Melissa A. Click and Suzanne Scott, 18–26. New York and Oxon: Routledge.
Jenkins, Henry. 1992. *Textual Poachers: Television Fans and Participatory Cultures.* New York and Oxon: Routledge.
Jenkins, Henry. 2012. "'Cultural Acupuncture': Fan Activism and the Harry Potter Alliance." In "Transformative Works and Fan Activism," edited by Henry Jenkins and Sangita Shresthova, special issue, *Transformative Works and Cultures* 10. https://doi.org/10.3983/twc.2012.0305.
Kassabian, Anahid. 2013. *Ubiquitous Listening: Affect, Attention, and Distributed Subjectivity.* Berkeley and Los Angeles: University of California Press.
Love, Courtney and Eric Erlandson. 1994. *Violet.* Performed by Hole [CD] Recorded at Triclops Sound Studios. (Geffen Records GEC 24631).
Paasonen, Susana. 2013. "Grains of Resonance: Affect, Pornography and Visual Sensation." *Somatechnics* 3 (2): 351–368.
Petersen, Line Nybro. 2017. "'The Florals': Female Fans over 50 in the *Sherlock* Fandom." In "Sherlock Holmes Fandom, Sherlockiana, and the Great Game," edited by Betsy Rosenblatt and Roberta Pearson, special issue, *Transformative Works and Cultures* 23. https://doi.org/10.3983/twc.2017.0956.
Rachael. 2011. "How to Be a Fan of Problematic Things." *Social Justice League* (blog), September 18. https://socialjusticeleaguenet.wordpress.com/2011/09/18/how-to-be-a-fan-of-problematic-things/.
Russo, Julie Levin. 2017. "Femslash Goggles: Fan Vids with Commentary by Creators" (multimedia). In "Queer Female Fandom," edited by Julie Levin Russo and Eve Ng, special issue, *Transformative Works and Cultures* 24. http://dx.doi.org/10.3983/twc.2017.1026.

Sedgwick, Eve Kosofsky. 2003. *Touching Feeling: Affect, Pedagogy, Performativity*. Durham, NC: Duke University Press.
sisabet. 2007. "New Vid! Women's Work." *sisabet* (blog), August 15.
Stanfill, Mel. 2018. "The Fan Fiction Gold Rush, Generational Turnover, and the Battle for Fandom's Soul." In *The Routledge Companion to Media Fandom*, edited by Melissa A. Click and Suzanne Scott, 77–85. New York and Oxon: Routledge.
Star Wars: Episode VII – The Force Awakens [feature film] Directed by J.J. Abrams. Lucasfilm & Bad Robot, USA, 2015. 136 min.
Stein, Louisa Ellen. 2010. "'What You Don't Know': *Supernatural* Fan Vids and Millennial Theology." *Transformative Works and Cultures* 4. https://doi.org/10.3983/twc.2010.0158.
Stein, Louisa Ellen. 2015. *Millennial Fandom: Television Audiences in the Transmedia Age*. Iowa City: University of Iowa Press.
Stevens, Charlotte. 2015. "Exploring the Vid: A Critical Analysis of the Form and Its Works." PhD thesis, Warwick University.
Supernatural [television programme] Created by Eric Kripke. The WB Television Network & The CW Network. 2005–present.
The Cell [feature film] Directed by Tarsem Singh. New Line Cinema, Caro-McCleod & Radical Media, USA, 2000. 107 min.
Turk, Tisha. 2015. "Transformation in a New Key." *Music, Sound, and the Moving Image* 9 (2): 163–176. *Project MUSE*, muse.jhu.edu/article/608349.
Wilson, Anna. 2016. "The Role of Affect in Fan Fiction." In "The Classical Canon and/as Transformative Work," edited by Ika Willis, special issue, *Transformative Works and Cultures* 21. https://doi.org/10.3983/twc.2016.0684.

PART III

Offence, Media Ethics and Regulation

CHAPTER 9

Blocked Access: When Pornographers Take Offence

Susanna Paasonen

Pornographers are traditionally assumed to cause rather than to take offence, yet porn video aggregator sites, production studios and individual professionals alike have recently engaged in protests against proposed work safety regulation, internet policy and legislative measures connected to sexual equality, especially in the US. In many instances, this has involved porn companies protecting their own financial interests, whereas the economic rationale has remained less lucid in others. Focusing on moments of pornographers acting out in protest, this chapter examines the political economy of offence connected to contemporary pornography.

More specifically, this chapter explores how porn companies, and video aggregator sites in particular, make use of social media visibility to articulate their case, how their forms of protest function as PR, and how the shift of porn distribution to online platforms has changed the political stakes in all this. I first briefly contextualise the politics of offence connected to pornography, before moving on to recent examples of two

S. Paasonen (✉)
University of Turku, Turku, Finland
e-mail: suspaa@utu.fi

major video aggregator sites, xHamster and Pornhub, blocking user access as a form of protest, and inquire after the political and financial stakes that such seemingly paradoxical moves involve. This is followed by a discussion of xHamster's and Pornhub's sexual health and social responsibility campaigns as brand-building activities within the framework of social media. Pornography occupies an uneasy position within this economy, as content that is deemed inappropriate and undesirable in terms of the targeted advertising around which the flows of profit rotate. Further considering the political implications of the centralisation of porn distribution for independent and fringe operators, I then move on to examine the current UK internet filtering policy that makes MindGeek, Pornhub's parent company, a national gatekeeper of sexually explicit content—and in so doing to operate in porn production, distribution and regulation. The concluding section asks how articulations of offence are shifting in the course of porn's becoming a business of data, and how considerations thereof can help in thinking through the regularly paradoxical political economy of pornography.

Histories of Offence

It may seem odd for pornographers to express outrage over social justice or policy issues, especially if one subscribes to the repeated view that porn only involves the intent of turning people on and its only motivation is to make money. The tendency to separate the work of pornography from political interests and aims beyond the promotion of sexism and violence against women—a connection insisted on in anti-pornography initiatives—can be linked to the genre's assumed preoccupation with a singular intent of sexual stimulation that excludes, or at least sidetracks, social, political or artistic interests, merits or goals (see Strub 2010; Wilkinson 2017). There is certainly no reason to underestimate the centrality of financial profit as a motivation for the production and distribution of pornography, from either a historical or a current perspective, yet it does not follow that other intents, aims or purposes are absent.

As a media genre, pornography has throughout its modern history been defined as offensive in contravening codes of decency, moral norms and varying principles of appropriate and inappropriate sexual desires, acts and pleasures (Kendrick 1996). Its displays of body parts, orifices and secretions have broken with standards of good taste ever since the term pornography was coined in the nineteenth century—and even before, as in mass-produced eighteenth-century prints and literature mocking the clergy, aristocracy and other powers that be. Many scholars have seen the later popular attraction of pornography as owing to its bawdy, unruly disregard for bourgeois aesthetic norms (for example, Kipnis 1996; Penley 2004). According to Linda Williams's (2004, 4) well-known argument, the obscene is by definition that which is to be put off-scene—out of public sight, circulation, display and discussion. Pornography's cultural position as that which is, on the one hand, abundantly available, but which needs, on the other hand, to be screened off, has afforded the genre a specific lure of forbidden fruit. In Annette Kuhn's (1985) phrasing, pornography's titillating attraction requires disapproval, acts of censorship and policing. Following this line of thinking, if pornography fails to be offensive to someone, at least, its historically construed cultural position and function will somehow unravel. The gesture of pornographers taking offence and acting out for social causes remains particularly effective in contexts where pornography is equated with a social ill. In other words, its scent of forbidden fruit thrives in the gardens of Puritanism.

Pornography has literally been a terrain of offence, since the genre's legal position was long compromised in Europe and North America, and in a global context it remains so. For a large part of the genre's modern history, the production and distribution of pornography have been criminal offences and the position of a pornographer has been that of an offender. Following the decriminalisation of porn, starting with Denmark in 1969, its gradual and by now manifest 'onscenity' (Attwood 2009, xiv) has rendered it a topic of cultural debate and an object of mass consumption. In the course of this, much of pornography's default offensiveness seems to be evaporating. Porn taste cultures are increasingly shared topics of engagement, adult performers have entered the mainstream media as sex experts, and crossover celebrities are making diverse careers within the creative industries, while the constant accumulation of user-generated, amateur, semi-amateur and professional-amateur content has challenged assumptions concerning who makes pornography, how, and for whom (see, for example, Paasonen et al. 2007).

The protests addressed in this chapter are part of a longer continuum of pornographers engaging in debates both on freedom of speech and on advancing the rights and health of sex workers, with the notable difference that the most visible actors on the former have been producers, directors and publishers and on the latter porn performers themselves. The overall field of operation has nevertheless been drastically transformed during the past decade alone. With broadband connections, the video clip has become the predominant porn format distributed through video aggregator sites modelled after YouTube. Hosting porn video files in millions, these aggregator sites trade in sponsored content, premium membership fees and user data that is automatically collected, analysed for the purposes of targeted advertising, or sold to third parties. MindGeek remains the most formidable of current actors, owning the leading porn tube site, Pornhub, as well as most other key platforms, with the exceptions of xHamster and xVideos (Auerbach 2014). Porn circulates as data, the business of porn has grown inseparable from IT labour, and key players in the field are tech companies. All this pushes extant definitions of the porn industry and the politics of offence connected to it.

The increasing centrality of porn distribution and ownership, combined with the vastly lucrative markets of data, has notable ramifications. The profits of porn have shifted from production, DVD and magazine retail to key video aggregator sites, giving select players unprecedented control over audience access to adult content on a global scale. Pornhub and xHamster are both pornographers by proxy, in the sense that they do not produce or direct the videos they host and stream. As corporate players, aggregator sites focus on distribution, which, in the current technological context, means running servers and managing massive data traffic. In doing so, they have control over what content comes up in users' internet searches, what gets 'amped up' in visibility, and what may disappear in their constantly accumulating reservoirs of data. Aggregator sites hold a different kind of power and agency than any singular porn publisher or distributor—individual or corporate—has to date. Even if Pornhub does not make porn as such, MindGeek has bought up a range of high-profile studios that were suffering from the fall of the DVD economy and the easy accessibility of pirated content on the tube sites it owns. The ensuing system is both centralised in terms of ownership and dispersed in terms of profession and agency. A MindGeek-owned studio such as Brazzers employs producers, who then employ performers and other staff to create the desired scenes. As this 'gig economy' has become standard, fees have dropped and porn careers have grown increasingly precarious (Berg 2016).

Pornhub in particular has been actively branding itself as a lifestyle and media company, through media stunts that aim to reframe it as a socially responsible actor that is simultaneously more than naughty enough to titillate. The company's PR gestures, addressed below and ranging from donating money to various charities and giving out scholarships to support women in the tech industry, may easily come across as haphazard attempts at whitewashing a public image that is bound to be spotty and shady, given the poor reputation that the porn industry continues to enjoy in terms of gender and racial inequality, workplace safety and the overall lack of transparency in its flows of labour, finance, income and profit. These gestures, like the cultural visibility and popularity of aggregator sites internationally, run in parallel to and conflict with anti-pornography agendas that have notable visibility in the US, UK and Australia, and have contributed to the framing of pornography as a public health risk, or crisis, necessitating stricter online policy, filtering and regulation (see Attwood 2018, 1). The trajectories or policies of offence involved in the current traffic of porn are, in sum, convoluted, and inseparable from both the online attention economy and the business of data that this builds on.

BLOCKING AND THE VISIBILITY OF DATA

On 16 April 2016, the Cyprus-based xHamster, which has long supported Planned Parenthood by collecting voluntary donations on its site, blocked access for users from the state of North Carolina in protest against the newly introduced Public Facilities Privacy & Security Act. More commonly known as the 'bathroom bill', this law limited trans people's access to toilets and changing rooms of their own preference and choosing. Instead of gaining access to pornographic content when visiting xHamster, North Carolinian users were faced with the following notification, which the company also shared on their Twitter account:

> The Incredible Hypocrisy of North Carolina
> The Land where Homophobia is Law
> 2016 North Carolina GAY categories views 319 907
> 2016 North Carolina SHEMALE categories views 491 295
> 2016 North Carolina searches contain GAY 50 612
> 2016 North Carolina searches contain SHEMALE 48 585
> North Carolina! Stop Your Homophobic Insanity!

In their statement to the *Huffington Post*, the company further explained the ban: 'Judging by the stats of what you North Carolinians watch, we feel this punishment is a severe one' (quoted in Moye 2016). While the annual number of views and searches reported from the state is by no means extraordinarily high—and while the company's chosen category of 'shemale' for transgender porn fails to be among the most politically correct denominators available—the political point and the object of the protest were clear enough: xHamster objected to the politics of gender and sexuality that the 'bathroom bill' had emerged from. More specifically, the company was voicing its disapproval of the law and aimed to render visible the discrepancy between the conservative, heteronormative community standards that politicians deployed in justifying it and the not-strictly-straight porn preferences within the said community, as illustrated by their data traffic.

The tracking of user locations and actions, as facilitated by internet protocol (IP) numbers and cookies ever since the advent of the Web, is routine on virtually any site, be it commercial or not, even as user data has grown increasingly central as the fuel of social media that is collected, analysed and sold. xHamster, for example, collects cookies, IP addresses, geographic location and other session data 'in order to increase Your (and other Users') experience according to tracked interests, to analyze and target potential new markets, and for other marketing purposes' (xHamster 2018). The default tracking of users makes it easy to block content for visitors from specific regions, as well as to analyse and render public regional search and viewing patterns, trends and preferences. In their protest against the bathroom bill, xHamster relied on a combination of these.

The company's comment on the protest was somewhat grandiose: 'We blacked out the access to our website because we wanted to draw the attention of millions of people to patterns of human rights violations, and we are glad that our voice has been heard across the globe' (quoted in Tourjée 2016). This expression of offence gained international attention, largely due to its unorthodox rationale (it makes sense for any commercial site to attract, rather than to intentionally ban, users). Since porn companies are not generally considered paragons of civic virtue, even one protest for social justice comes across as unusual.

Porn companies are rarely associated with struggles for social justice, except when these are directly connected to initiatives threatening their flows of income. It was therefore less surprising when several major porn studios, including Vivid, Evil Angel, Treasure Island Media and Kink, blocked Californian users' access to their sites in protest at Proposition 60 in October 2017. Dubbed 'the condom bill', Proposition 60 demanded mandatory use of condoms in all porn films for reasons of occupational safety. The proposition was deemed a liability for the overall profitability of the industry, as well as itself a health hazard—the use of condoms in penetrative sex over several hours is likely to cause abrasions and their mandatory introduction was opposed by female performers in particular. The proposed initiative was no less problematic in requiring porn performers to make public their personal information, including legal name, date of birth and home address. Had the bill passed, it would have given any resident of California the right to sue pornographers for scenes performed 'bareback', with the possibility of receiving 25% of the fines awarded. Since US porn production remains largely based in the San Fernando Valley, studios sought to pressure local voters to oppose the proposed legislation. For its part, Vivid, once a leading studio for glossy DVD porn, allowed users with Californian IP addresses access only to a black screen with the text: 'Harassment is not a California value: NO ON 60', while a coalition of studios threatened to permanently block all access for Californians, should the law pass.

The technical tactics deployed in the two protests described above were nearly identical—blocking access to users from certain US states in order to comment and have an impact on legislative measures. Yet they differed clearly from one another in their motivations and purposes. Proposition 60 was directly aimed at transforming the working practices and, consequently, the revenues of the porn industry. Permanently barring access for Californians would have been a pre-emptive measure against potential lawsuits (Kokura 2016). As a form of protest, pre-vote blocking served the self-interest of the industry while also helping to attract attention to the proposition and its less discussed features. Although the proposed bill was justified on the grounds that it would improve work safety within the industry, it involved risks to the health, wellbeing and overall privacy of performers. For its part, the bathroom bill involved transgender rights and was in no direct way connected to the working practices, operating possibilities or business models of xHamster.

Although the act of blocking access from North Carolina would seem to be against xHamster's best interests, it benefited the company's brand-building by projecting a liberal, socially engaged public image. With the exception of Twitter, most social media platforms exclude sexually explicit content, which is consequently subject to flagging and banning. Facebook, for example, does not allow users to directly share links to porn sites, or adult companies to pay for targeted advertising or sponsored content. Amplified through online news articles and clickbait links reiterating its details, xHamster's bathroom bill protest gave it free, widespread and positive publicity on platforms from which it is otherwise banned. News items such as *The Next Web*'s 'XHamster Blows a Load of Justice on North Carolina Over Anti-LGTB bill' (Clark 2016) and *Broadly*'s 'Ejaculating Justice: The Porn Company Protesting Anti-Trans Law Speaks Out' (Tourjée 2016) aimed to attract clicks, views and shares with their catchy double entendres and intriguing subject matter. Within the attention economy of social media, these stories benefited all parties involved: xHamster's brand got a lift, the news sites gained visitors, and social media platforms such as Twitter and Facebook, through which the news links were shared, attracted traffic translating as corporate value.

In 2017, both xHamster and Pornhub, similarly to more mainstream tech and social media companies like Google, Facebook, Amazon, Netflix, Github, Imgur and Reddit, protested for the protection of net neutrality in the US—the principle whereby service providers are not allowed to block access to sites, to slow down traffic to them or to charge users more for accessing them. On 12 December, major sites joined in the 'Break the Internet' protest by adding information on net neutrality to their front pages in formats impossible for users to miss. Pornhub, for example, presented a largely black interface with the text, 'SLOW PORN *SUCKS:* join Pornhub in the fight to save net neutrality'. The motivation was explicitly a financial one: if net neutrality was overturned, nothing would stop US internet service providers (ISPs) dividing traffic into different speeds so that either porn companies or porn consumers would need to pay for the better-quality service required for streaming video. The ruling would also alter the ways in which user data can be mined, analysed and sold. By cancelling the ban on ISPs selling user data, such as browsing history or app use, or sharing it with third parties, the ruling would make it possible for ISPs to trade in users' porn search and browsing habits. Even if people make use of Google's anonymous browsing mode, Incognito, their motions remain visible to ISPs, which, in this novel context, could use the information as they like. The combined ramifications of repealing net neutrality may eventually challenge the viability of tube business models based on free porn.

These protests relate to the self-interest of tube sites vis-à-vis legal initiatives, without being entirely reducible to these. Actions against Proposition 60 have extended to ethical concerns about worker privacy and safety, while net neutrality involves the broad principles of internet freedom. In instances such as the North Carolina user ban, protest has expanded into registers of moral complaint, even while remaining part and parcel of xHamster's brand management and promotional social media pursuits. Circulating across social media, the coverage of Pornhub's and xHamster's protests helped to bolster the companies' public image as liberal and socially engaged. While Pornhub has a considerably more extensive track record in promotional stunts than xHamster, their brand-building pursuits have similarities.

Socially Responsible Pornographers?

In 2017, Pornhub launched its sex education site, Sexual Wellness Center, providing information on reproductive health, STDs and relationships, in the name of public good. The same year, xHamster protested against the State of Utah voting not to fund sex education, by giving users from the state the option of visiting non-explicit sex ed videos on YouTube by explaining that Utahns watch more porn per capita than any other state, but have some of the lowest levels of sexual education. Here, xHamster called out—and in fact to a degree shamed—the residents of Utah for their ample porn consumption and, in providing links to sexual education content on YouTube, directed traffic out from its own site.

For its part, Pornhub's sexual education campaign was not targeted against any particular state or educational policy, nor was the company interested in directing users elsewhere in search of information. By incorporating sex education into its palette of free service, Pornhub seemed to be covering all possible angles of consumer interest. Pornography has generally been framed as a dangerously poor source of sexual pedagogy in education, journalism and public debate (see Albury 2014). These two initiatives, even if emanating from porn sites themselves, seem to support this claim by pointing to educational resources external to their own core content. At the same time, this move helped to brand both companies as socially responsible enough to fill the gaps in sexual education left by the formal educational system.

The Sexual Wellness Center, as personified in its female director, Dr. Laurie, is an attempt to bolster Pornhub's image of public responsibility. As such, the initiative is far from an isolated one. The company has a steadily growing history of publicity stunts, such as the 2014 crowdsourced campaign for an advert encapsulating the company's brand, which gained broad clickbait coverage, or the idea, introduced in 2015, of the 'Wankband', a hypothetical wearable device generating energy through the motions of masturbation. Pornhub has also engaged in charitable actions, from the 'Save the Boobs' campaigns, collecting money for breast cancer research through views of its 'big tit' and 'small tit' categories, to the 'Pornhub Gives America Wood' campaign (2014), which involved planting a tree for every hundred 'big dick' videos watched, or the 2015 'Save the Balls' testicular cancer awareness campaign. Since 2015, Pornhub has been giving out scholarships to support underprivileged undergraduate student (see Paasonen et al. 2019).

Pornhub's wittily titled campaigns efficiently orient the eyeballs of users on online news hubs, blogs, Twitter and Facebook. Presented under the heading, 'Pornhub Cares', they provide virtually free publicity while helping to frame the company as committed to making the world a better place. This further involves mainstreaming of Pornhub as a lifestyle and entertainment brand, and even a household name of sorts. This branding exercise necessitates a redefinition of pornography's default offensiveness, on which the genre's cultural status and central attraction have depended. Pornhub's social responsibility campaigns contribute to the onscenity of pornography by increasing the brand's visibility in a range of mainstream social media outlets. Similar cross-platform circulation or presence does not, however, extend to the video content that the site hosts and makes money from: a gap remains.

In its PR efforts, Pornhub takes its cue from *Playboy* and *Hustler*, both brands of mainstream fame—or, depending on perspective, infamy—which some decades ago extended their operations into casinos and retail outlets trading in t-shirts, coffee mugs and jewellery (Osgerby 2001; Gunelius 2009; McKee 2016). Pornhub followed suit by opening a Manhattan SoHo pop-up store on 'Black Friday' in 2017. A *New York Times* report lamented the lack of raunch in Pornhub's commodity display, where most of the merchandise consisted of 'branded goods like hats, underwear, hoodies and even socks'. Rather than either revitalising the local sex shop tradition that had disappeared in the course of gentrification, or presenting any of Pornhub's streaming video content in a semi-public social context, the boutique presented purely brand promotion (see Nir 2017).

The intentional, yet volatile, decoupling of the Pornhub brand from the content it operates with finds support in the company's overall principle of operation. Like all video aggregator platforms, Pornhub does not produce its own porn, although it may reward select content producers for their efforts, and although it distributes the content that its parent company, MindGeek, produces and owns (Auerbach 2014). As Tarleton Gillespie (2010, 356), points out, the notion of a platform functions as a legal strategy protecting the company from liability for the content it hosts and for the activities of its users. Writing on YouTube, Gillespie examines the diverse discursive functions of the platform as:

> computational, something to build upon and innovate from; political, a place from which to speak and be heard; figurative, in that the opportunity is an abstract promise as much as a practical one; and architectural, in that YouTube is designed as an open-armed, egalitarian facilitation of expression, not an elitist gatekeeper with normative and technical restrictions. This fits neatly with the long-standing rhetoric about the democratizing poten-tial of the internet, and with the more recent enthusiasm for user-generated content (UGC), amateur expertise, popular creativity, peer-level social networking and robust online com-mentary. (Gillespie 2010, 352)

Emulating YouTube's principles of operation in the context of pornography, Pornhub taps into the diverse layers, promises and possibilities of a platform. Although commercially produced content dominates, as the most viewed content on YouTube and Pornhub alike, a certain vernacular promise of openness remains key to both. The discursive dimension of the platform as an egalitarian place to speak and be heard from resonates with protests against legal initiatives seeking to limit the rights of sexual minorities, to regulate the working practices of porn and to facilitate slower or more expensive access to sexually explicit content. Within this framing, a platform is that which enables and promotes sexual diversity and democratic self-expression.

When video aggregator sites are understood as platforms, pornographers remain actors apart, who nevertheless share their produce through the platform provided and, in doing so, contribute to its overall brand value. Despite running numerous porn video aggregator sites and owning a range of studios, MindGeek has consistently branded itself as a tech company, 'A Leader in Web Design, IT, Web Development and SEO [search engine optimization]' detached from the content and labour of pornography. In a deeply paradoxical line of development,

MindGeek both owns video aggregator sites that are, in Gillespie's terms, 'designed as an open-armed, egalitarian facilitation of expression, not an elitist gatekeeper with normative and technical restrictions', and expands its operations into this very realm of gatekeeping and technical restriction. This latter move, discussed below, very much undermines any simultaneous protests against internet regulation.

Pornographers as Gatekeepers

It remains crucial to note the obvious, namely that minority-interest, queer and feminist pornographies do not thrive in the tube economy, which is premised on free downloads and centralised on a few key aggregator sites. As Eleanor Wilkinson (2017, 982) points out, Web 2.0 operating principles of easy and inexpensive publishing allow for the hosting and dissemination of 'post-capitalist, non-capitalist, anti-capitalist, or "only slightly capitalist" pornographies', and 'global pornography corporations exist alongside myriad local place-based DIY alternatives, including sole producers, couples, groups and cooperatives'. This does not, however, result in an even playing field in terms of the different actors' visibility, agency or income. In fact, the 'Web 2.0' business models of MindGeek, based on free content and the mining of user data, present an explicit threat to independent pornographers wishing to financially support themselves through their work.

The denominator of mainstream pornography is slippery by definition, given the striking diversity of acts, aesthetics and scenarios that are already available on any aggregator site. Yet if one were to map out the current state of the mainstream, it would be most aptly represented by the content that Pornhub pumps up to its front page in the form of most viewed, most popular, most recommended, sponsored and hot content targeted to consumers according to their country of location and their past history of searches and views. Despite the staggering volume of available videos, the default content available on the front page tends to be representative of the logic of sameness in the performers' body styles and aesthetics, as well as in the choreographies and scenarios that they act out. Less viewed and less highly rated content easily remains buried in the data archives and, when viewed, is unlikely to yield profits for the people making it.

In the UK, the position of independent pornographers has been rendered even more difficult by government efforts to ban, in films produced in the country, acts deemed obscene, such as face-sitting, spanking, penetration with any object, physical restraints, water sports, humiliation, menstruation, public sex and female ejaculation (Hooton 2014a). No similar constraints have been introduced on viewing such content produced elsewhere and the policy, relaxed in 2019, drastically curbed the operating possibilities of local dominatrixes and other kink porn practitioners, whose position within the porn industry is a marginal one to start with. In December 2014, sex workers and other campaigners gathered in London outside the Houses of Parliament to protest against the newly introduced regulation. Realised as an ironically British spectacle, the sit-in featured female pornographers dressed in tweed, riding boots and bondage gear seated on male partners' faces. Some participants sipped tea while others sang Mounty Python's 'Sit on My Face'. In addition to expressing outrage over a policy directly resulting in their loss of income, protesters highlighted the explicit double standard at play. They took offence at the fact that the policy primarily targets acts foregrounding female sexual pleasure, such as female ejaculation, and of female sexual dominance, such as face-sitting, as dangerous, obscene and offensive (Hooton 2014b).

Introduced in the name of child protection, these legal measures are merely one part of a larger British anti-pornography policy that extends to filtering and compulsory blocking of adult content by ISPs. The Digital Economy Act 2017 aims at bringing online content under similar regulation to other media, through compulsory age verifications. Since this task is well beyond the scope of the British Board of Film Classification, to which it has been allocated, the most viable solution at the time of writing was to purchase the age verification system from MindGeek—the very same company that has close to a monopoly position in global porn distribution. Unlike the US Motion Picture Rating System, which was introduced in 1968 as the film industry's system of self-regulation, to mark out displays of sex and violence, this government plan would outsource filtering to MindGeek, which would block access for millions of domain names unless these subscribe to their AgeID system and pay for the service according to their volume of traffic.

As the ban takes effect on the 15th of July, 2019, internet users will need to hand over their names and email addresses to MindGeek, via AgeID, which will then verify the user's identity through third-party sources such as social media accounts, ID card or credit card information. AgeID will also 'log which pornography websites are visited and store them', effectively creating a register of porn use (Burgess and Clark 2018). The system will be compulsory for anyone wishing to access adult content from a British IP address: the 'gatekeeper will have the right, and duty, to demand you show proof of age, or else refuse you access. In addition, the body will be able to impose fines and enforcement notices on those who either neglect or circumvent the policy' (Cooper 2017).

MindGeek will be given the licence to charge adult sites for using their compulsory verification system in ways that further eat away at the profit margins of independent producers while unavoidably and considerably profiting the monopoly in question. Despite the scale and nature of the new law, protest largely remained on the level of newspaper articles critical of the privacy risks involved. Independent queer pornographer Pandora Blake remained one of the most vocal critics: 'The Government has written MindGeek a blank cheque. Once age verification is in effect, smaller sites like mine will effectively have to pay a "MindGeek tax" to our biggest competitor, who has established market dominance by pirating our content' (Blake 2017; Cooper 2017). As the dominant company within the porn industry becomes a national gatekeeper for sexually explicit content, it is within the realm of possibility that it will promote its own business over that of competitors, marginal independent entrepreneurs included.

As this example makes evident, narratives of the sexualisation or pornification of culture as a result of the generally increased social accessibility, availability and acceptability of sexually explicit content, as debated in journalism, scholarship and activism for the past decade and more, are simply not allowing for consideration of the nuances and frictions that the 'onscenity' of sexually explicit content involves (see Smith 2010; Attwood 2018, 61–81). This onscenity is met with governmental censorship in countries such as China, Saudi-Arabia and the UK, whereas the repeal of net neutrality makes corporate blocking a viable possibility in the US. In all these instances, pornography—either in all its forms or in some niches deemed obscene—retains an aura of offensiveness that its onscenity would otherwise seem to do away with. The rationale of the Digital Economy Law 2017 is firmly lodged in the offensiveness of pornography, which renders content filtering and mass-scale blocking issues of public good—even if executed by the same parties that facilitate the flow of offensive content to begin with.

Diverse, Scattered Politics

After net neutrality was repealed in December 2017, the xHamster blog elaborated on the possible effects, making readers aware that '[W]ithout net neutrality, the company that you get your internet from can outright block any site they want, including xHamster'. xHamster highlighted how social conservatives across the world put governments more under pressure to censor or block adult sites and how larger corporations control now not only our devices but also the content that you can access. 'If pressure intensifies from the ISPs', they conclude, 'you'll likely see adult content pushed off of Twitter, Reddit and Tumblr' (xHamster 2017). This warning turned out to be true in December 2018 when Tumblr permanently banned adult content from its platform after it was removed from Apple's iOS App Store.

Citing the company's vice president, Alex Hawkins, the blog continues: 'In a time of corporate censorship and conservative crackdowns, we think that making sex videos is a revolutionary act, and we're glad to be able to lend our support to the fight for Net Neutrality'. In the final line, xHamster makes a plea for keeping 'the sexual revolution going'. To argue that shooting a porn film is a revolutionary act, independently of its particular content, is certainly a hyperbolic, debatable claim that smacks of Hugh Hefner's 1970s sexual freedom rhetoric. All in all, the statement reads as somewhat anachronistic for something written in late 2017, given the degree to which this moment can be characterised by the mundane and abundant availability and casual consumption of sexually explicit content, be it categorised as pornography or not. Around this time, xHamster was the 76th most visited site globally, according to Alexa rankings, while Pornhub held 35th place. As highly successful, indeed predominant, actors within the tech industry, these companies are not so easy either to ignore or to position as revolutionary agents.

At the same time, the effacement of sexually explicit content from social media remains a viable concern connected to corporate ownership and its centralisation. The combined corporate power of Google, Apple and Facebook in regulating access to applications and online content according to their community norms and terms of use is overpowering, and none of these companies is known for being amicable towards pornography. As *Wired* reporter Cade Metz (2015) points out, 'The big tech companies behind the big platforms control not only the gateway services (the iPhone app store, Google Search, the Facebook social network), but the gateway devices (the iPhone, Android phones, Google Chromecast, the Amazon Fire TV, the Oculus Rift virtual reality headset). And for the most part, they've shut porn out'.

Should the repealing of net neutrality in the US lead to ISPs blocking porn sites, or to users being charged more for access, sexually explicit content will be further effaced from view. The almost default shutting out of porn by key tech and social media companies is premised on its default offensiveness, which mainstream commodity brands—such as Nike, McDonalds or Starbucks—are unlikely to want to be associated with in their targeted advertising initiatives. It is Google's policy to ban sexually explicit content from its advertisements in all countries 'as an effort to continually improve users' experiences'. There is little that Pornhub's brand-building exercises can do to influence such default blocking. At the same time, compulsory age verification in the UK makes MindGeek, as the leading global porn company, an official gatekeeper of pornographic content that can make money both from distributing porn and from controlling access to it. In a deeply paradoxical solution to pornography's both becoming increasingly present in culture and necessitating regulation and censorship in order to retain its forbidden allure, the same company will be in a position both to massively distribute pornography and to curb access to it. This paradox is in fact key to understanding the stakes involved in the contemporary political economy of porn.

In resisting limitations to their operations through acts of public protest, pornographers are self-evidently protecting their own trade. Yet, motivated by self-interest as such efforts may be, they cannot be separated from broader social, political and financial stakes. Pornography has been identified as 'the canary in the coalmine of free speech', as the first freedom to die (see, for example, Hooton 2014b). Here, historical parallels certainly remain numerous, given the extent to which debates on public access to pornography in the US alone have been inseparable from those concerning freedom of expression. First Amendment rights and their connection with pornography have been a primary focus in much scholarship concerned with the genre (see Strub 2010), even if this emphasis does not extend to, or define, public debates and political investment internationally. The drama of pornographers fighting censorship has been equally key in popular porn historiography, as in the 1996 film *The People vs. Larry Flynt*, which details the multiple anti-censorship court cases of *Hustler*'s publisher, Larry Flynt (see Petersen 2007), and the 2005 documentary *Inside Deep Throat*, which focuses on the cultural resonances of the 1972 pornographic feature film *Deep Throat*. In these, male pornographers engage in a heroic and tragic battle against the powers that be, and in protecting their own smut, they protect the freedom of all.

The political economy involved in contemporary pornographers' expressions of offence is considerably more convoluted and embedded in struggles over data, in ways that afford no easy heroes. The actors expressing outrage against changes in policy are largely corporate brands with mainly invisible figureheads and spokespeople whose fields of responsibility are detached from the fleshy labour of porn production itself. These corporate actors mine user data in ways impossible for individuals to affect or know, while limiting the operating possibilities of independent porn entrepreneurs with their market domination and business models. To the degree that they fail to acknowledge hierarchies among pornographers, narratives of sexualisation, pornification and the onscenity of porn make it possible to overlook the diverse, and mutually conflicting, interests and operating principles involved, from the corporate IT entity of MindGeek to kink practitioners running their own pay sites, and the different ways in which legal measures regulating appropriate and inappropriate, permissible and obscene, sexual representation condition their spaces of agency.

Pornography has never been a singular object or industry, but more of an umbrella term bringing together diverse actors with varying interests and aesthetics. It then follows that the political passions and projects connected to this have come in all kinds of shapes and forms, from gay porn promoting safe sex (Patton 1991) to that celebrating the breeding and seeding of HIV in queer kinship-building (Morris and Paasonen 2014), from couples porn bringing spice to monogamous matrimony to videos advancing promiscuous lust, spirituality and veganism. The politics of contemporary pornography range from the macro-level of civil liberties to the politics of representation connected to gender, race and class, the micro-level of body politics connected to desires, orientations and shapes, data ownership, privacy and access. In addition to pornography's being a perennial object of political debate in feminist and value-conservative activism, its political registers expand to sex-worker rights activism, queer and feminist politics. As the discussion above indicates, the interests of different stakeholders—be these financial or other—are by no means mutually compatible.

This incompatibility is currently more striking than ever, as tech companies have not only increased their presence within the porn industry but largely come to own it. Tech companies provide the necessary infrastructure for streaming video while simultaneously transforming the principles of how porn is made and how this work is compensated. Detaching their activities from content production, tech companies retain mainstream credibility as business partners that have relatively fluid agency to operate in web hosting and search engine optimisation outside the realm of pornography. If porn is understood as data, then the work connected to it is no different than any other form of data labour. A company such as MindGeek produces, distributes and filters out pornography, limiting the spaces of agency available to other entrepreneurs in the process, and possibly eating away at their possibilities of operation. As the IT labour connected with online porn has grown ever more specialised, it is increasingly difficult for independent pornographers to make their content known and seen. Even if they have the necessary financial resources in site design and hosting, which is not always likely, the traffic dominance of aggregator sites means that content hosted elsewhere lags behind in top search results.

Independent pornographers like Pandora Blake have novel possibilities for public outreach via social media platforms such as Twitter, yet their voices do not have the same reach as those of key corporate players whose campaigns easily gain viral lift through clickbait sites. Expressions of offence among pornographers come with vested interests and hierarchies of visibility, just as their focus has expanded from workplace safety to pornography as data that is governed, owned, displayed, processed, leaked and sold. In this hierarchical and somewhat disjointed landscape, different agents taking offence have different resonances, and the voices of individual performers and independent producers may fail to have much resonance at all.

References

Albury, Kath. 2014. "Porn and Sex Education, Porn as Sex Education." *Porn Studies* 1 (1–2): 172–181. https://doi.org/10.1080/23268743.2013.863654.

Attwood, Feona. 2009. "Introduction: The Sexualization of Culture." In *Mainstreaming Sex: The Sexualization of Western Culture*, edited by Feona Attwood, xiii–xxiv. London: I.B. Tauris.

Attwood, Feona. 2018. *Sex Media*. Cambridge: Polity.

Auerbach, David. 2014. "Vampire Porn: MindGeek Is a Cautionary Tale of Consolidating Production and Distribution in a Single, Monopolistic Owner." *Slate*, October 23. http://www.slate.com/articles/technology/technology/2014/10/mindgeek_porn_monopoly_its_dominance_is_a_cautionary_tale_for_other_industries.html.

Berg, Heather. 2016. "'A Scene Is Just a Marketing Tool': Alternative Income Streams in Porn's Gig Economy." *Porn Studies* 3 (2): 160–174.

Blake, Pandora. 2017. "Do You Trust PornHub with a Database of Your Sexual Preferences?" *Pandora Blake* (blog), November 16. http://pandorablake.com/blog/2017/11/do-you-trust-pornhub-with-a-database-of-your-sexual-preferences.

Burgess, Matti, and Liat Clark. 2018. "The UK Will Block Online Porn From April. Here's What We Know." *Wired*, February 9. http://www.wired.co.uk/article/porn-block-ban-in-the-uk-age-verifcation-law.

Clark, Bryan. 2016. "XHamster Blows a Load of Justice on North Carolina Over Anti-LGTB Bill." *The Next Web*, April 12. https://thenextweb.com/insider/2016/04/11/xhamster-blows-a-load-of-justice-on-north-carolina-over-anti-lgbt-bill/#gref.

Cooper, Daniel. 2017. "Pornhub Owner May Become the UK's Gatekeeper of Online Porn." *Engadget*, November 11. https://www.engadget.com/2017/11/23/pornhub-mindgeek-age-verification-ageid-digital-economy-uk-online-porn/.

Gillespie, Tarleton. 2010. "The Politics of 'Platforms'." *New Media & Society* 12 (3): 347–364. https://doi.org/10.1177/1461444809342738.

Gunelius, Susan. 2009. *Building Brand Value the Playboy Way*. London: Palgrave.

Hooton, Christopher. 2014a. "A Long List of Sex Acts Just Got Banned in UK Porn." *The Independent*, December 2. http://www.independent.co.uk/news/uk/a-long-list-of-sex-acts-just-got-banned-in-uk-porn-9897174.html.

Hooton, Christopher. 2014b. "Porn Censorship Ruling to be Protested with Mass 'Face-Sitting' Outside Parliament." *The Independent*, December 10. http://www.independent.co.uk/news/uk/porn-censorship-to-be-protested-with-mass-face-sitting-at-parliament-9914354.html.

Kendrick, Walter. 1996. *The Secret Museum: Pornography in Modern Culture*, 2nd ed. Berkeley: University of California Press.

Kipnis, Laura. 1996. *Bound and Gagged: Pornography and the Politics of Fantasy in America*. Durham, NC: Duke University Press.

Kokura, Joe. 2016. "Prop16 Could Take Away All Porn in California." *Thrillist*, November 7. https://www.thrillist.com/sex-dating/san-francisco/proposition-60-condom-law-porn-industry-california.

Kuhn, Annette. 1985. *The Power of the Image: Essays on Representation and Sexuality*. London: Routledge.

McKee, Alan. 2016. "Pornography as Creative Industry: Challenging the Exceptionalist Approach to Pornography." *Porn Studies* 3 (2): 107–119. https://doi.org/10.1080/23268743.2015.1065202.

Metz, Cade. 2015. "The Porn Business Isn't Anything Like You Think It Is." *Wired*, October 15. http://www.wired.com/2015/10/the-porn-business-isnt-anything-like-you-think-it-is/?mbid=social_fb.

Morris, Paul, and Susana Paasonen. 2014. "Risk and Utopia: A Dialogue on Pornography." *GLQ: A Journal of Lesbian and Gay Studies* 20 (3): 215–239. https://doi.org/10.1215/10642684-2422656.

Moye, David. 2016. "Porn Site Bans North Carolina Users Due to State's Anti-LGBT Laws." *The Huffington Post*, April 11. https://www.huffingtonpost.com/entry/porn-site-bans-north-carolina-users-due-to-states-anti-lgbtlaws_us_570bd057e4b0885fb50d9a92.

Nir, Sarah Maslin. 2017. "At PornHub Pop-Up Shop, a Hint of New York's Dirty Days." *The New York Times*, November 28. https://www.nytimes.com/2017/11/28/nyregion/pornhub-pop-up-shop-soho.html.

Osgerby, Bill. 2001. *Playboys in Paradise: Masculinity, Youth and Leisure-Style in Modern America*. Oxford: Berg.

Paasonen, Susanna, Kaarina Nikunen, and Laura Saarenmaa (eds.). 2007. *Pornification: Sex and Sexuality in Media Culture*. Oxford: Berg.

Paasonen, Susanna, Kylie Jarrett, and Ben Light. 2019. *NSFW: Sex, Humor, and Risk in Social Media*. Cambridge: MIT Press.

Patton, Cindy. 1991. "Visualizing Safe Sex: When Pedagogy and Pornography Collide." In *Inside/Out: Lesbian Theories, Gay Theories*, edited by Diane Fuss, 373–386. New York: Routledge.

Penley, Constance. 2004. "Crackers and Whackers: The White Trashing of Porn." In *Porn Studies*, edited by Linda Williams, 309–331. Durham, NC: Duke University Press.

Petersen, Jennifer. 2007. "Freedom of Expression as Liberal Fantasy: The Debate Over *People vs. Larry Flynt*." *Media, Culture and Society* 29 (3): 377–394. https://doi.org/10.1177/0163443707076181.

Smith, Clarissa. 2010. "Pornographication: A Discourse for All Seasons." *International Journal of Media and Cultural Politics* 6 (1): 103–108.

Strub, Whit. 2010. *Perversion for Profit: The Politics of Pornography and the Rise of the New Right*. New York: Columbia University Press.

Tourjée, Diana. 2016. "Ejaculating Justice: The Porn Company Protesting Anti-Trans Law Speaks Out." *Broadly*, April 12. https://broadly.vice.com/en_us/article/mgmzkv/ejaculating-justice-the-porn-company-protesting-anti-trans-law-speaks-out.

Wilkinson, Eleanor. 2017. "The Diverse Economies of Online Pornography: From Paranoid Readings to Post-capitalist Futures." *Sexualities* 20 (8): 981–998.

Williams, Linda. 2004. "Porn Studies: Proliferating Pornographies on/Scene: An Introduction." In *Porn Studies*, edited by Linda Williams, 1–23. Durham, NC: Duke University Press.

xHamster. 2017. "Net Neutrality: What's Next?" https://fr.xhamster.com/blog/posts/737444.

xHamster. 2018. "Privacy Policy." Modified 24 May. https://xhamster.com/info/privacy.

CHAPTER 10

Regulatory Expectations of Offended Audiences: The Citizen Interest in Audience Discourse

Ranjana Das and Anne Graefer

INTRODUCTION

In this chapter we analyze fieldwork carried out with 90 people in the United Kingdom and Germany, exploring the perceptions and expectations audiences articulate about the regulatory processes behind provocative media content they find offensive. Across the political spectrum, from liberal to conservative positions, a popular view remains that offence and feeling offended by things in the media is the price of living in a liberal society. Voices within the right and far-right seem to champion the

---

A version of this chapter has been previously published in: *Communication, Culture and Critique* 2017, 10 (4): 626–640.

R. Das (✉)
University of Surrey, Surrey, UK
e-mail: r.das@surrey.ac.uk

A. Graefer
Birmingham Centre for Media and Cultural Research, Birmingham City University, Birmingham, UK
e-mail: anne.graefer@bcu.ac.uk

cause of rescuing the right to not be bounded by so-called political correctness. The populist press in the United Kingdom, with denunciations of "political correctness gone mad," or right-wing populist movements in Germany, such as Patriotic Europeans Against the Islamization of the West (PEGIDA), offer a remedy against a Lügenpresse (lying press) that is ruled by a set of powerful, unnamed actors, who are trying to control everything people do and think. At antipodal ideological positions too, for entirely different reasons, we have a long-standing liberal defense of free speech. Despite this public visibility of offence, audience voices continue to be unheard, or assumed, and very often spoken for, in many of these debates. Audiences are often painted as the gullible and easily affected recipients of media content by tabloid newspapers, or not sufficiently and substantially heard and included within regulatory processes.

OFFENCE AND "TASTE CULTURES" IN THE UNITED KINGDOM AND GERMANY

We set our scene in the United Kingdom and Germany, two Western democracies sharing a unique combination of contemporary cultural politics. Both countries have, for a while now, been ruled by conservative governments driving austerity measures. There has been in both countries a national focus on diversity and multiculturalism, and both have witnessed in recent years growth of populist groups and movements expressing concerns about increasing levels of migration. Traditionally, both countries have shared an emphasis on public service media (PSM), with the British Broadcasting Corporation (BBC) having served as the blueprint for Germany's public broadcasting system after the First World War. Both British and German broadcasters import U.S. entertainment programming, which guaranteed that research participants in both countries would tend to be familiar with some of the same TV programs. Yet Germany and the United Kingdom differ significantly in terms of their relationship to the European Union (EU), their demographic and economic makeup, and their television industry. While the United Kingdom successfully exports a range of TV programs and formats, German domestic television production is limited, and broadcasters rely on imports to fill their schedules. Moreover, and this is crucial for this project, the United Kingdom and Germany can be seen as having different "offense cultures." While some research has been conducted on different taste cultures (Hofstede 2001), very little is known about offence in cross-cultural contexts. The differences between the United Kingdom and Germany can be seen in everyday encounters, where German "directness" may be experienced as hurtful and offensive in a British context, or, on the other hand, instances of British "polite restraint" read in a German context as aloof and unengaged (Evans 2011; House 1996).

Furthermore, different histories and demographic makeup lead to different understandings of offence and political correctness. For instance, in Germany there is little of the critical awareness of the Black struggle against White supremacy that we find in the United States or even in the United Kingdom. This is why we can find a White actress (Katia Riemann) sporting dreadlocks in a German public broadcasting film production ("Freundinnen," ARD 2016). Riemann's hairdo was not critiqued for cultural appropriation, but rather lauded by the press as a great look. In a documentary about German actress Uschi Glas, she referred to herself as a "kleines Negerlein" ("little negro") (ARD Mediathek 2016). Glas tried to explain how she had often felt excluded as a child due to her black curly hair, and how other White kids used to call her by such names. But the expression "Negerlein" was not problematized, either in the interview situation or afterward by the wider media. Examples like this demonstrate that words and symbols that would not go unnoticed in other cultures such as that of the United Kingdom may very well do so in Germany.

In the United Kingdom, the populist press has recently been in the spotlight, with Wikipedia, as this article was being written, banning the use of the Daily Mail as a source of information, and the Stop Funding Hate campaign on social media frequently citing a range of media outlets for headlines believed to incite hate. The sources cited argue, in the face of this, that these are all attempts to stifle the telling of truth. On the other hand, it also seems to be the case that some popular comedians in the United Kingdom, for instance, Ricky Gervais or Jimmy Carr, often build jokes or comedy routines around race, ethnicity, or even incest or pedophilia—and this usually from individuals who identify as very liberal. These examples go to underline our earlier point that a dismissal of the very category of offence rests, for widely differing reasons, at the heart of both sides of the political spectrum in the United Kingdom. Nonetheless, discussion of media content as having arguably crossed a line frequently punctuates public life, whether in a celebratory tone (e.g., in 2016, The Independent published a compilation of Ricky Gervais's most provocative moments) or in a context of potentially requiring greater regulation (e.g., the BBC enquiry into tastes and standards in 2009, cf. Livingstone and Das 2009).

THE IMPLIED AUDIENCE AND THE CITIZEN–CONSUMER IN GERMAN AND BRITISH TELEVISION REGULATION

In this article we pay attention to the literature that has developed around media regulation to distil theorizations of regulatory roles, and use these as a backdrop against which to read the perceptions and expectations audiences articulate about media regulators. We turn here to Livingstone and Lunt's work over the last decade (2007, 2011, 2012) on making sense of the UK media regulator's work and its relationship as a "quango" (quasi-autonomous nongovernmental organization) with the British public. Juxtaposing neoliberal visions of a receding, small state with diminished or diminishing regulatory responsibilities against social democratic visions of a state that seeks to participate in, engage with, and enhance the public interest, Livingstone and Lunt distinguish between the consumer interest and the citizen interest thus:

Livingstone and Lunt use four criteria from Habermasian public sphere theory to ask whether the British media regulator "(a) recognises when it is dealing with issues of public concern, (b) recognises through its principles and practices that it represents one institution among many, (c) gives equal recognition to effectiveness and legitimation, and (d) respects rather than undermines the right to self-determination of citizens" (Livingstone and Lunt 2011, 9). These underlie, they argue, the citizen interest in media and communications, where audiences are conceptualized as publics and where media institutions function with key social and democratic responsibilities, rather than the consumer interest where audiences are conceptualized as self-regulating consumers.

The pairing of German and British national contexts in this project has been particularly insightful to trace the citizen interest against the consumer interest for a few reasons. In both countries, the arrival of the Internet and on-demand television has posed significant challenges to audio–visual regulation of "offensive" content. There has been, in both cases, a shift from top-down prohibitions toward self-management and self-regulation, creating an audience of self-regulated viewers in the context of a rapidly fragmenting and Internet-dominated environment. PSM in Germany has been developed largely along the lines of the BBC in the

United Kingdom, with widely social democratic ambitions behind its existence, and aspirations that it would be free of vested interests, performing a key role in German public life, and governed by a body of stakeholders representing a wide variety of professions and expertise from public life. The intentions behind this constitutional and legal role of PSMs have historically been an interest in the transparent, bureaucracy-free, independent sociodemocratic role of media institutions, and the furthering of what Livingstone et al. have called the "citizen interest" (Livingstone et al. 2007). In reality, however, this has run into a range of difficulties in Germany, including a range of economic and political pressures German PSMs, and in particular, smaller public broadcasters, have been under, ranging from substantial amounts of public unwillingness to pay the required license fee (GEZ) to a lack of transparency in terms of the interface between media institutions, regulatory mechanisms, and audience participation. As this project was conducted, the newest debate surrounding broadcasting in Germany has been the role of the second largest PSM—the channel ZDF—and whether its broadcasting council composition is in alignment with the constitutional mandates. As Horz (2016) demonstrates succinctly, the role of the audience was often "implied" (spoken for and assumed) in the process in certain states, and in general, barely represented (see also Eilders et al. 2006; Webster and Phalen 1994).

While this article does not permit us to delve deeply into the recent controversy surrounding ZDF and regulatory reform, a few things stand clear. First, Germany enshrines, legally, the citizen interest in public broadcasting, with ambitions to preserve PSMs as free of vested interests and serving social and democratic functions for its audiences to contribute to a rich and fair public life. Second, the picture in reality is intersected by conflicting approaches across the federal states, economic and political pressures around the nonpayment of license fees (which links to public perceptions of media institutions and PSM channels), and a lack of audience voice in regulatory mechanisms (Hasebrink 2011; Horz 2016; Puppis et al. 2007). The author doing fieldwork for this project in Germany approached media institutions as a member of the public, and ran into substantial difficulties in establishing clear and transparent information on regulatory processes, debates, or even a record of audience complaints. When she explained to a former employee of Medienanstalten (media authorities) in Munich that organizations she had contacted were not willing or able to tell her which programs viewers complained about the most, he said that he was not surprised, and if they did not want to give any detailed information, then he would not either if he was approached to be interviewed. An employee of Radio Deutsche Welle (Germany's international public broadcaster) said, similarly, that she was not surprised that regulators were not keen on sharing their insights for this study. An employee of Progammbeschwerde.de (program complaints), an online portal where people can go online and complain about something they have seen on a private broadcasting channel, said that they do not collect this data, as "this would not make any sense." When contacted again—a year later—he referred us to a report that was, at best, vague. We cite these instances from fieldwork to make the case that, in keeping with recent regulatory literature about German television broadcasting, the citizen interest, while enshrined in the constitution, is insufficiently reflected in practice, and audience voices are insufficiently incorporated into the regulatory process, staying "implied" (Livingstone and Lunt 2012), assumed, and spoken on behalf of. As Horz remarks, "It is a peculiarity of the German system that an organization like the British Voice of the Listener and Viewer (VLV) does not exist, although the German PSM system is comparable to the BBC" (2016, 357).

Since 2003 British broadcasting has been regulated by the Office of Communications (Ofcom), the country's media regulator, and a greater deal of transparency might be noticed in the United Kingdom compared to Germany. Setting aside the work of organizations representing the voices of audiences such as VLV, Ofcom has performed a central role in terms of collecting and responding to public complaints. This is clearly and readily accessible on the Ofcom website, and Ofcom themselves were open and welcoming to us when approached at the start of this project to listen to early findings and share insights. However, an analysis of the political purposes that underlie the relationships between media institutions and audiences, conducted succinctly by Peter Lunt and Sonia Livingstone in their work on the British media regulator (Livingstone and Lunt 2012), reveal a tendency for the citizen interest to lose out, still, on many occasions, to the consumer interest. Lunt and Livingstone frame this against the backdrop of two parallel philosophies behind regulation, that is, the liberal—pluralistic model that calls for largely individual control and decision-making in a self-regulatory process, and the social democratic model of protecting citizens's interests, regulating against unfair treatment of individuals and discriminatory representations. They map these two approaches on to the consumer interest and the citizen interest, "ultimately concluding that, in cases where there is a conflict of interest, the citizen interest—and the civic republican vision that underpins it—tend to lose out to the consumer interest" (Livingstone and Lunt 2012, 39).

So, how does the United Kingdom respond to "offensive" television content? In 2009, one of us coauthored a review of the literature for the BBC on public attitudes, tastes, and standards (Livingstone and Das 2009). The review revealed gaping limitations in empirical audience research, in terms of its insufficiency to inform public policy. And yet, British policymakers continue to be both interested and often plagued by concerns about offensive content. The British broadcasting code (Office of Communications [Ofcom] 2013) makes the "protection of under-18s" a clear priority, with the responsibility for such protecting presumably shared with those who look after children and young people (see also young people's response to the consultation on the code; Office of Communications [Ofcom] 2005). The British communications regulator also aims to ensure that generally accepted standards are applied to the content of radio and television services to provide protection from harmful or offensive material (section "Offense and 'Taste Cultures' in the United Kingdom and Germany"). In much of the research that exists for policy purposes (British Board of Film Certification [BBFC] 2005; Cumberbatch et al. 2003), two kinds of contexts seem to be studied—the programming context and the viewing context. Findings from such sectors are useful—indeed, they provide quantitative analyses correlating demographic attributes to whether or not somebody finds something offensive (for more on this, see Livingstone and Das 2009). These findings have historically been mirrored in Germany with its system of state media authorities (Landesmedieananstalten) at the federal level that hold primary responsibility for evaluating viewer complaints and also legal authority to monitor issues arising when a complaint is upheld. Similar to the United Kingdom, in Germany, too, as Hasebrink noted, complaints have historically related mostly to "protecting the vulnerable" from violent and sexually graphic content—enshrined in the Ofcom broadcasting code in the United Kingdom. Crucial to note here is that the historical claim made in Germany—that the "interests and needs of the viewers are hardly definable" (Hasebrink 1994, 32)—is as valid and applicable to both countries today, whereby, despite the more recent shift to racism and sexism in addition to violent content or swear words, much about audiences continues to be implied and assumed. As Horz (2016, 352) notes, "These results correlate with the 'implied image' from regulators of the audience-as-consumers rather than citizens in media regulation: the audience seems to accept its consumer role and has difficulties in identifying itself as citizens, especially when it comes to partaking in media policy debates."

Methodology

"Although offensive material is, in principle, distinguished from that which is illegal (obscenity, child abuse images, incitement to racial hatred, etc.), it remains difficult to define the boundaries in a robust and consensual fashion" (Millwood Hargrave and Livingstone 2009, 25). Generally, media content is judged to be offensive when it is too graphic or explicit in style and content (Attwood et al. 2012). Intrusive images of suffering, or racist, classist, or sexist depictions that contribute to stereotyping, or bias and inaccuracy in news reports and documentaries is also often reported as offending audiences (Millwood Hargrave and Livingstone 2009). Academic work has focused on so-called "body genres" (Williams 1991) that might cause offence because they display and move the body in controllable ways—the horror film (Brottman 1997; Carroll 1980; Janovich 2002), comedy (Lockyer and Pickering 2009), and pornography (Paasonen 2011; Williams 2004), as well as screen violence to the body (Abel 2009; Hill 1997; Schlesinger 1992; Schlesinger et al. 1998). We contribute to this body of literature through interviews and focus groups with over 90 participants in the United Kingdom and Germany. We investigated not only what kind of television content is perceived as offensive, but also what expectations people have toward media regulators and producers in regulating offensive media content. Each author was responsible for conducting half of these fieldwork encounters. We each conducted focus groups with 4–5 members in each group for 25 audience members and 20 individual interviews using an open-ended interview guide. Before each focus group or interview the authors and participants watched a selection of daytime television clips from what audiences themselves "recommended" or complained about as offensive. Our interviews were anonymized, audio recorded, fully transcribed, and analyzed using NVivo before being analyzed thematically, read over and again while assigning codes. The strand of analysis in focus in this article investigates people's expectations of actors and institutions. We note here that in the fieldwork we worked with the broadest possible definition of regulation. Here, the definition of regulation forwarded by Livingstone and Lunt (2012) proves useful as they employ the term regulation "to refer to the relations between power and the ordering of social behavior at all levels of society from the nation state up to the transnational organization and down to the subnational organization or community and, even, the individual" (p. 4). Our findings grouped into two key categories across a scale—from an alignment with a self-managed and self-regulated approach to controversial content (the consumer interest) to an alignment with an approach where institutions had critical roles to play in public life (the citizen interest). But the real analytical issue that emerged for us, however, was in reading people's positions on this scale at face value. Most people who seemed to align with an individual-led approach to regulating problematic content were also the people who interpreted regulatory intervention as heavy-handed top-down censorship (often citing instances of totalitarian regimes), and on probing, they revealed a closer alignment with a more negotiated position, actually closer to the citizen interest.

THE (APPARENT) CONSUMER–AUDIENCE OF PROVOCATIVE SCREENS

Our clearest category emerged with a sizeable majority of people arguing for a completely individual-led and self-monitored approach to "provocative" television content. However—and this is very crucial to note—this group was also the least clear on what the alternative to this was. This group assumed time and again, that the only possible alternative to switching off the TV, throwing away the remote, or making similarly drastic choices, was to embrace heavy-handed censorship—something that one respondent described as "the North Korean alternative." Embodying the sentiments of many at this end of the spectrum, we therefore cautiously interpret the strongly voiced, but thinly understood, support for the self-regulating audience of offensive screens. Kerry, a school teacher and mother from the United Kingdom, said:

> We have to look at ourselves because they wouldn't be putting it out there if we weren't watching, and we have an off button … we do ultimately have a control over what we … what technology we choose to access. I find I don't watch many programmes because of that any more. I just turn it off.

When questioned about what she feels would be a useful alternative to this switching off, and if she is aware of the mechanisms through which audiences might be consulted on such matters, Kerry responds strongly that she believes firmly in free speech. This dichotomy, or indeed dilemma that this group of audiences posited—between free speech and censorship—distracted from a conversation on the nature and purposes for which documents like the broadcasting code are written. This is because it sets up the conversation on a dialogue about provocative/offensive content as an irresolvable struggle between the champions of free speech on the one hand, and the heavy-handed scissoring of all things spoken or broadcast on the other. Umesh, an Indian man in his sixties, living in the United Kingdom, provides an excellent demonstration of this point:

> I think once you get the state involved in sensitizing anything, then where do you draw the line with that? What …? Who, within government, has the right to say, this is offensive, so we're not going to broadcast this, and then you're restricting somebody's … You know, then all of a sudden you end up like North Korea and you can't see anything.

Among a substantial section of audiences at the self-regulating end of the spectrum, there also worked a misunderstanding of the regulatory process as such, even if they did not contrast self-regulation with the alternative of a totalitarian state, as above. Some struggled with the idea that full responsibility for any risks or harm associated with problematic media content should lie with individuals, but it still must, they said, because the idea of the alternative was far too uncomfortable. This idea, as it turns out, does not bear any resemblance to how, for instance, the media regulator would operate in the United Kingdom. A doctoral student in the United Kingdom, Sally, provides an example of this:

> Individuals should make a decision what you are going to buy or to watch because again you are paying for this so you're not going to pay for those things because you don't want to see it. I do not think that the responsibility lies with those who are drawing up laws and rules because the only reason why they have to do this is because others are not reacting in a responsible way.

When asked what she envisions the alternative would look like, she said "I think unfortunately it would have to be some out-dated, out-of-touch government institution who's setting up a law and saying those things are okay and those things are not—unfortunately." The "unfortunately" here is key, for such work is indeed done, but the use of the word "unfortunately" corresponds with the perceived out-datedness of these bodies. The apparent out-datedness of these bodies that are no longer needed in times of endless choice through television on demand is rooted in a neoliberal ideology in which individuals manage themselves and official intervention is seen as liming freedom.

One of our youngest participants from Germany, for example, made their case for self-regulation when faced with offensive material—"because artistic freedom is important." His fear is that "censorship gets quickly out of hand. Who has the authority to draw the line?" In Germany people often made reference to the United States, where swearwords are censored. They saw themselves as responsible individuals who did not need this kind of regulation:

> Censorship never paid off. And I think that it is quite ridiculous that in many other countries, such as the US, you are not allowed to use swear words on TV. As if people wouldn't know these words just because they aren't shown on TV. I am actually really happy that we do not beep these words over, except for programmes before 6 pm maybe … (Marina)

Interviews demonstrated again and again that regulation was equated with heavy-handed censorship, and was thus seen as patronizing rather than furthering public interests. Even when speaking about vulnerable audience members or children, responsibility was again placed on the individual (the parent). As Wolfgang pointed out in Germany:

> No, in this respect (censorship) we in Germany are much more relaxed than other countries. Because we think that parents have the responsibility to look after their children and make sure that they only look at appropriate TV programmes. Nowadays every TV has a parent-code where you can limit what your child can watch.

We returned repeatedly to a vision of regulation as heavy-handed censorship that automatically created its desirable opponent—the self-regulating audience. A teacher who runs a small Face Project community as its moderator uses her own role that she describes as "very light-touch" to illustrate that even if images are very graphic, and abhorrent, she would rather walk away than "embrace—I don't know—totalitarian bureaucracy." Dawn continued:

Table 10.1 Citizen interests and consumer interests (from Livingstone and Lunt 2007)

Consumer interest	Citizen interest
Wants	Needs
Individual	Society
Private benefit	Public benefits
Language of choice	Language of rights

> So you see, I think nobody has the right to be protected from being offended but everybody has the right to reply, you know, in order to … to, you know, yes, if you like, if you'd have presented me with images of Ku Klux Klan and BNP [British National Party], I would have found that quite abhorrent. But it is on me to walk away.

These voices of our seemingly consumer–audience, the vast majority of our audiences offended by provocative screens, should not, therefore, be read at face value. We should not assume that these people are vastly against the placing of any responsibility about offensive material at all in the hands of producers and regulators, for their reasons are guided by a heavy-handed vision of a scissor-wielding bureaucratic censor. These findings remind us of the parallel story emerging from Livingstone and Lunt's focus groups with audiences in 2007 where, although not speaking about the matter of offensive media content, they found "an initial barrage of antiregulation views" were largely to do with red tape and bureaucracy "were qualified further into each discussion" and "alternative views emerged" (Livingstone and Lunt 2007, 11) (Table 10.1).

THE CITIZEN–AUDIENCE OF PROVOCATIVE SCREENS

In analyzing responses that argued for a clearer role of institutions to better serve the needs of audiences, when it came to the production and regulation of content they found problematic, we found a closer alignment with the democratic ideals behind the media and media institutions' responsibilities. This applied not simply, or even at all, to the blanket use of categories such as censorship (which in itself is, of course, highly nuanced), but rather, to the broader role that others in the media audience relationship—those not holding the remote—might play in the process. Here, too, we note that it is not easy, or indeed not even accurate, to read off the surface of these responses as calling for limits to artistic freedom, or the freedom of expression in general. As is evident below, these responses speak more about ideals and expectations placed on institutions acting for, speaking for, and on behalf of audiences and publics.

Ernie, a middle-aged LGBT (Lesbian, Gay, Bisexual, Transgender) activist who lives in inner-city London, speaks of his views on offensive content as content that lies outside what is captured on screen, that is, content that is conspicuous by its absence, or shallow treatment, making one of the key arguments we try to make in this project, that "offensive" material, as a category, needs more expansive thinking through than a list of clear red flags. Ernie speaks of the responsibilities of those behind these screens—aligning clearly with the second column attributes in Table 10.1, presented earlier:

> There was always a very small amount of disability programming ... and I think they were all kind of early 1990s BBC initiatives that were interesting but a little bit ... I don't know. I've always found that with identity programmes anyway that ... identity programmes are problematic because it specifies something, but you kind of need to do it until we can get to the place where people have gone past that into more proper inclusion if that makes sense. That never happens ...

These views are mirrored by the vast majority of audiences who speak about the responsibilities of institutions rather than audiences, and here, it is very clear that public broadcasters and state, or part-autonomous, institutions have a different range of expectations placed on them than private players in what is clearly identified by people as a market. Amy, who lives in the Midlands in the United Kingdom, describes it thus:

> I would have ... it's higher expectations of ethical standards, really, from public bodies who deal with the media. As for the Internet—it's almost like you've sold your ... if you go on the Internet, you've sold your soul, so it's, kind of, pointless, so ... but which is a bit defeatist, I suppose.

In both countries we found that not only genre (news vs. comedy), but also the type of broadcaster (public or private) had a significant influence on whether offense was taken or not. Paul, a young professional from Munich, remarks:

> Well, I also find this kind of language quite problematic. This was shown on a public service broadcaster, ZDF, they shouldn't use this kind of language ... such as "fuck" and "shit" ... I don't know, it's just not right because these channels have such a wide outreach, many people can see this. You can talk like this privately, but it creates a weird public image if this kind of language is used by public broadcasters.

In Germany people became angry if public service broadcasters violated borders of media ethics because, in their understanding, these channels are paid by the taxpayer to produce valuable, neutral and nonoffensive content, as Klaus, a nurse and part-time DJ, expresses:

> But I sometimes really wonder what I get for my 17 Euros a month. You are forced to pay for an institution that is separated from the state, and has its own administration, but is still highly propagandistic.

In the United Kingdom a significant minority was also critical of the conditions within and against which media institutions operate. Many were mindful of the fact that austerity regimes were likely to have an impact on PSM, that the representation of minorities on the screen was likely to be linked to contemporary sociocultural atmospheres instead of solely being a question of individual creative eccentricities. Ella points out:

> Even the BBC, and the BBC will probably suffer in addition to all public bodies really, given what's happening, but even the BBC is a body of relative power and there are countless voices never heard, faces never represented.

Jackie, a disabled LGBT activist living in London, mirrors these views, as she tries to understand institutions, including producers and regulators, as part of a map where race, gender, and sexuality continue to draw lines, in her view, just as in the world she works and lives within:

> There's so much, so much when it comes to TV, that is held by white men who are part of a certain ... And they're not ... it never ... that sort of thing never touches them, they never have to worry about the consequences of people coming up to people in wheelchairs and saying, oh, you're just like, when Ricky Gervais had a series recently about somebody with a mental health illness, is it "Derek"? You look at the BBC website about all their equality things and everything and you just think, no, no you're not.

Jackie remembers e-mailing Ofcom about a phone-in program she had a complaint about, and says that it felt good to speak about concerns she felt nobody had listened to, but the reply she received, was "far too generic." Like Jackie, Beth, who has recently transitioned from male to female, complained about the representation of trans issues on Little Britain (a TV program). She, too, said she got a generic response acknowledging that she had sent in a complaint, but little beyond. Rebecca, in the United Kingdom, speaks of a similar story when she found a response to a complaint very generic, and even addressing her wrongly: "And the funniest thing was, I complained about something and they wrote back to Mr. Gilmore." These voices demonstrate a clear alignment with the social democratic visions of media institutions in public life, but equally display a sense of disappointment in their programming and processes.

RED HERRINGS AND THE IMPLIED AUDIENCE

Three conclusions stand out to us. First, in the context of a long-standing conversation on the roles of broadcasters and regulators on protecting the public from harmful and offensive material, a further nuancing of what qualifies as offensive material is now required, over and above the recent shift to include racism and sexism in addition to previous red flags. Our recent fieldwork has shown us that we should not only focus on those complaints that make it to the regulator. Contrary to what we expected, swear words, bad language, and inaccurate facts were not always what people wanted to talk to us about. Rather, people were concerned with wider issues, around the construction of characters or the relative power and positions of the actors/creators behind characters.

Second, in investigating people's expectations of actors and institutions in their responses to television content that startles, upsets, or just offends them, it is crucial, we find, to treat a conversation on free speech and censorship with caution. Often, as it seemed to us, this issue showed up as a red herring—misleading people to conflate regulation with censorship, and to interpret regulation as a monolith of high-profile, totalitarian, often religiously motivated shutting down of art (take, for instance, the banning and burning of projects in certain countries). The real conversation, instead, was about the expectations people felt able to place (or not) in the institutions acting on their behalf, and whether they will continue to do so. So, we were keen to discover whether theorizations of regulatory responsibilities map on well to the framework of expectations publics as audiences articulate when they speak of television content that offends them. What kinds of expectations are articulated, what responsibilities are placed on media itself and on those who regulate it, and what division of responsibility between regulators, producers, broadcasters, and individuals, do people adhere to? The answers are of interest because they signal not just the public "mood" on long-standing debates about free speech and censorship, but also because they are a lens into the unarticulated yet nonetheless present ideological underpinnings of citizens' expectations of televisual media and the national frameworks within which it operates.

Third, as readers of this article from other countries may identify, what is at stake in a conversation about material perceived to be offensive is, we argue, the citizen interest. This is because, in the end, the "implied audience" (Livingstone and Lunt 2012) prevails across many media institutional frameworks, as the voices of audiences are far too often assumed and spoken for. In the recent legal controversy surrounding a German public service broadcaster (ZDF), for example, only two contributors are bottom-up audience groups (Publikumsrat and Ständige Pub-likumskonferenz), and only one statement was sent by an individual citizen (Horz 2016). This speaks volumes of the relationship being encouraged and built between individuals and institutions in the media sphere, where, on the one hand, in a digital, international media framework, audiences have apparently greater visibility and voice, such voice often being written into institutional frameworks, and on the other hand, regulatory processes still do not adequately involve the audience to inform the regulatory process, from conceptualizations and definitions to policy-making. Some form of public consultations already exist, of course—we note, for instance, the Broadcast and On Demand Bulletins in the United Kingdom, which reveal a useful mechanism in place for audiences to communicate their grievances, and a process for documenting the ways in which the regulator responds to these complaints. This process is far less straightforward in the federal system of Germany. Improvements to both these contexts are possible, although speaking to the public is expensive and time-consuming. We hope that academic research, such as ours, can continue to stay grounded in the political purposes lying behind the role of media institutions in public life and that it can perform its critical role, using the conceptual pairing of the citizen consumer, to access, interpret, and communicate audience's expectations, and to argue for the social democratic citizen interest over the neoliberal self-regulating consumer interest.

References

Abel, Marc. 2009. *Violent Affect: Literature, Cinema and Critique After Representation*. Lincoln: University of Nebraska Press.
ARD. 2016. Freundinnen—Alle für eine | Filme im Ersten Video | ARD Mediathek. ardmediathek.de. Retrieved 4 May 2017 from http://www.ardmediathek.de/tv/Filme-im-Ersten/Freundinnen-Alle-f%C3%BCr-eine/Das-Erste/Video?bcastId=1933898&documentId=40606276.
ARD Mediathek. 2016. Uschi Glas—Ich weiß, wo ich herkomm' | Lebenslinien Video | ARD Mediathek. ardmediathek.de. Retrieved 4 May 2017 from http://www.ardmediathek.de/tv/Lebenslinien/Uschi-Glas-Ich-wei%C3%9F-wo-ich-herkomm/BR-Fernsehen/Video?bcastId=14913740&documentId=38937414.
Attwood, F., V. Campbell, and I. Q. Hunter. 2012. *Controversial Images: Media Representations on the Edge*. Basingstoke, England: Palgrave.
British Board of Film Certification (BBFC). 2005. *Public Opinion and BBFC Guidelines*. London: BBFC.
Brottman, M. 1997. *Offensive Films: Toward an Anthropology of Cinema Vomitif.* Westport, CT: Greenwood Press.
Carroll, N. 1980. *The Philosophy of Horror or Paradoxes of the Heart*. New York, NY: Routledge.
Cumberbatch, G., S. Gauntlett, and V. Littlejohns. 2003. *A Content Analysis of Sexual Activity and Nudity on British Terrestrial Television*. London, England: BBC, BSC, and ITC.
Eilders, C., U. Hasebrink, and A. Herzog. 2006. "Das aktive Publikum. Instituionalisierung zivilgesellschaftlicher Kontrolle des Fernsehens auf europäischer Ebene." In *Europäische Öffentlichkeit und medialer Wandel*, edited by W. Langenbucher and M. Latzer, 330–351. Wiesbaden: VS Verlag.
Evans, S. 2011. "What Paddington Tells Us About German v British Manners—BBC News." BBC News. Retrieved 24 February 2017 from http://www.bbc.co.uk/news/world-europe-13545386.
Hargrave, A. Millwood, and S. Livingstone. 2009. *Harm and Offence in Media Content: A Review of the Evidence*. LSE Research Online. Bristol: Intellect Books. Retrieved from http://doi.org/10.1007/s11616-007-0058-2.
Hasebrink, U. 1994. "Country Report Germany." In *Television and the Viewer Interest: Explorations in the Responsiveness of European Broadcasters*, edited by J. Mitchell, J. G. Blumer, P. Mounier, and A. Bundschuh, 25–46. London, England: John Libbey.
Hasebrink, U. 2011. "Giving the Audience a Voice: The Role of Research in Making Media Regulation More Responsive to the Needs of the Audience." *Journal of Information Policy* 1: 321–336.

Hill, A. 1997. *Shocking Entertainment: Viewer Response to Violent Movies.* Luton, England: University of Luton Press.
Hofstede, G. 2001. *Culture's Consequences.* 2nd ed. Thousand Oaks, CA: Sage.
Horz, C. 2016. "The Public: Consumers or Citizens? Participatory Initiatives and the Reform of Public Service Media Regulation in Germany." *Comunicação e Sociedade* 30: 349–366.
House, J. 1996. "Contrastive Discourse Analysis and Misunderstandings: The Case of German and English." In *Contrastive Sociolinguistics,* edited by M. Hellinger and U. Ammon, 345–363. New York, NY: Mouton de Gruyter.
Janovich, M. 2002. *Horror: The Film Reader.* New York, NY: Routledge.
Livingstone, S., and R. Das. 2009. *Public Attitudes, Tastes and Standards: A Review of the Evidence.* London, England: BBC.
Livingstone, S., and P. Lunt. 2007. "Representing Citizens and Consumers in Media and Communications Regulation." *Annals of the American Academy of Political and Social Science* 611: 51.
Livingstone, S., and P. Lunt. 2011. "The Implied Audience of Communications Policy Making: Regulating Media in the Interests of Citizens and Consumers." In *The Handbook of Media Audiences.* Global Media and Communication Handbook Series (IAMCR), edited by V. Nightingale, 169–189. Oxford, England: Blackwell.
Livingstone, S., and P. Lunt. 2012. *Media Regulation: Governance and the Interests of Citizen and Consumers.* London, England: Sage.
Livingstone, S., P. Lunt, and L. Miller. 2007. "Citizens, Consumers and the Citizen-Consumer: Articulating the Citizen Interest in Media and Communications Regulation." *Discourse & Communication* 1 (1): 85–111.
Lockyer, S., and M. Pickering. 2009. *Beyond a Joke: The Limits of Humour.* New York, NY: Palgrave Macmillan.
Office of Communications (Ofcom). 2005. *Language and Sexual Imagery in Broadcasting: A Contextual Investigation.* London: Ofcom.
Office of Communications (Ofcom). 2013. *The Ofcom Broadcasting Code.* London: Ofcom.
Paasonen, S. 2011. *Carnal Resonance: Affect and Online Pornography.* Cambridge: MIT Press.
Puppis, M., L. d'Haenens, and F. Saeys. 2007. "Broadcasting Policy and Regulatory Choices." In *Western Broadcast Models: Structure, Conduct and Performance,* edited by F. Saeys and L. d' Haenens, 61–78. Berlin, NY: Mouton.
Schlesinger, P. 1992. *Women Viewing Violence.* London, England: British Film Institute (BFI).
Schlesinger, P., R. Haynes, and R. Boyle. 1998. *Men Viewing Violence.* London, England: Broadcasting Standards Commission (BBC).

Webster, J. G., and P. F. Phalen. 1994. "Victim, Consumer, or Commodity? Audience Models in Communication Policy." In *Audiencemaking: How the Media Create the Audience*, edited by J. S. Ettema and D. C. Whitney, 19–37. London, England: Sage.

Williams, L. 1991. "Film Bodies: Gender, Genre and Excess." *Film Quarterly* 44 (4): 2–13.

Williams, L., ed. 2004. *Porn Studies*. Durham, NC: Duke University Press.

CHAPTER 11

Negotiating Vulnerability in the Trigger Warning Debates

Katariina Kyrölä

INTRODUCTION

Since around 2012, the use of trigger warnings (TW) or content warnings (CW) has spread all over the Internet and, to some extent, academic classrooms. Warnings about content that may be upsetting, offensive or that could trigger post-traumatic stress responses abound online, particularly in contexts where the addressed include people or groups deemed marginalised, disadvantaged or traumatised. Trigger or content warnings have most commonly been linked to online images and texts explicitly depicting sexual violence, mental illness, or sexist, racist, ableist, cis-sexist or heterosexist subordination.

These warnings have unsurprisingly elicited heated debate in academic circles: debate pieces appear on a regular basis in scholarly journals and

---

A version of this Chapter has appeared in Anu Koivunen, Katariina Kyrölä and Ingrid Ryberg (eds.) 'The power of vulnerability. Mobilising affect in feminist, queer and anti-racist media cultures'. 2018, Manchester University Press.

K. Kyrölä (✉)
Åbo Akademi University, Turku, Finland
e-mail: kkyrola@abo.fi

blogs, such as *Inside Higher Ed*; the feminist journal *Signs* has assembled a digital archive of resources[1] on trigger warnings; and the first book-length collection of essays about them, *Trigger Warnings: History, Theory, Context*, appeared in 2017. The online magazine *Slate* declared the year 2013 as the 'year of the trigger warning' (Marcotte 2013). To a large degree, views have become polarised into 'against' and 'for' camps. At the same time, in many feminist, queer and anti-racist social media groups and discussion forums, the use of TWs or CWs has become standard practice and is taken as a necessary part of online discussion in spaces that are dedicated to fighting marginalisation and abuse based on gender, sexuality, ability, race or ethnicity. Trigger warnings have become expected and normalised in what are called safe—or safer—spaces online.

The point of departure for this chapter is my own initial doubt, even confusion, about trigger warnings. As a feminist media scholar long involved in interrogating 'bad feelings', and convinced they serve a purpose in challenging unjust power structures (Kyrölä 2015, 2017), I felt such warnings ring disconcertingly of avoidance—and it seems that this point of departure is shared by most feminist, queer and critical race studies scholars who have participated in the public debate so far. However, something about the strong dismissal of TWs bothered me as well, since they obviously serve an important purpose to those who request them, which led me to investigate the debate more thoroughly and to question my own initial reservations. This chapter thus examines first and foremost the *online debates* about TWs or CWs during the last few years, providing a mapping of the discourses around them, while another important aspect of the debate, namely the educational or classroom aspect, is not at the centre of focus. My aim here is not to argue against or for trigger warnings per se, but to invite readers to re-evaluate their own stances, as I have done, and understand what exactly we oppose or side with, when we oppose or side with trigger warnings. I do argue that it is essential to carefully analyse how trigger warnings are being used in various contexts and how they mobilise varying understandings of vulnerability, since they can be and are being used for completely oppositional political purposes—both to create alternative worlds where the marginalised set the pace, and to ridicule and offend feminist, queer and anti-racist efforts.

---

[1] The *Signs* digital archive on trigger warnings is available at: http://signsjournal.org/currents-trigger-warnings/#digitalarchive (accessed 4 June 2018).

The figure of the trigger warning currently seems to circulate most intensely in three key contexts: (1) feminist discussion forums and peer support communities where the use of TWs or CWs is a desired, required and normalised practice; (2) feminist, queer and anti-racist academic critique of trigger warnings which emphasises the pedagogical value of negative affect such as offence and discomfort; and (3) anti-feminist online spaces where TWs are seen as a condensation of how 'feminism has gone too far' in 'policing' what can and cannot be said. For feminist discussion forums, I use the rules for a Finnish closed Facebook group called the 'Laid-back Feminist Group' (in Finnish, 'Rento feministiryhmä') as an example, alongside some public online and academic debate pieces, including Sara Ahmed's. For the feminist, queer and anti-racist opposition of TWs, I examine a selection of key texts by, for example, Jack Halberstam and Roxane Gay. For the anti-feminist ridicule of trigger warnings, I exemplify broader tendencies in the discourse through selected online articles. In each of these contexts, I aim to show that vulnerability is understood in somewhat different but overlapping ways: as a standpoint that both prohibits and enables; as a necessity to life that must be embraced; and as a paradoxical position where claims to power are made through claims of disempowerment.

In feminist and peer support discussion forums, trigger warnings have been seen as protection for vulnerable groups, an attempt to create safer spaces for those living with trauma or societal stigma. The intention of giving a trigger warning is usually to make apparent that the giver of the warning cares for the well-being of their audience members and wants to protect them from encountering potentially offensive content without warning or preparation. It is less important whether that content is actually experienced as offensive or traumatising by anyone, and more important to signal what the content may entail as well as perform the gesture of care. From this perspective, trigger warnings enable people to make informed choices about when, how or whether to engage, instead of being bombarded without warning with content that can produce emotional distress and therefore prohibit engagement (Carter 2015; Cecire 2014).

For the feminist anti-trigger warning public debaters, the same warnings have been seen as extensions of a culture of overprotection and paradoxical celebration of victimhood, focusing on individual psychology rather than oppressive structures. From the opposing perspective, the proponents of trigger warnings infantilise themselves and unwittingly pathologise the reading and watching practices of already marginalised groups, as if they were unable to take a critical distance from what they see, hear and read. Those opposing argue that trigger warnings can repress discussion and the representation of difficult or hurtful matters, when a feminist, queer and anti-racist stance to the world almost always means dealing with very hurtful matters—and hurt, pain and anger can have great value as feminist tools. Furthermore, the things that can trigger actual post-traumatic stress are usually unpredictable, such as a sound, a colour or an arbitrary word or image, and even if triggers were known and obvious, avoidance is not effective treatment (Gay 2012; Friedersdorf 2015; Freeman et al. 2014; Halberstam 2014a, 2017).

Even more recently, trigger warnings have become the latest favourite target of mockery for anti-feminists and some white liberal feminists alike, as well as for those opposing 'excessive political correctness' in the era of Donald Trump and the rise of right-wing nationalism in many European countries. In this context, trigger warnings have dismissively been called another symptom of 'generation snowflake'—the generation that came into adulthood in the 2010s, presumably more fragile and easily offended than the previous ones (GQ 2016; Hartocollis 2016). I bring this context into focus not to present it as a perspective among others but to examine how some of the language used in feminist contexts has been disconcertingly adopted into the anti-feminist discourse. Scholars, activists and public debaters should be aware of the potential allegiances they may build, even if inadvertently, with anti-feminist voices, or white supremacist, trans-exclusionary feminist discourses.

While the debate and the division between pro and anti camps have most forcefully taken place in the North American context, the same debates are also happening in other parts of the world like the Nordic countries, the location from which I am writing. Academic culture in the Nordic countries is different from the US and Canada, for example in terms of the cost of education, but online cultures and practices of communication spread quickly across the world, like trigger warnings have. As many students and staff members participate in online communities, the online debates at the focus of this chapter cannot be held fully separate from educational contexts. Regardless of one's location and stance to trigger warnings, the question of how to deal with potential trauma and the varying backgrounds and identifications on university courses and online communities alike is a pertinent one.

Trigger warnings have been connected to an 'ethos of vulnerability' (Brunila and Rossi 2017) in contemporary Western culture, where a shared vulnerability, in terms of shared experiences of trauma, oppression and victimhood, is underlined by the 'vulnerable' themselves as a key basis for claims to rights, recognition and voice. At the same time, and as pointed out in the introduction to this volume, vulnerability has a long history of being used as an authoritative concept, justifying the management and control of groups and populations from the 'outside' because they are deemed vulnerable. Both ways of employing vulnerability have further been linked to the rise of therapy culture where, it has been claimed, individual and psycho-emotional approaches to trauma and oppression are easily prioritised over structural, political and policy efforts (Brunila and Rossi 2017, 2–3; Brown 1995).

In many ways, the debate about trigger warnings concretises key questions about vulnerability. This chapter asks how the varying uses of trigger or content warnings in online debates negotiate vulnerability and agency in relation to media content. Whose and what feelings matter in debates on trigger warnings? What bodies become vulnerable in various contexts, how is vulnerability understood in them, and how does it relate to agency—how subjects seem to gain and lose agency through vulnerability?

RESPECTING VULNERABILITY—TRIGGER WARNING POLICIES IN FEMINIST ONLINE COMMUNITIES

The background of trigger warnings has been identified as lying, on one hand, in online peer support and therapeutic forums and message boards for people with eating disorders, experiences of rape or sexual assault, or mental illness ever since the 1990s—members of these communities often (although not exclusively) being women or members of various marginalised groups (Washick 2017). In the late 1990s, trigger warnings also began to appear on feminist website message boards and blogs such as on *xoJane* and the *Ms. Magazine* forum, signalling care and safe spaces (Vigliano 2014). In this sense, the history of trigger warnings can be connected to the simultaneous rise of cyber-feminist utopias about the Internet: how it could enable a different kind of world that would function based on the needs of the marginalised, and free us from identity-based hierarchies and oppression (for an overview see Bromseth and Sundén 2011).

On the other hand, the background has been located in fan fiction (Lothian 2016), where content warnings were also used in the 1990s. In fan fiction, however, the purpose of trigger warnings was not only to turn away those who did not want to encounter, for example, homosexual content or suicidal ideation, but also to lure in those who took pleasure in engaging with precisely that. The use of content warnings was community created and community driven, or, as Lothian (2016) phrases it, about queer world-making practices outside the world of the mainstream and more broadly acceptable pleasures. Into the 2010s, the terms 'content warning' or 'content note' have become more popular in fan fiction communities (Washick 2017, 90), while the term 'trigger warning' has been saved more for explicitly shocking or violent content. As all these terms have become popularised, they are regularly used interchangeably.

In feminist, queer, anti-racist or disability activist groups and forums online, the rules and guidelines often direct participants in using trigger or content warnings. More often than not, these online spaces are moderated by a group of peers. The place of warnings is in the beginning of a post or a share, sometimes with empty space in between the warning and actual content, so that the content is hidden from appearing simultaneously with the warning. The aim is to create a non-discriminatory, safe or safer space for the participants—in other words, warnings can be seen as a part of such forums' feminist world-making practices, with the acknowledgement that the world at large is not and will not be as accommodating.

World-making, according to José Esteban Muñoz (1999, 195–196), is not only about alternative views of how the world could or should be, but about reordering, reshaping and decomposing, creating a space where different things are possible as compared to the 'real world' while using the real world as raw material. World-making practices are about potentiality, imagining what could be outside of the hegemonic order, building alternate realities. Trigger or content warnings, as they appear in feminist, queer and/or anti-racist online forums and groups, participate in such world-making in the sense that they transform a world which functions on the terms of the privileged, where the hurt of the marginalised is constantly normalised and swept aside, into a world where the marginalised and the hurtfulness of structures and practices that subordinate them are highlighted and prioritised. Trigger or content warnings can be seen as one of the starting points for such world-making that ultimately aims to build an alternative reality, whether that is called a 'safe space' or something else.

For the purposes of this article, I received permission from the moderators of the Finnish Laid-Back Feminist Group, a closed group on Facebook, to use their collectively created rules (a document within the group last edited 13 November 2017) as research material.[2] I have been a member of the group for some time but have not participated beyond an infrequent 'like', only quietly observing. By applying to the group, members agree to follow the rules, which include not sharing content from the group to other websites or people outside the group. Feminist groups and publically vocal feminists overall tend to be targets of intense anti-feminist trolling and harassment, thus this rule is meant to not only protect the privacy of the participants, but also protect them from online and offline attacks. Such policies are typical of closed feminist, queer, anti-ableist or anti-racist forums and groups, which poses challenges for studying online community formation in them (Association of Internet Research 2012). The rules document, however, can be seen as an anonymous, collectively formed and continuously developing text which can exemplify some of the principles by which such feminist online groups can function, without specifically jeopardising the privacy or safety of any of its members. Nevertheless, the rules also acknowledge and warn members about sharing anything too personal, since the moderators cannot guarantee that no one in the group of thousands will share content elsewhere.

The group's name includes the adjective 'laid-back' because, as the rules document states, it is a group inclusive of people interested in learning about feminism who are not necessarily well versed in feminist thought and discourse yet. The rules explain that inadvertent mistakes with language use or such are fine as long as members are willing to learn and correct themselves. That said, the rules also state that the group does not tolerate anti-feminist behaviour, which includes racism, ableism,

---

[2] I contacted the moderator who created the document in November 2017, explained the purposes of the research and the article, and requested permission to use the rules document in my research, with the understanding that the moderators would check and, if needed, correct the article before publication. The moderators gave permission for this. In early February 2018, I sent a pre-proofread article draft for them to check, and on February 8 they gave permission to move forward with the publishing process without corrections.

cis-sexism, homophobia, and sexism, and if a member does not correct themselves after a warning, or does not follow the rules otherwise, the moderators will expel them from the group. Typical posts to the group include sharing links to and thoughts about media examples, political decisions, articles, or current events, as well as requests for advice in various situations.

The rules also require trigger or content warnings (with the abbreviation TW, CW or SV, the last one for the Finnish word 'sisältövaroitus', that is, 'content warning') before disturbing content. What counts as disturbing content is left open, but examples given include 'TW animal torture' and 'TW violence against children'. Warnings can be requested by moderators or participants if the person posting did not include them, and the rules instruct that requests should be followed. In practice, it is relatively common to see warnings before posts in the group, but many posts come without warnings, which means, after a while, that they were not requested either.

Notably, the 'Laid-back Feminist Group' functions through what the rules call 'the principles of safe space, where we prioritise listening to the oppressed. Before you comment, find out about your privileges'. The rules document also explains that moderators can close a comments section to people other than those oppressed by the matter at hand. I interpret this to mean, for example, disallowing white people from commenting on a racist incident, or prioritising trans voices when discussing cis-sexism. While the principle can raise questions about identity, such as definitions of a non-white identity and the fluidity of gender identification, it clearly recalls a standpoint feminist epistemological stance. Importantly, feminist standpoint theories (Harding 1993; Collins 2009) have demanded accountability for the specificity of knowledge producers' viewpoints, with a broader goal of challenging how the white, male perspective often cloaks itself as a 'universal' or 'neutral' perspective, dominating discussion and knowledge about marginalised groups from the 'outside'. Instead, standpoint feminisms place particular value on the experiences, voices and knowledge of subjugated groups and people broadly, and specifically about issues that concern them.

Similarly, in the Laid-back Feminist Group, what counts as vulnerability to various forms of oppression, a lack of a voice or a disadvantage in the world outside is turned into a prioritised voice, a demand for explicit recognition, respect and space. What is at stake, then, is not so much the individual possibility of being triggered into post-traumatic stress or anxiety, but the gesture by the community that it will function on the terms of those that are most fragile within the group and ask for care, that it will make space for the marginalised, the traumatised; that it will not allow the dominant to dominate, even if the dominant are the majority. Vulnerability becomes the basis of this standpoint feminist stance, which can be seen as a powerful world-making process. The risk is that it will inevitably estrange and exclude some people, groups and feminists, but that is the price for a collective space where the privileged do not speak for others but concretely step aside (Alcoff 1991).

On the other hand, by setting the possibility of trauma as the norm and bottom line, this stance does place everyone within the group as vulnerable unless-otherwise-proved, implementing a kind of equality of vulnerability. As Valeria Souza has argued in the blog post 'Triggernometry' (2014), trigger warnings can be seen as progressive from a disability perspective since they assume mental disability as the default state rather than able-mindedness or able-bodiedness. Angela Carter (2015) takes a similar perspective, framing trigger warnings as a question of access and making spaces accessible, not a question of safety or coddling all-too-fragile egos. The issue of prioritising access for those potentially disabled by trauma connects back to the history of trigger and content warnings in the peer support and therapy-focused online groups. However, the Laid-back Feminist Group does not assume or require any shared experiences or identity (such as 'survivor' or 'woman') from its participants in order to allow access, only a shared politics of intersectional feminism before anything else, as defined in the rules. These shared politics then lead to shared practices, including warnings.

At the same time, there can be 'dark' sides to this world-making and standpoint-based, default disability-assuming community building. For example, acceptable participation demands learning the rather specific language and discourse—including the correct use of trigger warnings—of feminist activism. Those who have not yet spent much time in feminist, queer and/or anti-racist contexts, and who have not taken gender studies classes or read feminist books, might not master the rules of the activist community quickly enough, and in those instances they risk being seen as unwilling to learn and are expelled. Learning the culturally and linguistically specific intersectional feminist discourse, and adopting the 'good feminist discussant' position and voice, may be more challenging and time-consuming than the rule of expulsion-from-the-second-warning allows.

Furthermore, online discussions overall tend to quickly escalate into debates and even full-blown conflicts where affect runs intense (Paasonen 2015). In order to keep the community functional and de-escalate a conflict, it might sometimes be necessary to shut down discussions either by removing a participant or closing a chain of comments, and the moderators of the Laid-back Feminist Group reserve the right to do this in the rules—a right which they have also exercised in the group. However, again, the wiggle room for marginalised subjects to express emotion is broader, according to the rules, than for the privileged: the rules forbid tone policing, which refers to intervening or policing the tone in which the oppressed talk about their own experiences of oppression. As an example, the rules mention a situation where an oppressed person is instructed to stay calm when they are being oppressed.

The discourse in an activist-oriented feminist community is not entirely similar to academic feminist discourse, at least not in the form familiar to me: despite my study and work history of two decades in feminist thought and theorising, the regular inclusion of content warnings and the typical ways of phrasing posts and comments took me some time to get used to and learn. What has to be noted here is that groups that function according to the principles of safe space similar to the Laid-back Feminist Group are already most likely to stay around for a while, which also means that the language of trigger and content warnings is already here to stay. Regardless of the reservations or the outright rejection of warnings by many academic feminists, which I will discuss in the next section, many feminist, queer and anti-racist scholars and students participate in, learn and want to follow the principles of similar activist groups and communities, and by doing so are passionately involved in alternative world-making. Trigger warnings in these spaces are not about the avoidance of difficult issues or creating a false sense of safety, but about showing care and recognition, and enabling access and informed engagement to potential and actual participants living with trauma.

Sara Ahmed (2014a), in an essay called 'Feminist Hurt/Feminism Hurts' on her blog *Feminist Killjoy*, points out how the hurt expressed by those who have been traumatised by sexism or racism is often heard as imposition. This hurt, this imposition, can take the form of, for example, a trigger warning—which is then claimed to limit someone else's freedom to speak without one. But Ahmed turns the issue around: even if the requests or demands for warning may feel like an imposition or are turned into censorship, they are in fact not asking for limitations in the sense of less, but are about asking for more: more consideration for the context, the situatedness and the affective force of the material, and thus more complexity.

Yet, even if trigger warnings are understood as feminist standpoint practices, as radical alternative world-making, as an expression of the need to situate and complicate the affective force that the world can grab us through, the question remains about when and in what context to use trigger warnings. Their predecessors, like content labels on consumer products, began to be used in the US in the 1930s and since spread from food, alcohol and tobacco to cultural products, first in the form of film classification and age ratings (Souza 2014). These labels and ratings, just like trigger warnings, seem to most often concern relatively easily identifiable things like (presumably) harmful substances, clear physical or emotional violence and eating disorders or suchlike, but problems arise immediately, when they are—or are not—used with finer and deeply normalised structures of oppression or marginalisation addressed, maintained or produced. For example, most contemporary media content and political decision-making functions according to the binary and heteronormative gender system, dividing all bodies into either men or women, and despite that system's violent reduction of all gender and sexual expressions and identifications into two categories, would it be necessary to add a trigger warning about cis-sexism and/or heterosexism to all examples of them when shared in a safe space or a classroom context? I will return to the question of when to use and not use trigger warnings in the next section, as the difficulty or impossibility of answering the 'when' question is one key motivation for those who choose not to give warnings.

Another difficulty arises from the possibility and reality that any feminist idea, principle or practice can (and often will) be taken out of its original context and used for purposes precisely opposite to what the idea or principle was created for (see Gill and Elias 2014). Trigger warnings have also been de-rooted and appropriated to various contexts at the same time as claims of vulnerability have gained more ground as claims to rights and voice that cannot be silenced. In these cases, vulnerability becomes something that anyone experiencing hurt can 'claim' for themselves, whether that hurt derives from the momentary loss of structural privilege or from structural oppression. Therefore, it has become possible for Trump supporters to ask for safe spaces on liberal campuses (Hartocollis 2016), or Christian conservative students in the US to ask for (and receive) a trigger warning for (or be excused from engaging with) sexually explicit content or homosexual themes on university syllabi through claiming vulnerability to religion-based oppression, when their religious beliefs are against homosexuality (Cooper 2014; Levinovitz 2016).

The language of triggers has furthermore been adopted in trans-exclusionary feminist demands to exclude transwomen from 'women-only safe spaces' because even the potential presence of a penis can, they claim, be triggering for rape survivors—who, within this logic, can only be cis-female (Phipps 2016). The discussion becomes entirely something else and shockingly violent, when the very existence of a person and a gender identity becomes named as 'triggering', when a body, not a text or image, becomes a 'trigger' by its mere presence. Such practices stand in radical contrast to the principles of safe space in communities such as the Laid-back Feminist Group, which explicitly prohibits trans-exclusionary feminist practices within its discussions. This only goes to show how the language of triggers can be used for entirely different, and indeed oppositional, purposes.

Embracing Vulnerability—Academic Feminist Anti-trigger Warning Arguments

The feminist anti-trigger warning arguments have mostly been made in the context of higher education, touching upon the use of such warnings online and in activist communities only in passing. The majority of such writing and engagement has simultaneously expressed compassion and concern for students struggling with racist, sexist, heterosexist and cissexist or ableist marginalisation, as well as mental health issues and sexual harassment and violence (Freeman et al. 2014; Gay 2012; Halberstam 2014a, b, 2017). Next, I want to look more closely at some key arguments of the anti-trigger warning camp. They are, firstly, the unpredictability of how trauma and PTSD work; secondly, the difficulty or impossibility of deciding when to warn and when not to in terms of media material; and thirdly, the value of staying with discomforting and overwhelming—or perhaps especially discomforting and overwhelming—reactions and affect.

In her essay 'The Safety of Illusion/The Illusion of Safety' (2012), the well-known black feminist public intellectual Roxane Gay argues that there is no trigger warning that could guarantee anyone's safety, that they are about an illusion of safety that may function contrary to its purpose. Gay's essay is spotted with sentences that begin 'when', such as 'when I smell Polo cologne' and 'when someone comes up behind me unexpectedly', signalling moments that function as triggers for her, as she has publically relayed her own complicated struggles with post-traumatic stress disorder from having been gang-raped as a young girl. According to Gay, there can never be trigger warnings for all that might trigger a post-traumatic stress reaction for a rape or sexual assault survivor, because such triggers are unpredictable, even to those experiencing them. Anything can be a trigger for someone—furthermore, trigger warnings can also make things more appealing, just like age restrictions for media content can make it all the more attractive for some. However, Gay also states that, regardless of how ineffective and impractical she considers trigger warnings, the illusion of safety they produce can be powerful and important, even if it is an illusion. The voice she uses is that of someone who has much experience of becoming triggered, a voice from the 'inside'; an empathetic, even if suspicious, voice that unequivocally argues that vulnerability will always be a part of life and corporeality as well as media consumption, and that pain has value, even if a cost too.

Trauma therapists, similarly, have argued that PTSD cannot be treated effectively with the avoidance of possible triggers, which trigger warnings might enable—if such triggers can even reliably be identified (Waldman 2016). A group of prestigious gender, queer and critical race studies faculty (Freeman et al. 2014) also point out in their statement about why they see trigger warnings as flawed in that university faculty are not therapists nor trained in treating PTSD. Therefore, resources should be directed to offering sufficient professional care to students who suffer from mental health issues and disabilities, since trigger warnings can never substitute treatment.

Here, a differentiation between a trigger warning and a content warning becomes important, although their meanings slide into each other after much interchangeable use. The term 'trigger' connects particularly to PTSD and the sudden, potentially violent and disabling reactions to 'triggers' like images, sounds, smells, words, and touch that may recall a traumatic event. Also, the argument against trigger warnings from a PTSD perspective is, like Gay's, highly convincing—after all, it does seem futile to try to fight complex trauma with the simple addition of the letters 'TW'. However, it seems that in their contemporary activist uses, trigger or content warnings are not really used with post-traumatic stress disorder sufferers in mind—more so, the use of terms like 'trigger' and PTSD in these contexts appears to lend the warnings more legitimacy in the therapy cultural context. When warnings are seen first and foremost as a call for recognition of and care for the suffering that racist, sexist, hetero and cis-sexist hegemonic structures produce for members of subordinated groups, then the argument against TWs as ineffective treatment loses much of its meaning.

The argument indeed recalls the critiques that feminist consciousness-raising and political therapy groups in the 1960s and 1970s faced in terms of the investment in the personal as political. Carol Hanisch (1969), who is usually credited with the well-known feminist slogan, actually argued that dismissing such groups as therapy or focused on personal problems is to dismiss their political dimension, since they do not aim to solve personal problems by offering personal solutions. Their focus is on seeing both problems and solutions as political, as in having to do with oppressive structures, not individual successes or failures in dealing with them. Similarly, trigger and content warnings in groups such as the Laid-back Feminist Group are not so much for those who suffer personally or are diagnosed with PTSD, but those who are structurally oppressed and carry the trauma of that oppression.

The more important question thus becomes: what counts as content that warrants a warning in a world that is so thoroughly structured by unjust norms and hierarchies—hierarchies that feminist, queer and critical race studies teachers and online communities are dedicated to revealing and unravelling? Jack Halberstam, in his several texts about trigger warnings (2014a, b, 2017), has addressed precisely this difficulty of when and where to warn as a key reason why trigger warnings are, according to him, counterproductive, as they seem to set representations and practices in a flawed hierarchy of oppressiveness based on affective reaction. In the essay 'Trigger Happy' (2017), Halberstam gives the example of how silence and invisibility—the complete lack of representation—can potentially be just as traumatising or discomforting as an explicit representation, such as the exclusion of issues of race, gender or class altogether from philosophy or political science classes. Another example that Halberstam discusses is a course he taught on the Holocaust, where he showed the film *Night and Fog* (1955, dir. Alain Resnais), with brutal imagery of dead, naked, piled-up bodies, to the students' shock, while they were captivated by and wanted to see more of

The Triumph of the Will (1935, dir. Leni Riefenstahl), a film specifically meant to make Nazism aesthetically and ideologically appealing through veiling it in visual pleasure. Indeed, it is of essential importance to question why seemingly inconspicuous and pleasurable to watch content usually does not warrant a warning, even if it is ideologically deeply disturbing, just as it must be asked why the lack of representation does not warrant a warning. However, while Halberstam considers this an example of why trigger warnings do not make sense overall, I suggest that the difficulty of deciding 'when' could just as well necessitate more questioning, careful contextualisation and collective consideration of why, when and if to warn.

Indeed there was a time when feminist, queer and critical race studies scholars were much more worried about the treacherousness of pleasure than about pain and hurt. For example, in the 1980s Mary Ann Doane (1982) interrogated the ways Hollywood cinema constructs the female body as an idealised and pleasurable spectacle. Through a recognition and pull of similarity, the female spectator has no choice but to over-identify with the image, unless she fully rejects it. The reward is pleasure and idealisation, and the price is submission to a patriarchal structure of gendered subordination where women are reduced to beautiful surfaces. According to feminist psychoanalytical film theory approaches, such as Doane's, it is pleasure that makes spectators unwittingly and unavoidably vulnerable and open to identifying with power structures that will keep them subordinated, whereas in the pro-trigger warning arguments, subordination is often taken up as something that is easily recognisable in representation and discourse through viewers' and readers' upset reactions.

On the other hand, one of the key critiques directed at feminist psychoanalytical approaches is that they have often assumed a rather stable similarity between the gendered spectator and the image of a gendered human form to be a prerequisite for the 'suction' into the image. The impossibility of predicting reactions based on such an assumed similarity is also one of the key feminist anti-trigger warning arguments: that it is impossible to say, for example, that seeing explicit racism is more triggering than silence about racism for those that live with the trauma of everyday racism, or that every black person would be equally upset or anxious about a representation of racism. Such 'competitions' of what kind of content wounds more, or who are the ones most vulnerable to potentially triggering content, come up easily when trigger warnings become standard practice, Halberstam (2017) points out. On the other hand, these 'competitions' that Halberstam critiques are also direly necessary in order to not accept or condone the claims to victimhood by members of structurally privileged groups, such as white men in right-wing and white nationalist movements habitually do, or to not claim a false symmetry between all levels and forms of structural subordination, for example that between trans women of colour and white cis women.

I tried to tackle these complications around shock and normalisation, pleasure and trauma, when to warn and when not to, in my own teaching in Finland in 2015 on a course about media and the body. One of the course themes was trigger warnings and sexually violent content (see also Kyrölä 2019). The students read blog texts advocating for and against trigger warnings, as well as the main points of an empirical study by Martin Barker et al. (2007), who had been commissioned by the British Board of Film Classification (BBFC) to study audience reactions to five films that depict sexual violence. One of those films was *À ma soeur!* (*Fat Girl*, France, 2001, dir. Catherine Breillat), which we watched for class. The students were then asked to compare their own reactions and reflections to those of Barker and his group's respondents, as well as form an opinion of whether trigger warnings or censorship were necessary in relation to the film.

Fat Girl ends in a notorious rape scene that has been the film's most debated feature, and has been censored in some countries. In this scene, a 12-year-old girl Anaïs (Anaïs Reboux) is raped in the woods by a nameless male attacker after he has brutally killed her sister with an axe and strangled her mother at a rest stop by a highway. The students were given access to the censored version of the film, and separately to the rape scene (about five minutes long)—with my explicit warning that the scene would include rape. I did not require them to watch it, but all of them chose to do so. However, instead of the rape scene, many of the students wanted to discuss the more insidious sexual abuse elsewhere in the film, particularly a lengthy (25-minute) scene earlier in the film where a young man pressures Anaïs' 15-year-old sister Elena (Roxane Mesquida) to have intercourse with him with Anaïs in the room. To the students, it seemed hypocritical that the scene which directly portrayed rape was censored and accompanied by warnings, while the scene about sexual pressuring and abuse was not. Many reviews of the film even discussed the lengthy scene as one of seduction, not abuse. The students broadly agreed that the film was very discomforting to watch overall, but that was precisely how it should be, given its topic of sexual abuse and gendered sexual agency.

Today, in the post #MeToo world, I would very likely make the choice to give a content warning about the whole film, not only the explicit rape scene, and the possibility for an alternative assignment. However, this example testifies to how the lines of what warrants a warning—or when, or if—are necessarily changing according to how gendered, racialised and sexual power structures shift in culture and society. Should we include a TW or CW about sexual abuse to all films or other content that include a scene of heterosexual 'seduction' or a woman reluctantly 'giving into desire'—one of the most common tropes representing female desire according to Linda Williams (1989)? That might have seemed ridiculous only a little while ago, but no more, as sexual harassment and the blurry lines of consent and abuse around sex have finally become high-profile topics.

The feminist anti-trigger warning arguments, or perspectives suspicious of the effectiveness and purpose of trigger warnings, seem to have one thing in common: they place great value on feelings of offence, discomfort and even hurt as necessary parts of pedagogy and learning, and they take vulnerability as an unavoidable condition of embodied life, which should be embraced rather than rejected. This view of vulnerability, that can be characterised as phenomenological and ontological (Butler 2004; Shildrick 2002), does still take into consideration the ways in which the basic human and non-human openness to the world, the porousness and fragility of corporeality, are distributed unevenly between groups of bodies. This allows some groups to maintain the privilege of relative safety, despite it being a fragile illusion, while others are deemed exceptionally vulnerable and thus disposable or subjected to paternalistic management measures. The feminist anti-trigger warning stance sees warnings as a measure to create such an illusion of safety, which in this logic easily translates into a paradoxical position of privilege that students who are unwilling to be uncomfortable exercise. Black feminist professor Brittney Cooper (2014), in her argument against trigger warnings, suggests that being and staying comfortable is actually at odds with the very foundation of what it means to get an education, especially in the gender and critical race studies classroom. Cooper also sees this tendency as understandable in the context of a broader results and test focused neoliberal educational culture and the financial pressures to get a college degree, regardless of what one actually learns in the process. The more effective strategy for changing the world, for Cooper as well as other feminist trigger warning critics, is to stay with the discomfort and deal with vulnerability even when it is almost unbearable, since it will become more endurable through learning feminist tools of analysis and critique.

In my teaching and research I have also studied and argued for the ethical and political value of feeling bad, uncomfortable, guilty, disgusted, and angry when engaging with problematic media materials from a feminist, queer studies and critical race studies perspective, a stance that has long roots in these critical traditions (Kyrölä 2015, 2017). I no longer think, though, that the use of trigger or content warnings would be at odds with such an approach which embraces vulnerability and so-called bad feeling. Many proponents of trigger warnings in fact argue that such warnings can be a prerequisite for the ability to engage with discomfort and bad feeling, since without warning that ability might be compromised (Carter 2015). But it matters deeply who or what instance asks for a warning and in what context, as trigger warnings can surely become a tool of condescending, paternalistic control, just as their refusal and the suggestion to just 'suck it up' and take a critical distance can seem condescending and paternalistic.

Mocking or Appropriating Vulnerability—Anti-feminist Anti-trigger Warning Discourse

The most disconcerting way in which trigger warnings have been mobilised today concerns the anti-feminist stances which see them as ridiculous symptoms of a culture of victimhood, or how 'whiny', overly protection-oriented and narcissistic young people, particularly feminist and queer youth and students of colour, have become. For example, the magazine *GQ* (2016) ridicules 'Millennials' who have become 'Generation Snowflake: a collective that quivers at the slightest breeze and dissolves at the slightest upset'. The deployment of the term 'Generation Snowflake', or 'snowflake' more broadly, appears regularly in distinctly anti-feminist contexts, where complaints against using insensitive words, such as racist or sexist slurs, are seen to limit freedom of speech. The *GQ* article is accompanied by an image of students of colour protesting with a sign saying 'Decolonise Education: Rhodes Must Fall', in reference to the student-led campaign which started in South Africa to remove statues of white imperialist oppressors from university campuses, and to produce cultural counter-memory (see e.g. Bosch 2016).

The article asks where to draw the line—if the presence of imperialist oppressors is perceived as triggering, should the faces of all oppressors, like Hitler and Mussolini, be removed from books and museums too? The image seems an odd choice, since the Rhodes Must Fall campaign never actually utilised the language or triggering or warnings, but the campaign has repeatedly been taken up as an example of the 'cult of the victim' (O'Neill 2015). 'Snowflakes' are rarely white in this discourse that mocks trigger warnings, which points towards its investment in white supremacy and white patriarchal sense of disenfranchisement. The vulnerability of easily triggered 'snowflakes' is seen as a false claim of victimhood, which has the barely hidden purpose of gaining power and unwarranted privilege through sinister calls for compassion and care.

Those feminists who mobilise the problematic figures of the 'snowflake' and 'overly fragile students' in debating TWs should seriously reconsider their use of such figures, since they can easily play into the anti-feminist and white supremacist discourses that ridicule and seek to silence marginalised voices seeking change. Feminists opposing trigger warnings may want to be extra careful about the tone with which they discuss trigger warnings and those who request them, if they want to avoid siding with anti-feminist and white supremacist voices. Disquietingly, the feminist and anti-feminist critics of trigger warnings often share a humorous and mocking tone, perhaps accompanied with a meme or a text about being 'triggered by trigger warnings', popular in the anti-feminist blogosphere, but found in Halberstam's first blog post about TWs too (2014a). This tone leaves the proponents of trigger warnings with no other role than that of feminist killjoy.

The white, masculinist anti-feminist anti-trigger warning stance intersects with the feminist anti-trigger warning stance also in the claim that this is an issue of generational differences, and that the previous generation was not as fragile (Halberstam 2014a). Transfeminist writer and activist Julia Serano (2014) has indeed critiqued Jack Halberstam for too broad strokes and simplifications about feminist generations and for dismissing the younger activists for their oversensitivity and 'killjoy' or 'no fun' approaches. Serano argues that the activist strategies of previous generations often cease to work for the next, as the world has also changed drastically through social media. However, women and marginalised people who 'take things too personally' have also been around as figures of concern for decades, and the vocal worry about complainers turning the nation into a narcissistic well of oversensitivity is not something that characterises our time alone. For example, Imogen Tyler (2007) has pointed out that the narcissistic, self-centred feminist was in fact already a popular figure in the anti-feminist discourses in the 1970s and 1980s—and then, too, it was argued that such feminists are a part of a new, broader narcissistic malaise.

The feminist-mocking anti-trigger warning discourse has even adopted other arguments of the feminist anti-trigger warning camp. Another one is the approach to vulnerability and the inevitable cruelty of this world: that vulnerability is an ontological condition of existence, and in order to be able to live in the world as a mortal who will experience hurt, one must learn tools to 'suck it up'. Yet a further similar argument concerns the difficulty of drawing the line between when to warn and when not to, and what to show and what not to: both feminist and anti-feminist critics of trigger warnings agree that the line is impossible to draw.

However, the important difference is that, in the anti-feminist discourse, there is very little if any recognition of the political dimensions of vulnerability and the ways it becomes asymmetrically lived, managed, assigned and made palpable for various groups in global and local power structures. The subordinated groups that ask for trigger warnings are seen as ridiculous, their requests for recognition of their suffering unjustified and whiny, claiming that those who do not 'submit' to such requests are victims of harassment and falsely accused of racism or sexism. The feminists opposing trigger warnings disagree with trigger warning proponents about the effectiveness of warnings, but agree about the existence of injustices and the goal of a world free of oppression. The anti-feminists opposing warnings see no real or deep structures of oppression, just a world that is an equally cruel and trying place for all. However, as Marilyn Frye (1983) stated in the 1980s in response to anti-feminist claims that everyone suffers, and thus everyone is oppressed: 'This is nonsense. Human beings can be miserable without being oppressed, and it is perfectly consistent to deny that a person or group is oppressed without denying that they have feelings or that they suffer'.

Paradoxically, trigger warnings themselves can also be used for anti-feminist, racist and transphobic purposes that completely defy their original purpose, as mentioned in this chapter in relation to trans-exclusionary feminists. Freeman et al. (2014) argue that the complaints made about the lack of appropriate trigger warnings tend to be disproportionately directed towards faculty who teach critical race studies and feminist and queer theory. The material that educators in these critical fields ask students to engage with is most often upsetting by nature, and the ways we ask students to engage with that material is meant to unsettle normative, ordinary and perhaps comfortable ways of thinking. The irony is that trigger warnings are not asked—or expected—from people or groups that are already assumed to not care. They are asked of those who are assumed and expected to care, but the risk is that disagreement about how to show that care can result in divisiveness, even the adoption of anti-feminist discursive figures like 'snowflakes' or (other) feminists as narcissists.

Vulnerable World-Making

Vulnerability has, in the contexts discussed above, been understood as a structurally produced disadvantage that can be countered by a standpoint epistemological privileging of the voice of and care for the vulnerable; an ontological, necessary condition which should be explored and embraced head-on in order to fight the way it is used for managerial politics; or a false claim of disempowerment and thus a false attempt to gain more power.

Two of the contexts I have discussed, the feminist trigger warnings policies and the feminist anti-trigger warning arguments, can be seen to participate in feminist world-making, following Muñoz's (1999) reflections on queer of colour performance as world-making—even if they suggest different routes and strategies. For those feminists who support trigger warnings, their absence produces a barrier or a wall that restricts or prevents their mobility (Ahmed 2014b), or the mobility of those they want to show they care about. Their alternative world-making, enabled by trigger warnings, concerns a world where the marginalised could roam free without the barrier of fear, without constantly, accidentally, and without warning running up against the wall of sexism, racism, cis-sexism or heterosexism. In this sense, groups like the Laid-back Feminist Group in part recall the feminist separatist groups of the 1970s in terms of alternative world-making and rules different from those of the 'outside' world. For feminist separatist groups, the best way to not only imagine but practice how to build a world free from white capitalist patriarchal oppression was to detach from it, create barriers that shield from it, break down everyday practices that define it, and exclude people who benefit from it (Valk 2008).

The anti-feminist and white supremacist voices that oppose trigger warnings do not see or recognise walls or structural oppression in the world, but prioritise an equally shared, ontological vulnerability and suffering. For them, the world is an even playing field, and trigger warnings are yet another symptom of how 'whiny' people of colour, queers and feminists are in the face of unavoidable pain. This discourse includes a paradox though, since trigger warnings also get to represent walls that could restrict the movement and 'free speech' of the privileged, the claimed 'victims' of 'trigger warnings'. One of the most disconcerting findings of my mapping of the discourses around trigger warnings is the extent of how much feminist anti-trigger warning language intersects with and is co-opted by anti-feminist and white supremacist contexts.

The feminists who oppose warnings, just like those who support them, see that the world, as it is now, is structured by barriers that produce marginalisation and privilege, distributing vulnerability asymmetrically. However, their suggestion is to push up against such barriers and trust that this pushing will not break those who push, instead of turning away from the barriers through practices such as warnings. But feminist support for warnings is not quite the opposite of pushing either, as evidenced by the fierce opposition that trigger warnings have encountered: it takes another kind of pushing to make space for and turn towards an alternative world. The difference is perhaps rather the difference between pushing with one's back and pushing head first—a matter of which direction you face. The advantage of a community facing inwards while pushing is that it then might be easier to glimpse an alternative, although fragile and complicated, world where the currently marginalised have the power, where their voices are privileged, and where gestures of care towards them abound. It is important, however, that both 'sides' of the debate recognise the value and effort of how the other side pushes, since the alternative worlds we long to inhabit may not be that different.

References

Ahmed, S. 2014a. "Feminist Hurt/Feminism Hurts." *Feminist Killjoys*, July 21. Accessed December 17, 2017. https://feministkilljoys.com/2014/07/21/feminist-hurtfeminism-hurts.

Ahmed, S. 2014b. "Atmospheric Walls." *Feminist Killjoys*, September 15. Accessed February 4, 2018. https://feministkilljoys.com/2014/09/15/atmospheric-walls.

Alcoff, L. 1991. "The Problem of Speaking for Others." *Cultural Critique* 20: 5–32.

Association of Internet Research. 2012. *Ethical Decision-Making and Internet Research*. Accessed June 4, 2018. http://aoir.org/reports/ethics2.pdf.

Barker, M., E. Mathijs, J. Sexton, K. Egan, R. Hunter, and M. Selfe. 2007. *Audiences and Receptions of Sexual Violence*. London: British Board of Film Classification.

Bosch, T. 2016. "Twitter Activism and Youth in South Africa: The Case of #RhodesMustFall." *Information, Communication & Society* 20 (2): 221–232.

Bromseth, J., and J. Sundén. 2011. "Queering Internet Studies: Intersections of Gender and Sexuality." In *The Handbook of Internet Studies*, edited by M. Consalvo and C. Ess, 270–300. Chichester: Wiley & Blackwell.

Brown, W. 1995. *States of Injury: Power and Freedom in Late Modernity*. Princeton, NJ: Princeton University Press.

Brunila, K., and L.-M. Rossi. 2017. "Identity Politics, the Ethos of Vulnerability, and Education." *Educational Philosophy and Theory*, June 26. https://doi.org/10.1080/00131857.2017.1343115.

Butler, J. 2004. *Precarious Life: The Powers of Mourning and Violence*. London: Verso.

Carter, A. 2015. "Teaching with Trauma: Trigger Warnings, Feminism, and Disability Pedagogy." *Disability Studies Quarterly* 35 (2). Accessed December 17, 2017. http://dsq-sds.org/article/view/4652/3935.

Cecire, N. 2014. "On the 'Neoliberal Rhetoric of Harm'," July 7. Accessed December 17, 2017. http://nataliacecire.blogspot.fi/2014/07/on-neoliberal-rhetoric-of-harm.html.

Collins, P. H. 2009 [1990]. *Black Feminist Thought: Knowledge, Consciousness and the Politics of Empowerment*. New York: Routledge.

Cooper, B. 2014. "No Trigger Warnings in My Class: Why You Won't Find Them on My Syllabi." *Salon.com*, May 20. Accessed December 17, 2017. https://www.salon.com/2014/05/20/no_trigger_warnings_in_my_class_why_you_won%E2%80%99t_find_them_on_my_syllabi/.

Doane, M. A. 1982. "Film and the Masquerade: Theorising the Female Spectator." *Screen* 23 (3–4): 74–87.

Freeman, E., B. Herrera, N. Hurley, H. King, D. Luciano, D. Seitler, and P. White. 2014. "Trigger Warnings Are Flawed." *Inside Higher Ed*, May 29. Accessed January 14, 2018. https://www.insidehighered.com/views/2014/05/29/essay-faculty-members-about-why-they-will-not-use-trigger-warnings.

Friedersdorf, C. 2015. "The Rise of Victimhood Culture." *The Atlantic*, September 11. Accessed 17 December 2017. https://www.theatlantic.com/politics/archive/2015/09/the-rise-of-victimhood-culture/404794.

Frye, M. 1983. "Oppression." In *The Politics of Reality: Essays in Feminist Theory*. Trumansburg, NY: The Crossing Press. Accessed February 4,

2018. https://feminsttheoryreadinggroup.wordpress.com/2010/11/23/marilyn-frye-the-politics-of-reality-oppression.

Gay, R. 2012. "The Illusion of Safety/The Safety of Illusion." *The Rumpus.net*, August 27. Accessed December 17, 2017. http://therumpus.net/2012/08/the-illusion-of-safetythe-safety-of-illusion.

Gill, R., and A. S. Elias. 2014. "'Awaken Your Incredible': Love Your Body Discourses and Postfeminist Contradictions." *International Journal of Media and Cultural Politics* 10 (2): 179–188.

GQ. 2016. "Millennials: Stop Being Offended by, Like, Literally Everything." *GQ*, August 12. Accessed December 17, 2017. http://www.gq-magazine.co.uk/article/millennials-created-generation-snowflake.

Halberstam, J. 2014a. "You're Triggering Me! The Neoliberal Rhetoric of Harm, Danger and Trauma." *BullyBloggers*, July 5. Accessed December 17, 2017. https://bullybloggers.wordpress.com/2014/07/05/you-are-triggering-me-the-neo-liberal-rhetoric-of-harm-danger-and-trauma.

Halberstam, J. 2014b. "Triggering You, Triggering Me: Making Up Is Hard to Do." *BullyBloggers*, July 15. Accessed December 17, 2017. https://bullybloggers.wordpress.com/2014/07/15/triggering-me-triggering-you-making-up-is-hard-to-do.

Halberstam, J. 2017. "Trigger Happy: From Content Warning to Censorship." *Signs: Currents*. Accessed December 17, 2017. http://signsjournal.org/currents-trigger-warnings/halberstam.

Hanisch, C. 1969. "The Personal Is Political." In *Writings by Carol Hanisch*. Accessed February 3, 2018. http://www.carolhanisch.org/CHwritings/PIP.html.

Harding, S. 1993. "Rethinking Standpoint Epistemology: What Is 'Strong Objectivity'?" In *Feminist Epistemologies*, edited by L. Alcoff and E. Potter, 49–82. New York and London: Routledge.

Hartocollis, A. 2016. "On Campus, Trump Fans Say They Need 'Safe Spaces'." *The New York Times*, December 8. Accessed December 17, 2017. https://www.nytimes.com/2016/12/08/us/politics/political-divide-on-campuses-hardens-after-trumps-victory.html.

Knox, E. J. M. 2017. "Introduction: On Trigger Warnings." In *Trigger Warnings: History, Theory, Context*, edited by E. J. M. Knox, xiii–xxi. Lanham: Rowman & Littlefield.

Kyrölä, K. 2015. "Toward a Contextual Pedagogy of Pain: Trigger Warnings and the Value of Sometimes Feeling Really, Really Bad." *Lambda Nordica: Nordic Journal on LGBTQ Studies* 1/2015: 131–144. http://www.lambdanordica.se/wp-content/uploads/were-here2.pdf.

Kyrölä, K. 2017. "Feeling Bad and *Precious* (2009): Black Suffering, White Guilt, and Intercorporeal Subjectivity." *Subjectivity* 10 (3): 258–275.

Kyrölä, K. 2019. "Squirming in the Classroom: *Fat Girl* (2001) and the Ethical Value of Extreme Discomfort." In *Unwatchable*, edited by N. Baer, M. Hennefeld, L. Horak, and G. Iversen. New Brunswick: Rutgers University Press.

Levinovitz, A. 2016. "How Trigger Warnings Silence Religious Students." *The Atlantic*, August 30. Accessed January 14, 2018. https://www.theatlantic.com/politics/archive/2016/08/silencing-religious-students-on-campus/497951.

Lothian, A. 2016. "Choose Not to Warn: Trigger Warnings and Content Notes from Fan Culture to Feminist Pedagogy." *Feminist Studies* 42 (3): 743–756.

Marcotte, A. 2013. "The Year of the Trigger Warning." *Slate*, December 30. Accessed December 17, 2017. http://www.slate.com/blogs/xx_factor/2013/12/30/trigger_warnings_from_the_feminist_blogosphere_to_shonda_rhimes_in_2013.html.

Muñoz, J. E. 1999. *Disidentifications: Queers of Color and the Performance of Politics*. Minneapolis: University of Minnesota Press.

O'Neill, B. 2015. "Never Mind Rhodes—It's the Cult of the Victim That Must Fall." *Spiked*, December 28. Accessed June 4, 2018. http://www.spiked-online.com/newsite/article/never-mind-rhodes-its-the-cult-of-the-victim-that-must-fall/17762#.WxZkVO6FPIU.

Paasonen, S. 2015. "A Midsummer's Bonfire: Affective Intensities of Online Debate." In *Networked Affect*, edited by K. Hillis, S. Paasonen, and M. Petit, 27–42. Cambridge: MIT Press.

Phipps, A. 2016. "Whose Personal Is More Political? Experience in Contemporary Feminist Politics." *Feminist Theory* 17 (3): 303–321.

Serano, J. 2014. "Regarding 'Generation Wars': Some Reflections Upon Reading the Recent Jack Halberstam Essay." *Whipping Girl* (blog), July 13. Accessed January 14, 2018. http://juliaserano.blogspot.fi/2014/07/regarding-generation-wars-some.html.

Shildrick, M. 2002. *Embodying the Monster: Encounters with the Vulnerable Self*. London: Sage.

Souza, V. M. 2014. "Triggernometry." *It's Complicated* (blog), May 21. Accessed June 1, 2015. http://valeriamsouza.wordpress.com/2014/05/21/triggernometry.

Tyler, I. 2007. "The Selfish Feminist: Public Images of Women's Liberation." *Australian Feminist Studies* 22 (53): 173–190.

Valk, A. M. 2008. *Radical Sisters: Second Wave Feminism and Black Liberation in Washington, D.C.* Chicago: University of Illinois Press.

Vigliano, A. 2014. "How the 'Trigger Warning' Took over the Internet." *BuzzFeed*, May 5. Accessed December 17, 2017. https://www.buzzfeed.com/alisonvingiano/how-the-trigger-warning-took-over-the-internet?utm_term=.bukOOAxb9#.cbXNNly1n.

Waldman, K. 2016. "The Trapdoor of Trigger Words: What the Science of Trauma Can Tell Us About an Endless Campus Debate." *Slate*, September 5. Accessed January 14, 2018. http://www.slate.com/articles/double_x/cover_story/2016/09/what_science_can_tell_us_about_trigger_warnings.html.

Washick, B. 2017. "An 'App' for That: The Case Against the 'Equal Access' Argument for Trigger Warnings." In *Trigger Warnings: History, Theory, Context*, edited by E. J. M. Knox, 86–120. Lanham: Rowman & Littlefield.

Williams, L. 1989. *Hard Core: Power, Pleasure, and the 'Frenzy of the Visible'*. Berkeley: University of California Press.

CHAPTER 12

Gruesome Images in the Contemporary Israeli Mediated Public Sphere

Tal Morse

INTRODUCTION

In the fall of 2015, Israelis witnessed yet another round of Palestinian resistance to the Israeli occupation of the West Bank. This was not the deadliest round of bloodshed between Israel and the Palestinians, but it was the most visually documented and therefore stirred a debate about the offensiveness of gruesome images, which started following the suicide attacks of the mid-1990s and early 2000s. In the course of these two decades much has changed—the nature of the attacks, the media ecology and the perceptions of gruesome images as offensive.

Violent death is integral to our political life. It reflects the power dynamics between the powerful and the powerless, between the oppressive and the oppressed. According to Murray (2006), death-related actions like killing, suicide or execution contain a rhetorical component and serve as an utterance in political debates. Murray encourages us to try to understand how contemporary public and violent death informs our political life, arguing that the use of suicide bombs changes the power dynamics between the oppressed and the oppressor. Chouliaraki

---

T. Morse (✉)
Hadassah Academic College, Jerusalem, Israel
e-mail: talmor@hac.ac.il

© The Author(s) 2019
A. Graefer (ed.), *Media and the Politics of Offence*,
https://doi.org/10.1007/978-3-030-17574-0_12

and Kissas (2018) develop this argument and take it to the realm of representation, arguing that it is not only the statement embodied in corporeal death that matters for understanding interrelations between hegemony and counter-hegemony, but that, in addition, the representations of death and the aesthetics of death play a pivotal role in how we understand power dynamics in contemporary political life. The making visible of gruesome death goes against the grain of the current trend in Western culture, which seeks to hide and conceal non-fictional violent, grotesque death, and it challenges dominant hierarchies of humanisation and dehumanisation.

Gruesome and gory images of violence are not uncommon in the Israeli mediated public sphere (Morse 2009). Over the years, Israeli media organisations and consumers have coped with an ongoing violent reality, some of it on remote battlefields and some in city centres. In the 1990s, journalists and media ethicists deliberated on the proper and ethical ways in which gruesome violence should be represented in the mass media, if at all. Gory images, it was argued, offend the public— they transgress norms of taste and decency, disrespect the dead and the bereaved families and may cause harm to the general public. Yet, at the same time, the perceived offensiveness of images depicting a violent reality, which have dominated the Israeli mediated public sphere, has lost its monopoly. The perceived offensiveness of gruesome images is now more ambiguous, and they are not always perceived as a threat that the public needs to be protected from. Gruesome images are circulated today via social media by political actors and internet users; users sometimes consume and share these images for various reasons that go beyond moral witnessing. These new practices call for a revisiting of 20-year-old norms and of the perceived functions governing the documentation and circulation of gory and gruesome images, and for an inquiry into how such images reshape contemporary Israeli visual culture and the politics of offence. This chapter argues that Israeli mediated *thanatopolitics*—or the use of representations of death in the service of political life—has changed, and that this change requires an updated understanding of offensiveness. It shows that the approach of news organisations to protecting those who are dear to 'us' from the offensiveness of gruesome death images has gradually been replaced by a non-journalistic approach that utilises such images in order give offence to 'them'.

This chapter first outlines the changes in the representation of gory images in the Israeli media and in their meaning over the last two decades, and how this has come to serve various and sometimes conflicting purposes. It begins with the contesting perceptions of Israeli journalists regarding the legitimacy of displaying gruesome images during a period of suicide-bomb attacks following the Oslo Accords in the mid-1990s. Gory images of mutilated bodies were perceived as offensive and unfit for public display despite the fact that scenes like this were part of public life. The discussion here then moves to another key moment in the debate about the representation of death following the *Itamar massacre* of 2011, and observes the involvement of politicians in distributing gruesome death images via digital social networks. In this round another consideration was put forward, namely the political motivation on the Israeli side to demonise the Palestinians. In its third part, this chapter discusses the rise of what can be defined as the introduction of user-generated content to the scene of gruesome images. In this phase, Israeli citizens, that is not professional journalists, have been engaged in documenting, circulating and framing gruesome images of dead Palestinians, and they use these to ridicule and mock the depicted dead and to find amusement in their fatal condition. This trajectory reflects not only a political 'change of guard', but also the new or renewed meanings and functions of gruesome images and the ambiguity around the representation of death.

One important caveat is in place, before I begin. This chapter explores issues of gruesome death images in the Israeli media. These gruesome death images are a political matter and their distribution always serves political goals. The images I discuss here emerged from numerous violent incidents between Israelis and Palestinians, which is yet another sad note in an ongoing violent conflict between the two parties. This chapter does not aim to delve into the origin or nature of the Israeli-Palestinian conflict, whose narratives are contested and in dispute. It does, however, deal with sensitive and controversial issues that have concerned *Israeli* politics over the years and have not yet been resolved. The chapter explores *the Israeli perspective* on these issues and uses *Israeli media terminology*, which has its own biases and is often one-sided.

Thanatopolitics and Visual Communication

Murray (2006) argues that suicide attacks like those committed by Palestinians in Israel in the 1990s and early 2000s have a rhetorical effect that challenges Western hegemony, since such attacks reintroduce death into the everyday, defy oppressive power on various levels and desecrate the sacredness of death itself. Chouliaraki and Kissas (2018) suggest that we need to study thanatopolitics—the politics of death—beyond its corporealness. It is not only the rhetorical effect generated by death-related actions, as Murray argues, but also the statement made by representations of death and the conditions of their appearance in the mediated public sphere. Therefore, in order to unpack mediated thanatopolitics, we need to look into the aesthetics of making death performances visible as political statements about hierarchies of lives and deaths.

The presentation of death has always served political purposes and always been a means to establish or confirm power relations (Seaton 2005; Sontag 2003). In the past, in Western societies, the representation of death and suffering was often associated with virtuous and moralising effects. Seaton explains that 'early Christians established the idea that contemplating images of suffering, torture and mutilation was good for the observer – and indeed good for the society as a whole' (Seaton 2005, 89). Practices of contemplating representations of suffering took place in churches and were associated with rituals of purification and atonement. Looking at and engaging with images of suffering even brought pleasure to the spectator, and Christian art has bundled images of the naked body together with images depicting the body in pain (Sontag 2003, 36–37).

It is commonly perceived that, like images of nudity and sex, imagery of savaged bodies and other representations of violent death have vanished since the nineteenth-century, but such representation never completely disappeared (Hanusch 2008). As in the case of nudity and sex, the public display of death is often considered a taboo in the West, and its visibility is regulated by its aesthetics:

> Death poses particular problems for visual culture. The imperative of visual media is to show rather than tell, but death confounds this agenda in significant ways ... Further, within Western culture, documentary ("real") images of the dead are conventionally taboo in public space, and their publication or screening subject to a nuanced economy of ethics, aesthetics and propaganda. (Tait 2009, 333)

Indeed, norms of taste and decency often govern the display of violent death by the mainstream media, and reports on violent events protect the public from horror imagery by removing images that can harm readers and viewers (Campbell 2004; Taylor 1998; Zelizer 2010).

Yet, representations of violent death do appear in the mainstream media, and when they do they are usually regulated by framing and contextualisation (Campbell 2004; Morse 2013) or by beautifying tropes (Chouliaraki 2009).

Tait (2008) delves into the analogy between death and nudity, and more specifically pornography, and shows that it emanates from the similarities around the authenticity of the imagery and the sense of transgression and even pleasure associated with its consumption. Both pornography and death objectify the human body, make visible what is commonly concealed and apply a mixture of pleasure and guilt for the observer. Yet Tait argues that the 'pornographic analogy misnames and elides the variety of looks engaged and their specific ethical implications' (Tait 2008, 107). Instead, she identifies four types of gaze—amoral, vulnerable, entitled and responsive—which ramify our understanding of engagement with the visual representation of death. I develop this point later.

Going back to the political use of death imagery, Seaton argues that '[s]howing pain is almost never neutral – it always has a purpose, and is part of arguments and strategies' (Seaton 2005, 84). In this regard, it is important to note the association between the public display of death images, questions of (de)humanisation and hierarchies of belonging. In the last two centuries, representations of violent death have been associated with demoralising effects. Whether these are postcards depicting dismembered bodies of lynched black men at the turn of the twentieth century, shortly after the invention of the camera (Wood 2011), or photographic practices in military prisons and war zones at the beginning of the twenty-first century, in the digital age (Apel 2012; Butler 2009), the visual representation of mutilated and dead bodies reflects the power dynamics and hierarchies of power. Death images in Western media are usually images of dead foreigners (Fishman and Marvin 2003; Fishman 2001; Hanusch 2010; Taylor 1998; Zelizer 2010)—a pattern that maintains the power relations between Western spectators and non-Western dead (Campbell 2004).

Azoulay (2008) takes the visibility of death beyond questions of aesthetics and representation to consider practices of watching and being watched. She theorises photography as a vehicle for the oppressed to make their oppression visible, and so to recruit spectators' solidarity and empathy with the sufferers. Contemporary discourse on bearing witness to atrocities often points to the moralising function of death imagery, which compels spectators to respond to human suffering and to act upon it (Chouliaraki 2009, 2010; Tait 2011; Rentschler 2004), although scholars in this field are aware of potential shortcomings and disfunctions (Zelizer 1998; Tait 2008).

In what follows, I explore the ambiguity of the offensiveness of gory images in the Israeli mediated public sphere, and argue that users of social media have abandoned *the economy of taste and decency* adopted by the news media and endorsed instead an *economy of display* (Campbell 2004) in three ramified manners that apply a forensic outlook, or dehumanise the dead, and reduce the corpse to a mere spectacle for political propaganda and for giving offence.

A SHORT HISTORY OF GORY IMAGES IN ISRAELI MEDIA

Taking Offence

A milestone for every discussion of gory images in the Israeli media was the 'Line 5 suicide attack'. On the morning of 21 October 1994, a Palestinian blew himself up on the upper deck of a line number 5 bus in the heart of Tel Aviv, killing 19 Israelis and injuring dozens of others. Such attacks, as Murray (2006) explains, affect not only those who were killed and injured, but a larger circle of spectators who thus encounter violent death in their living rooms. Indeed, the images that emerged from the scene were horrific—the dead body of the bus driver was recumbent on the steering wheel, mutilated and dismembered corpses were scattered around the broken bus, emergency teams were evacuating the bleeding and wounded passengers to ambulances, shop windows were shattered and debris was widely dispersed (Morse 2014). This destructive attack in a central urban setting was the first of its kind and it caught the Israeli media by surprise with no clear or resolute policy on how to cover mass violent death events. The images that emerged from the death scene were regarded as gruesome and as too graphic, and therefore as offensive and harmful for children and the general public to watch. Many enraged viewers filed complaints to the television channels, criticising and denouncing their decision to air such images repeatedly on daytime television (Rosenblum 1994).

In the following months and years, more such attacks followed. Since the *Line 5 attack*, journalists and media ethicists have delved into the ethical issues of news coverage of disastrous events (Morse 2009, 2014).

The bone of contention was whether and how news media should portray and convey violent and deadly events. There is an inherent tension between two contradictory values. On the one hand, a deadly attack in the centre of town is obviously newsworthy and fits within the public's right to know. On the other hand, the news media have a responsibility to protect the public from harmful images that can traumatise the viewer. This dilemma joins another consideration: the need to respect the dead and their families. Similar discussions took place in other countries (Taylor 1998; Hanusch 2008; Zelizer 2005; Griffin 2010).

According to the 'informing and displaying' approach, as its advocates argue, the mission of journalism is to inform the public so they can make a fair judgement of the political reality. In particular, the argument was that photojournalism had a mission to depict reality *as is*, no matter how gory or violent. In contrast, according to the 'taste and decency' approach, when the visual documentation of deadly events transgresses conventions of taste and decency these may harm viewers, disrespect the dead or hurt the feelings of their families. More specifically, it was argued that close-up images of corpses and amputated body parts were pornographic and did not serve the public's right to know; they dishonoured the dead and were regarded as too disturbing and even traumatising for the public to watch.

More suicide-bomb attacks followed the one described above. In practice, the gruesome imagery of these attacks led Israeli news organisations to abandon the journalistic slogan 'when it bleeds, it leads', and to adopt instead more restrained and responsible editorial guidelines for documenting and reporting on violent death events. As in other countries, these restrictive norms have been applied mostly to Jewish-Israeli deaths and not so much to foreign deaths (Morse 2014; Fishman and Marvin 2003; Taylor 1998).

In the Service of Hasbarah

The professional journalistic practice for the depiction of violent events was challenged in March 2011. On 11 March, two Palestinians broke into *Itamar*, a Jewish settlement in the occupied West Bank, and slaughtered in their sleep a family of five including three young children. The images that emerged from the scene were dreadful: images of bloodshed in children's rooms, including puddles of blood and butchered children. From a journalistic perspective, it had by then already been established that such images were unsuitable for public display since they violated the human dignity of the victims and offended the public. However, politicians were also engaged in a discussion about whether or not Israel should take advantage of these images and harness them for political purposes, a practice often called in Hebrew *Hasbarah*, which refers to Israeli efforts to influence global public opinion on political matters. This was not the first time political considerations informed such discussion,[1] but it was an unusual case that happened at a time when the news media had lost their monopoly over the circulation of information. Moreover, it was a rare case where the discussion took place in the (mediated) public sphere. So the public debate about the circulation of gruesome death images was evoked once again. This time journalistic norms were overruled by politicians, and the focus was not on questions of human dignity and respect for the dead, but on the potential political gain Israel could elicit by distributing horrific images of the victims.

On the one hand, left-wing politicians such as the member of parliament and minister for welfare Isaac Herzog (Labour Party) argued that using the images of bleeding corpses was disrespectful to the victims and undermined the sincere state of mourning the country was undergoing. Moreover, in terms of diplomacy, Herzog argued that using the images would be ineffective and convey a sense of panic (Somfalvi 2011a, b). On the other hand, right-wing politicians, including the minister for information and diaspora[2] Yuli Edelstein (Likud Party), advocated for circulating the images of the butchered children worldwide:

> I have often been asked why we are so sterile in the information we share. At some point the events accumulate and though we have personally been exposed to unmentionable horrors, everyone has that point that gets them. The decision wasn't an easy one, without the family's consent we would never have even considered the issue. The family said yes – under certain conditions. (Sofer 2011)

---

[1] See, for example, the case of the Jewish infant Shalhevet Pass (Barnea 2002, in Hebrew).

[2] The minister for information translates in Hebrew as the minister of *Hasbarah*, which means 'explaining', but is a euphemism for propaganda.

Similarly, Miriam Feirberg Ikar (mayor of Netanya, Likud Party) argued that

> We must use these disturbing images and make them known worldwide so that the world will be aware of the difficult reality we need to cope with ... By showing concern to the family in an excuse of sparing them the pain and horror, we keep the truth away from the world's eyes, we conceal the shocking reality we live in and do not expose the ugly faces of the creatures the world perceives as underdogs. (Feirberg Ikar 2011, *as translated by the author*)

Edelstein and others argued that Israeli diplomacy had to take advantage of the tragedy and exploit the graphic images for the Israeli political cause and against the Palestinians (Hasson 2011; Magnezi 2011; Sofer 2011). In other words, from the perspective of Israeli right-wing politicians, foreign audiences did not need to be shielded from what are commonly recognised in the West as disturbing images. On the contrary, as long as such images served the cause of Israeli diplomacy and helped to show the world how inhumane the Palestinian violence was, foreign audiences had to see these images.

The argument employed in this discussion resonates with the discourse of bearing witness, which deals with uncovering the truth and recruiting solidarity in the light of unfortunate reality. However, it does so in a rather cynical manner, since from an Israeli perspective the dead were effaced as human beings and reduced to a means to a political end. The Itamar massacre case shows that, from the perspective of the Israeli government, diplomatic gain overrides private grief and respect towards its own dead. Moreover, this case shows how death images serve in a competition over perceived victimhood in foreign eyes, as Israeli politicians addressed global audiences in an attempt to position Israelis as victims of Palestinian aggression.

Eventually, in this case, Israeli news media refused to display the images, since this would have violated their codes of ethics. Global news media were occupied with the earthquake and tsunami in Japan that took place at the same time in 2011, and so these images did not reach global audiences. In the absence of cooperative news media, the images were circulated eventually via digital social networks, and not via mainstream mass-media outlets.

Gruesome Images in an Age of Ubiquitous Media

In the Fall of 2015, Israeli civilians coped with a series of stabbing attacks by single Palestinians in city centres. These attacks, which Israeli media titled the 'Intifada of the individuals' or the 'knives Intifada',[3] took place within a different media ecology than the suicide bombings of the 1990s or the Itamar massacre in 2011. Due to mobile and digital technologies, Israelis literally witnessed the violent clashes between armed Palestinians and Israelis almost 'as is'. Almost every attack was documented by CCTV cameras or by bystanders using their smartphones, and the unedited, uncensored imagery of explicit violence, gunfire and blood was immediately shared and redistributed time and again in various social media groups on WhatsApp and Facebook.[4]

The rise of violent Palestinian resistance on Israeli streets in an age of portable digital media invoked once again the debate about the coverage of such events on mass news media. However, in this latest round of visually documented violence we can discern two main patterns of image distribution: an informative, forensic-type report by official news media organisations; and an inflammatory, sometimes inciting framing of dead or injured Palestinians being shot and disarmed during their attempts to harm Israelis. These two patterns ramify the economy of display (Campbell 2004) introduced earlier, which positioned spectators as investigators on a truth-finding mission, or enhanced feelings of superiority vis-à-vis the Palestinians. Either way, these patterns of displaying gory images of violence came at the expense of moral witnessing, in the sense that they did not make a moral claim to bear witness.

Forensics

In order to differentiate themselves from citizen-journalists, the professional news media were careful to frame the display of disturbing images in forensic terms. The stated policy was to show images from stabbing scenes, whether of the Israeli victim or the 'neutralised' Palestinian attacker, but to digitally blur the gory parts of the image. This way, the

---

[3] The latter was endorsed by the Palestinians too. Intifada means 'resistance' in Arabic.

[4] According to a report on the use of internet in Israel by Israel's main telephone company, in 2015, 42% of Israeli internet users self-reported to have been exposed to uncensored footage from terror-attack scenes, which contains explicit and graphic images of violence (Bezeq 2015).

audience could witness the actions on the ground, but the graphic evidence of blood or of shot bodies was hidden away. This exception for showing bleeding bodies or an actual shooting was justified as part of applying an investigative outlook in order to reveal what actually happened on site—a matter not always clear at first sight. Thus news media claimed to be fulfilling their role as educators of the public, informing them about the complexity of the events taking place, and allowing them to assess the actions on the ground for themselves ('Was the Line Between News and Snuff in Israel Crossed?' 2016; Assenheim 2016). Such reports employed an investigative discourse of truth-seeking, and were composed mostly of factual descriptions. This framing, it was claimed, contextualised the gruesome reality and ostensibly elided the offensive aesthetics of these images. And yet, such a perspective still makes violent death visible and allows a covert voyeuristic outlook which is commonly perceived as forbidden, but becomes legitimate under these circumstances.

The most discussed footage, which was displayed on Israeli media countless times, was the footage of an Israeli soldier, El'or Azaria, shooting a disarmed Palestinian after a stabbing attempt in Hebron, in the West Bank. This footage, captured by a Palestinian activist for a human rights organisation, stirred a massive debate in the Israeli public sphere, in which Israeli journalists, military experts and politicians, including the minister of defence and the prime minister, argued about whether or not the soldier's shooting was justified and within the army's instructions for opening fire, or whether it exceeded the law and military orders. In this incident, two Palestinians attempted to stab Israeli soldiers. They were shot and disarmed. Eleven minutes later, Azaria, an Israeli soldier who rushed to the scene, shot one of the disarmed Palestinians, who was lying wounded on the ground, in the head. The soldier claimed he suspected the Palestinian was carrying a bomb, but other evidence suggested this was a false claim, and that the shooting was not in line with the army's instructions on opening fire. Azaria was later convicted of manslaughter (Cohen 2017).

Uvda ('Fact', in Hebrew), a leading investigative journalism television programme, dedicated one of its episodes to investigating what happened that day in Hebron (Assenheim 2016). In a forensic-type manner, footage from various cameras was collected and analysed, minute by minute, frame by frame. The reporter's opening remarks were as follows:

> We all know how it ends. One shot of one soldier will shiver the entire country. A short footage of few seconds has made each of us to form their own opinion. But what do we really know about what happened here?

> ... Whether El'or Azaria is guilty or not, we will reveal here, second by second, the events of that day in Hebron ... To better understand what really happened we need to unpack the scene into minutes and seconds, into dozens of images and recordings that were never exposed. For the first time we will synchronize six video cameras that documented the event. The El'or Azaria case is now on. (Assenheim 2016, as translated by the author)

Indeed, throughout the report, we saw footage of the unfolding events, including the images of one dead attacker who was shot in the head, his blood oozes down the street, and the footage of Azaria shooting at the other attacker in the head and killing him. However, the wording and tone of the reporter was not furious. Rather, he employed informative language and applied a judicial-type tone to uncovering the facts, so that his audience could form an opinion on what had happened.

Thus, in this case, images of bleeding bodies were repeatedly displayed, but the purpose of showing these images was not considered pornographic, since it was properly contextualised. This was an outcome of a thoughtful journalistic practice, designed to inform the Israeli public on the circumstances of an incident that agitated, infuriated and divided them. The television programme applied an investigative outlook to this incident, allowing a voyeuristic gaze on a dead body as a byproduct of investigative journalism. In other words, professional news media do provide gruesome images for their audiences, yet they do so only when they believe these serve the public's right to know, and can generate and enrich public deliberation on matters of grave concern (like the ethics of armed fire in the complex conditions of a military occupation of a civilian population). In a way, this investigative outlook employed by mainstream media resonates with what Tait has identified as the entitled gaze employed by users of Ogrish.com, which provided access to body horror and various images and footage of non-fictional violence that the mainstream media would not show. This outlook justifies looking at gory images in the name of truth-finding, in order to see what really happened: 'the entitled spectator seeks to circumvent taboos pertaining to the destruction of bodies in order to acquire knowledge' (Tait 2008, 104). As we will see next, citizens with access to gruesome images applied a different approach.

Denigration and Scorn (or Giving Offence)

As described earlier, the series of knife attacks resulted, in a media-saturated environment, in a plethora of images depicting graphic violence.

The images were taken by CCTV, citizens and rescue teams, and they then reached the hands and eyes of other citizens with access to social groups on mobile digital platforms. And so, shortly after an incident occurred, unfiltered, explicit graphic images of the disarmed or dead attacker were widely spread online (Bezeq 2015). However, while the news media were relatively conservative in the kind of images they distributed, restricting these to imagery that could arguably educate and inform the public, the imagery that was distributed via social media served a different purpose, that of denigration and scorn. Social media users used digital social networks to inflame the public, to humiliate, ridicule and shame the 'enemy'.

In what follows, I focus attention on the Facebook profile of Yoav Eliasi,[5] also known as *HaTzel* ('The Shadow', in Hebrew), a former rap singer and right-wing political activist, who runs a very popular Facebook profile where he spreads his political viewpoint and expresses his opinion on various political matters. Eliasi has more than 340,000 followers and his account has accumulated a similar number of 'likes'. His posts are often political and provocative, transgressing what is commonly perceived as adequate and fair political deliberation. These posts are occasionally followed up by the mass media, which usually find his comments offensive and scandalous. It is beyond the scope of this chapter to determine whether or not discussions on Eliasi's Facebook profile are representative of the Israeli political atmosphere. However, these discussions do reflect one of the vibrant and vocal streams of Israelis' political viewpoint.

During the 'knives Intifada', Eliasi's Facebook profile was a source of information on various attacks, and Eliasi occasionally posted unfiltered and uncensored gory images of Palestinian attackers. In some cases, the images were digitally blurred to filter out the gruesome imagery or to conceal the identity of the attackers, but these posts were accompanied by links to the uncensored images. As illustrated next, this was not a mere attempt to inform the public. Rather, these posts aimed to denigrate and mock the attackers. Eliasi's followers complied with this approach and added offensive comments of their own. Needless to say, this framing of the gruesome images did not assume that these were offensive images or that the public needed to be shielded from such

---

[5] https://he-il.facebook.com/TheShadow69/.

sights. On the contrary, as in the case of photographs and postcards of lynchings in the US at the beginning of the twentieth century (Wood 2011), these images were deliberately circulated for amusement, malicious joy and gloating and to amplifying a sense of superiority.

For example, on 9 August 2015, Eliasi posted a fairly close-up shot of a Palestinian who was shot dead after attempting to stab Israelis. The image depicts the body of the attacker with some bruises on his face and his eyes half shut. Eliasi's followers' comments on this post referred to the appearance of the dead Palestinian, describing him as ugly: 'It is as if all Arabs are made of ugliness … Their faces are always defective',[6] one comment read. It was followed by another: 'Now I understand why they are willing to die. They look so ugly that no girl will look in their direction. Fuck them and I wish they all got cancer'.

On 20 October 2015, Eliasi's Facebook profile exhibited an image of a dead Palestinian attacker whose head lay in a puddle of blood. The comments on this post included swear words and referred to the attacker's looks: 'How can you tell that he is an Arab?', asked one of the comments, and the answer, accompanied by seven emojis of smiley faces, read: 'According to the fake *Lacoste* shirt he wears and the shabby Denim pants'. Another comment announced: 'I'm going to frame this picture and hang it in my room'. A similar comment was posted on 17 March 2016, next to an image of two dead Palestinians with bullets in their heads and knives in their hands: 'Beautiful pictures! I would make a poster out of them and hang it on the wall of my room'. Thus, not only did these users not find such images offensive or harmful, but, on the contrary, they found them amusing. They did not believe such images had to be hidden, but that they were to be put on a regular display, to 'decorate' one's home.

In the aftermath of some attacks, Israeli security forces on the ground stripped the attackers to verify they were not carrying a bomb on their bodies or wearing an explosive belt. Images of these attackers depict them naked or half-naked, sometimes revealing their genitals. Such images also appeared on Eliasi's Facebook profile, sometimes uncensored. Despite the norm of avoiding the public display of sex organs (which is also a breach of Facebook's policy) ('Community Standards', n.d.), such images were put on public display, and some of

[6]All quotes from Eliasi's Facebook profile are in Hebrew and were translated by the author.

the comments addressed the attackers' genitalia in a shaming manner. For example, an image that was posted on 23 December 2015 depicted a shot-down attacker lying naked on the ground with a bleeding wound on his torso and only a small piece of cloth covering his genitalia. Some comments on this post made fun of the attacker's shaved pubic hair: 'He probably prepared himself for meeting the 72 virgins waiting for him in the next world'. Furthermore, in some cases the image depicted the naked body surrounded by bystanders who took photos with their smartphones in a manner that resembled the (in)famous Abu-Ghraib prison images (Apel 2012). This act of picture-taking carries a meaning of its own, beyond the aesthetics of the picture, as it renders the alleged superiority of the victor over the dead and defeated enemy.

However, not all the comments on such gruesome images approved of this practice. As in the case of the mass news media that have appeared to be sensitive at least to Israeli-Jewish victims (Morse 2013, 2014), when Eliasi posted gruesome images of wounded Israelis, some followers criticised him and accused him of violating the dignity and privacy of the victims. For example, on 21 November 2015 Eliasi posted an image of paramedics treating a bleeding Israeli victim, and one of the comments accused him of being bloodthirsty. The person who posted that comment asked Eliasi 'to end the pornography of terrorism. Please pay some respect to the victim's privacy'. In another case, Eliasi's followers were critical of the practice of showing brutalised images of Palestinian attackers, not only Israelis. A comment to one such image read:

> Hey, bro! I usually respect your views, but in this case, I can't figure out what is the message you wish to convey. The more I see gruesome images of corpses the more I should hate Arabs? Perhaps this is just gloating, but given that you have many people who read your posts, including children, posting such images only enhances hatred … I think this is irresponsible.

On 22 March 2017, Eliasi posted two photos of a Palestinian boy—in one photo the boy looks at the camera and smiles, in the other he is dead, lying on bloodstained sheets. Eliasi's comment on this post read: 'Before and after the treatment the IDF gave to this terrorist who tried to put a bomb near Gaza's fence a few hours ago'. Again, together with supportive comments that rejoiced in the killing, one of the followers raised concern that the post undermined Israeli *Hasbara*, as it showed the world that Israelis celebrated the death of Palestinians.

Thus, the practice of circulating gory images is not common in Israeli mainstream media, and the public debates that take place on Facebook profiles like that of Eliasi show that not all Israelis approve of the distribution of such images. And yet, discussions on Eliasi's Facebook profile exemplify an approach of some Israelis who do not feel offended by looking at images of bleeding and mutilated bodies, or feel they need to be protected from these images. On the contrary, they find these images entertaining and even amusing, and use them to give offence to the Palestinian enemy.

Conclusions

Death imagery, and gruesome images in particular, are a political matter. The aesthetics of death, whether it is visible, and the conditions of its presentation, make a statement about power dynamics and hierarchies in life. More specifically, the sense of offensiveness contemporarily associated with gruesome death images that ignites and informs political debates and power struggles between rival parties. In the West, gory images are often perceived as disturbing and traumatising, as something the public needs to be protected from, something that does not comply with norms of taste and decency. And yet, as this chapter shows, in contemporary Israeli visual culture, death is visible even when it breaches norms of taste and decency. This visibility suggests that the Israeli public is not as vulnerable as journalists and media ethicists argue. The distribution and redistribution of gruesome death images in the Israeli mediated public sphere reflects an ambiguity around the offensiveness of such images.

The violent reality in Israel-Palestine makes death almost trivial. As Murray (2006) explains, the Palestinian thanatopolitics aspires to defy oppressive Israeli power by making death public and visible so that it can harm wide circles of society. However, in recent years the Palestinian corporeal thanatopolitcs has encountered an Israeli mediated thanatopolitics that uses the public visibility of gruesome death for its own purposes, namely to give offence to Palestinians. This practice challenges common perceptions of the offensiveness of death imagery and the ethics of its circulation.

This chapter has explored the evolution of death imagery in the Israeli mediated public sphere, from something that was perceived as offensive to viewers and readers to a symbolic weaponry utilised to give offence. Gruesome images of bodies in pain that were considered in the mid-1990s to be offensive and harmful have become, in some political circles, a political weapon for undermining and scorning the enemy, something that citizens share with one another and within growing social circles, something people brag about as trophy photographs. Accordingly, journalistic practices designed to protect the public have been replaced by a civic-journalistic *economy of display* (Campbell 2004).

The making visible of gory images serves multiple, sometimes contradictory, purposes: it fulfils the public's right to know and make sense of a violent reality, but it also feeds spectacular thanatopolitcs as it demonises and dehumanises Palestinians and facilitates a satisfying gloating and rejoicing over the defeat of the enemy. This trajectory of attitudes towards the representation of violent death in Israel demonstrates the changes in the dominance of the news media in governing and defining the properness of information for political deliberation, and showcases the gradual evolution and negotiation over the adequacy of death imagery as information and as symbolic political weaponry. As new technologies of communication change the mediated public sphere, so do the conventions on the legitimacy of death imagery change.

References

Apel, Dora. 2012. *War Culture and the Contest of Images.* New Brunswick, NJ: Rutgers University Press.
Assenheim, Omri. 2016. "One Shot in Hebron." *Uvda*, November 28, 2016. https://www.mako.co.il/tv-ilana_dayan/2017/Article-54705ecb25ca851006.htm.
Azoulay, Ariella. 2008. *The Civil Contract of Photography.* New York and Cambridge, MA: Zone Books; Distributed by The MIT Press.
Barnea, Nahum. 2002. "For Whom the Bell Tolls." *The Daily Eye*, May 1. http://www.the7eye.org.il/45729.
Bezeq. 2015. "Life in the Digital Age: Bezeq's Report on the Status of the Internet in Israel for 2015." *Bezeq*. https://www.bezeq.co.il/media/PDF/internetreport_2015.pdf.
Butler, Judith. 2009. *Frames of War: When Is Life Grievable?* London and Brooklyn, NY: Verso.
Campbell, David. 2004. "Horrific Blindness: Images of Death in Contemporary Media." *Journal for Cultural Research* 8 (1): 55–74. https://doi.org/10.1080/1479758042000196971.
Chouliaraki, Lilie. 2009. "Witnessing War: Economies of Regulation in Reporting War and Conflict." *The Communication Review* 12 (3): 215–226. https://doi.org/10.1080/10714420903124077.

Chouliaraki, Lilie. 2010. "Ordinary Witnessing in Post-Television News: Towards a New Moral Imagination." *Critical Discourse Studies* 7 (4): 305–319. https://doi.org/10.1080/17405904.2010.511839.

Chouliaraki, Lilie, and Angelos Kissas. 2018. "The Communication of Horrorism: A Typology of ISIS Online Death Videos." *Critical Studies in Media Communication* 35 (1): 24–39. https://doi.org/10.1080/15295036.2017.1393096.

Cohen, Gili. 2017. "Hebron Shooter Elor Azaria Sentenced to 1.5 Years for Shooting Wounded Palestinian Attacker." *Haaretz*, February 21. https://www.haaretz.com/israel-news/hebron-shooter-sentenced-for-shooting-wounded-palestinian-attacker-1.5489979.

"Community Standards." n.d. Accessed February 19, 2018. https://www.facebook.com/communitystandards#nudity.

Feirberg Ikar, Miriam. 2011. "Instead of 1000 Word—We Must Publish the Horror Images." March 13, 2011. https://www.makorrishon.co.il/nrg/online/1/ART2/221/442.html.

Fishman, Jessica M. 2001. "Documenting Death: Photojournalism and Spectacles of the Morbid in the Tabloid and Elite Newspaper." PhD Thesis, University of Pennsylvania. http://repository.upenn.edu/dissertations/AAI3003629.

Fishman, Jessica M., and Carolyn Marvin. 2003. "Portrayals of Violence and Group Difference in Newspaper Photographs: Nationalism and Media." *Journal of Communication* 53 (1): 32–44. https://doi.org/10.1111/j.1460-2466.2003.tb03003.x.

Griffin, Michael. 2010. "Media Images of War." *Media, War & Conflict* 3 (1): 7–41. https://doi.org/10.1177/1750635210356813.

Hanusch, Folker. 2008. "Graphic Death in the News Media: Present or Absent?" *Mortality* 13 (4): 301–317. https://doi.org/10.1080/13576270802383840.

Hanusch, Folker. 2010. *Representing Death in the News: Journalism, Media and Mortality*. Basingstoke: Palgrave Macmillan.

Hasson, Nir. 2011. "Why Did Israel Release Bloody Images of the Family Slain in Itamar?" *Haaretz*, March 15. http://www.haaretz.com/print-edition/features/why-did-israel-release-bloody-images-of-the-family-slain-in-itamar-1.349254.

Magnezi, Aviel. 2011. "Israel Distributing Itamar Massacre Photos." *Ynetnews*, March 14. https://www.ynetnews.com/articles/0,7340,L-4041557,00.html.

Morse, Tal. 2009. "Shooting the Dead: Photographs of Dead Bodies in Israeli Media." Haifa, Israel: University of Haifa.

Morse, Tal. 2013. "Shooting the Dead: Images of Death, Inclusion and Exclusion in the Israeli Press." In *Envisaging Death: Visual Culture and Dying*, edited by Michele Aaron, 140–156. Newcastle: Cambridge Scholars Publishing.

Morse, Tal. 2014. "Covering the Dead: Death Images in Israeli Newspapers—Ethics and Praxis." *Journalism Studies* 15 (1): 98–113. https://doi.org/10.1080/1461670X.2013.783295.

Murray, Stuart, J. 2006. "Thanatopolitics: On the Use of Death for Mobilizing Political Life." Special issue on "Biopolitics, Narrative, and Temporality", *Polygraph: An International Journal of Politics and Culture* 18: 191–215.
Rentschler, Carrie A. 2004. "Witnessing: US Citizenship and the Vicarious Experience of Suffering." *Media, Culture & Society* 26 (2): 296–304. https://doi.org/10.1177/0163443704041180.
Rosenblum, Irit. 1994. "Viewers Resented the Display of Horror Images in Television Broadcast." *Haaretz*, October 20, Sec. A.
Seaton, Jean. 2005. *Carnage and the Media: The Making and Breaking of News About Violence*. London: Allen Lane.
Somfalvi, Attila. 2011a. "Israel Mulling Publication of Shocking Attack Photos." *Ynetnews*, December 3. http://www.ynetnews.com/articles/0,7340,L-4041202,00.html.
Somfalvi, Attila. 2011b. "MK Herzog Slams Decision to Release Photos from Itamar Attack." *Ynetnews*, March 14. https://www.ynetnews.com/articles/0,7340,L-4041929,00.html.
Sofer, Roni. 2011. "Minister Hopes Images Will Shock World." *Ynetnews*, March 14. https://www.ynetnews.com/articles/0,7340,L-4042043,00.html.
Sontag, Susan. 2003. *Regarding the Pain of Others*. New York: Farrar, Straus and Giroux.
Tait, Sue. 2008. "Pornographies of Violence? Internet Spectatorship on Body Horror." *Critical Studies in Media Communication* 25 (1): 91–111. https://doi.org/10.1080/15295030701851148.
Tait, Sue. 2009. "Visualising Technologies and the Ethics and Aesthetics of Screening Death." *Science as Culture* 18 (3): 333–353. https://doi.org/10.1080/09505430903123016.
Tait, Sue. 2011. "Bearing Witness, Journalism and Moral Responsibility." *Media, Culture & Society* 33 (8): 1220–1235. https://doi.org/10.1177/0163443711422460.
Taylor, John. 1998. *Body Horror: Photojournalism, Catastrophe, and War: The Critical Image*. New York: New York University Press.
"Was the Line Between News and Snuff in Israel Crossed?" 2016. *The Daily Eye: Media File*. Israel: 23tv. http://www.the7eye.org.il/207434.
Wood, Amy Louise. 2011. *Lynching and Spectacle: Witnessing Racial Violence in America, 1890–1940*. New edition. Chapel Hill, NC: The University of North Carolina Press.
Zelizer, Barbie. 1998. *Remembering to Forget: Holocaust Memory Through the Camera's Eye*. Chicago: University of Chicago Press.
Zelizer, Barbie. 2005. "Death in Wartime Photographs and the 'Other War' in Afghanistan." *The Harvard International Journal of Press/Politics* 10 (3): 26–55. https://doi.org/10.1177/1081180X05278370.
Zelizer, Barbie. 2010. *About to Die: How News Images Move the Public*. New York: Oxford University Press.

Index

A
Abject, 8, 14, 77, 84, 110, 111, 116, 124, 131, 132, 134
Advertising, 10, 73, 98, 166, 168, 172, 180
Affect, 4, 14, 17, 50, 52, 61, 147–152, 158, 159, 181, 209, 216, 218, 238
Affective, 4, 8, 14–16, 52, 54, 58, 66–68, 70, 71, 75, 78, 82, 83, 85, 92, 109, 110, 115–118, 121, 124, 141, 149, 153, 158, 159, 217, 220
Affective publics, 52
Aggression, 48, 68, 83, 92, 154, 241
Amazon, 172, 180
Ambiguity, 238
Ambiguous nature of offence, 3
Anger, 4, 5, 8, 13, 47–51, 53–62, 66, 68, 75, 80, 82, 102, 150, 154–158, 210
Angry, 99
Apartheid, 14, 92, 96, 102, 104
Audience, 3, 5, 10–12, 14–16, 25, 27, 34, 35, 37, 39, 41, 50, 67, 83, 109–113, 115, 121, 123, 129, 131, 136, 138, 140, 141, 149–153, 155, 156, 158, 159, 168, 187, 188, 190–199, 202, 209, 222, 241, 243, 244
Authenticity, 30

B
Blogging, 51, 150
Body, 8, 13, 14, 36, 37, 39, 50, 52, 66, 70–74, 77–80, 83, 84, 93, 95–99, 101, 110, 112, 115, 117–119, 122, 166, 176, 178, 181, 191, 193, 194, 200, 218, 221, 222, 236–239, 244, 246, 247
Brand-building, 166, 173, 180
Brexit, 2

C
Carnivalesque, 66, 68, 69, 72–76, 78, 80, 83–85
Causing offence, 5, 8
Censorship, 3, 5, 9, 16, 67, 167, 178–180, 195–198, 201, 202, 216, 222

Citizen interest, 16, 190–193, 195, 198, 202
Consumption, 3, 109, 110, 120, 123, 167, 173, 179, 219, 237
Context, 2–4, 6, 8, 9, 11, 12, 14, 16, 23–25, 27, 28, 30, 31, 33–35, 37, 47–51, 54, 60, 66, 68–70, 74, 78, 80, 82, 85, 92, 95–97, 103, 140, 151, 154, 156, 167, 168, 172, 174, 175, 189, 190, 193, 201, 202, 207–211, 215, 217, 218, 220, 223, 224, 227, 228
Crazy Ex-Girlfriend (CXG), 15, 127–129, 131, 134–142

D
Death images, 17, 234, 235, 237, 240, 241, 248
Desensitised, 113
Digital Economy Law 2017, 178
Discrimination, 101
Disgust, 7, 8, 14, 79, 110, 111, 114–124, 132, 134, 139, 158, 224
Disturbing content, 214

E
Embarrassing Bodies (EB), 14, 109, 111, 113, 116, 118, 121, 124
Emotion, 4, 5, 8, 13, 15, 24, 47–62, 68, 80, 83, 134, 139, 140, 148–156, 158, 159, 209, 211, 216, 217
Emotional community, 48, 51–56, 58, 61, 62
Emotional labour, 57, 61
Entertainment, 12, 66, 110, 114, 122, 132, 174, 188
Ethnicity, 41, 189, 208
Excitement, 110

Exclusion, 13, 93, 100, 104, 124, 156, 210, 218, 220, 226

F
Facebook, 3, 33, 35, 70, 172, 174, 179, 209, 213, 242, 245, 246, 248
Fan, 15, 140, 147–151, 155–159, 212
Fandom, 147–152, 156–159
Fears, 119
Feeling, 3, 4, 6–8, 13–15, 47, 50, 51, 54–60, 66–69, 75, 80, 99, 110–116, 119–121, 124, 139, 140, 147–155, 158, 159, 187, 211, 223, 224, 226, 239, 242
Feels culture, 149, 152
Femininity, 73, 74, 83, 95
Feminism, 31, 41, 80, 130, 133, 209, 213–216
Feminist, 2, 15, 17, 41, 50, 51, 68, 75, 82, 84, 85, 95, 98, 128–133, 137, 142, 176, 181, 208–218, 220, 221, 223–228
Film, 5, 8, 48, 53, 93–95, 138, 147, 153, 171, 176, 177, 179–181, 189, 194, 217, 220–223
Freedom of speech, 7, 9, 10, 28, 35, 41, 167, 224
Free speech, 2, 7, 9, 10, 16, 28, 30, 38, 123, 180, 188, 196, 201, 202, 228
Frustration, 68, 75, 101–103, 129

G
Gaze, 237
Genitals, 121, 246
Germany, 11, 16, 188–194, 197, 200, 202
Gift economy, 149
Gig economy, 168

Github, 172
Giving offence, 6, 9, 17, 25–27, 234, 238, 244, 248
Google, 172, 179, 180
Gross-out humour, 128, 134
Gruesome images, 17, 233–235, 244, 245, 247, 248

H
Hate speech, 8, 9, 27, 100, 101
Hierarchie, 68, 85, 181, 182, 211, 220, 234, 236, 237, 248
Hutton, Dean, 14, 92, 97, 98, 100–103

I
Imgur, 172
Instagram, 3, 6, 13, 23, 66, 70, 71, 74, 82–84, 95, 134
Interpretive framework, 13, 51
Interview, 1, 14, 26, 109, 110, 114–116, 118, 119, 122, 123, 189, 194, 197

J
Jouissance, 8, 121
Joy, 4, 47, 57, 68, 110, 124, 130, 246

L
Language, 7, 9–11, 17, 24, 30, 31, 35, 38, 41–43, 50, 78, 95, 111, 129, 132, 198, 200, 201, 210, 213, 215, 216, 218, 225, 228, 244
Laughter, 73, 75, 78, 79, 129, 134, 140, 141, 243
Liberal feminists, 2, 210

M
Marginalised groups, 4, 50, 210, 211, 214
Marney, Jo, 33, 43
Masculinity, 13, 38, 66, 72–74, 81, 84, 96
The media, 1–5, 12, 50, 51, 67, 129, 142, 147, 187, 196, 198, 199, 202, 233
Media content, 2, 3, 5, 11, 12, 17, 67, 85, 111, 187–189, 194, 196, 198, 211, 217, 219
Media genre, 166
Mediated offence, 3, 9, 13, 15
Mental illness, 128, 129, 136–138, 142, 207, 211
#MeToo, 82, 223
MindGeek, 166, 168, 175–178, 180–182
Muholi, Zanele, 14, 92, 93, 103

N
Narcissistic crisis, 116, 117
Netflix, 172
Net neutrality, 172, 173, 178–180
Networked publics, 61, 62
Nudity, 10, 94, 95, 111, 236, 237

O
Offence, 1–17, 23, 24, 26–28, 30, 31, 33–35, 37, 39–41, 47, 48, 53–57, 59, 61, 92, 93, 97, 99, 102, 104, 110–113, 116, 118, 120–124, 128–130, 138, 141, 148, 151, 152, 154–159, 165–170, 177, 181, 182, 209, 223, 234, 248
Offensive, 1, 2, 4, 6–17, 24, 27, 28, 32, 34, 36, 40, 66–80, 82–85, 91–95, 101–104, 110, 111, 114, 119, 121, 123, 128, 129, 132,

140, 142, 155, 157, 166, 167, 177, 178, 187, 189, 190, 193–199, 201, 202, 207, 209, 233, 235, 238, 243, 245, 246, 248
Offensive humour, 13, 65
Offensiveness, 12, 15, 17, 23–25, 28, 31, 33, 35, 37, 39–41, 43, 128, 129, 167, 174, 178, 180, 233, 234, 238, 248
Online media, 5, 159
Outrage, 32, 49, 53, 60, 92, 101, 104, 166, 177, 181

P

Palestinian, 233, 235, 238, 239, 241–243, 245–249
Participation frameworks, 12, 24, 40
Patriarchy, 50, 75
Performance, 31
Performative, 9, 12, 13, 31, 40, 49, 52, 99, 101, 118
Performativity, 112
Pleasure, 10, 12, 14, 16, 37, 66, 75, 77, 80, 85, 110, 120–122, 124, 127, 134, 140, 141, 150, 166, 177, 212, 221, 222, 236, 237
Political change, 14, 43, 51, 66, 67, 69, 235
Political correctness, 2, 6, 7, 24, 27–31, 37, 38, 40–42, 123, 188, 189, 210
Political economy, 16, 165, 166, 180, 181
Politics of visibility, 33, 103
Popular culture, 12, 14, 15, 80, 98, 129
Populism, 13, 35, 51, 54
Pornhub, 166, 168, 169, 172–176, 179, 180
Pornographers, 16, 165–168, 171, 173, 175–178, 180–182

Pornography, 3, 8, 16, 92, 165–167, 169, 173–182, 194, 237, 247
Postfeminism, 15, 129, 131, 132, 134–136, 142
Power structures, 9, 67, 208, 221, 223, 226
Product, 2, 10, 11, 74, 133, 134, 217
Promotion, 2, 166, 173, 174
Provocation, 3, 14, 92, 97
Psychoanalysis, 14, 109, 110, 117, 120, 121
Public sphere, 12, 13, 17, 23–26, 39, 40, 42, 49, 50, 66, 73, 78, 79, 84, 93, 102, 103, 190, 234, 236, 238, 240, 243, 248, 249

Q

Queer, 14, 17, 50, 92, 94, 95, 97, 98, 102, 103, 176, 178, 181, 208–210, 212, 213, 215, 216, 219–221, 224, 227, 228

R

Race, 8, 29, 30, 33, 34, 79, 93, 98, 181, 189, 200, 208, 219–221, 223, 224, 226
Racism, 101
Reality television, 6, 11, 14, 114, 120, 123
Reddit, 172, 179
Regulation, 3, 5, 9, 11, 12, 16, 17, 30, 165, 166, 169, 176, 177, 180, 190, 192, 194, 195, 197, 198, 201
Resemiotisation, 33, 35, 37
Resistance, 42, 50, 52, 59, 61, 74, 80, 83, 85, 137, 151, 233, 242
Resonance, 148
Ridiculing, 111

S

Sensation, 4, 15, 115, 116
Sexism, 28, 29, 37, 128, 137, 138, 166, 193, 201, 214, 216, 226, 227
Sexist, 3, 10, 11, 34, 36, 67, 79, 111, 123, 127–130, 138, 194, 207, 218, 220, 224
Sexuality, 16, 73, 94, 95, 170, 200, 208
Shock, 4, 14, 47, 82, 95, 110–124, 156, 158, 212, 220, 222, 241
Silence, 4, 95, 101, 102, 137, 220, 221, 225
Social media, 3, 12, 16, 23, 25, 33, 34, 41, 42, 49, 51, 52, 55, 60, 66, 67, 69–71, 78, 80, 84, 92, 97, 123, 165, 166, 170, 172–174, 177, 179, 180, 182, 189, 208, 225, 234, 238, 242, 245
Social protest, 13, 74
South Africa, 14, 91, 93–97, 101–103, 224
Stereotypes, 111, 131

T

Taking offence, 5–7, 9, 14, 26, 39, 54, 55, 59, 130, 167, 182, 238
Target, 4, 6, 8–10, 12, 26, 27, 34, 35, 37, 39–42, 72, 77, 79, 80, 83, 170, 177, 210, 213
Taste cultures, 167, 188
Thanatopolitics, 17, 234–236, 248
Titillation, 4, 47, 68
Trigger warnings (TW), 17, 207–212, 214–217, 219–228
Trolling, 33, 61, 213
Trump, 31
Trump, Donald, 1, 13, 33, 47, 51, 66, 71, 124, 210
Tweet, 36–40, 47, 48, 53–56, 58, 60, 61, 76, 123, 124
Twitter, 1, 13, 23, 33, 36, 37, 52–55, 58, 62, 66, 70, 71, 74, 76, 78, 84, 93, 169, 172, 174, 179, 182

U

Unconscious desire, 116
United Kingdom (UK), 1, 11, 14, 16, 28–30, 32, 33, 36, 109, 166, 169, 176, 178, 180, 187–190, 192–196, 199–202
Unruly, 69, 80, 82–85, 167
Users, 3, 33, 54, 55, 67, 70, 71, 75, 76, 78, 82–84, 166, 168–177, 180, 181, 234, 238, 242, 244–246

V

Vid, 147
Vidding, 15, 147, 149
Viewers, 14, 91, 92, 94, 95, 99, 101, 109–111, 113, 114, 116–123, 128, 132, 141, 148, 154, 155, 158, 190, 191, 193, 221, 236, 238, 239, 248
Violence, 8, 11, 16, 24, 48, 68, 71, 92, 94–96, 99, 101, 103, 111, 124, 152, 154–157, 166, 177, 194, 207, 214, 217, 218, 222, 234, 241, 242, 244
Visibility, 32
Voyeurism, 14, 110, 120, 121

Vulnerability, 16, 17, 79, 94, 117, 208, 209, 211, 214, 215, 217–219, 223–228

W
WhatsApp, 242
White privilege, 96, 99, 101, 103
White supremacist, 210, 225, 228
Women's March, 13, 65, 66, 69, 70, 72, 76, 78, 80–82, 84, 85
Work, 3, 7, 8, 11, 14, 15, 17, 24, 30, 38–41, 50–52, 57, 59, 61, 67–70, 72–80, 83–85, 94, 95, 97–103, 147–150, 152, 153, 156, 159, 165, 166, 171, 176, 182, 190, 192, 194, 197, 200, 216, 218, 225

X
xHamster, 166, 168–173, 179

Y
Young, Toby, 36, 37, 39, 43
YouTube, 93

Printed by Printforce, the Netherlands